THE WALK-IN

A True Hollywood Story

Also By Brian Hunter,
Rising To Greatness: Fixing Your Life
And
The Hunter Equation

Rising To Greatness is a highly powerful and dynamic book that guides you through your very own process of transformation. *Rising To Greatness* is essential reading for those wanting a second chance at life, help re-booting their lives, or guidance with recovering from trauma and setbacks. Currently happy and successful people will find inspiring nuggets of information to help improve their life, relationships, and success. Topics include: Eliminating fear from your life, Living with Love, Mastering your emotions, Motivation and Discipline, Learning to believe in yourself, Becoming a master communicator and negotiator, Dealing with toxic and abusive people, Decision-making and problem solving, Finding and seizing opportunities in life, plus many other skills and topics. A favorite chapter for many demonstrates how to navigate the narcissists, sociopaths, and other toxic people in your life. *Rising To Greatness* goes into detail showing you how to use the new dynamic Universal equation known as The Hunter Equation.

Find out more about this unique formula which can transform your life in Brian's first book, *The Hunter Equation*. The Law of Attraction is incomplete and left many people disappointed with their results. Brian introduces his own Universal equation that more accurately reflects the reality and truth of the Universe. His realistic and common-sense alternative is more useful and effective. *The Hunter Equation* brings clarity and answers to the complicated questions and mysteries of the Universe, God, and Humanity. Topics covered include Death, Reincarnation, Destiny vs. Freewill, Soulmates, Karma, and How Psychics are Psychic.

www.brianhunterhelps.com

THE WALK-IN

A True Hollywood Story

By
Brian Hunter

First Edition

*Published by
Rainbow Wisdom
Ireland*

Copyright © 2020

All rights reserved.

No part of this publication may be reproduced, stored in a retrieval system, or transmitted, in any form or by any means, electronic, mechanical, photocopying, recording or otherwise without the prior permission of
Rainbow Wisdom or the author Brian Hunter.
This book is sold subject to the condition that it shall not, by way of trade or otherwise, be lent, re-sold, hired out, or otherwise circulated without the publisher's prior consent in any form of binding or cover other than that in which it is published and without a similar condition including this condition being imposed on the subsequent purchaser.

ISBN: 9781797938226

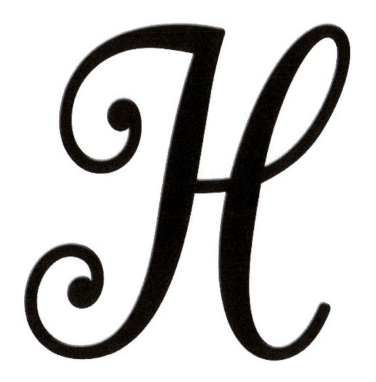

CONTENTS

PREFACE……………………................…..9

1 Childhood Tribulations…………......11
2 High School…………….....………….26
3 University Of Life……….....…………40
4 Building An Empire…….........………51
5 She Rocks My World……….........…..73
6 An Angel Is Born……………...........…90
7 That's Show Business…….........……108
8 Watch Those Dominoes Fall….......…119
9 Meet The Illuminati……..........………131
10 The Walk-In…………….........………146
   Christmas Mourning Poem…......……163
11 The Party I Never Had…….........……166
12 Brazil……………….....................……174
13 Stick A Fork In Me….........……………189
14 The Hustler……….........………………204
15 Star Trek Alien…….......………………223
16 Professional Psychic….......……………231

CONTENTS

17 European Adventures..................244

18 Forsaken..260

19 Is Murder Illegal?................................271

20 The Devil's Den....................................284

21 The Books...300

22 The Unexpected..................................313

23 Contemplation.....................................326

    Acknowledgments..............................332

    About The Author...............................333

DEDICATION

This book is dedicated to all those who feel they cannot go on any further, but continue on anyway.

I wrote this book for you.

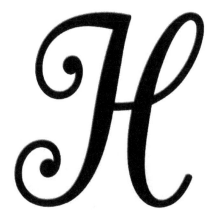

PREFACE

The Walk-In
A True Hollywood Story

This is my story. I am not telling my story to ruin anyone's life, call anyone out, or gain revenge against anyone. This story is entirely at my own expense, so that others may understand, learn, and grow. If anyone's life will be ruined or embarrassed by telling this story, it will only be mine. Thus, I have changed some names and fictionalized some details of events, in order to protect the guilty and innocent.

Furthermore, I apologize to anyone who may be offended by some of the content and events within this book. It is real life, and sometimes real life is not pretty. I also apologize to any family members, friends, or people close to me who may be offended or hurt by anything I am about to say. I would encourage anyone who knows me personally to NOT read the book (smile).

For everyone else who dares to continue, here is my truth as I see it. Here is what happened to me. Take from it what you will and use it to better your own life.

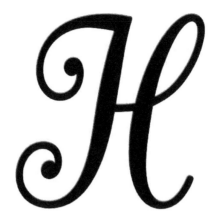

CHAPTER ONE

Childhood Tribulations

I am alone in the dark watching the shadows on the walls. Why are there shadows on the walls? Are they alive? What do they want? Are they coming to get me? Are they alone just like me? Why am I not afraid? Shouldn't I be afraid? I will just remain silent and watch them. Maybe they will talk to me.

This is my earliest memory. I think I was only two years old. Yes, I know that's usually too young for a memory, but the memory is faint, distant, very short, and concise. When I piece together what I see and feel, I am pretty sure it had to be around that age. To this day, I still do not know what the shadow people wanted. Or was it just a weird reflection? Does it matter? What matters is that I was alone in the dark, silently watching them, unafraid, and listening.

I spent lots of time alone in the dark listening.

A few years later, I would find myself alone again, in the dark, in another moment that is present for me. I lay motionless in my bed while tears slowly and gently run down the side of my face. I am a shy and quiet five-year-old little boy in a hospital alone without my mommy. Earlier, I asked the nurse to stay with me, but she said she couldn't. I asked for my blankie, but she can't find it and says it must be in the laundry. She turns out the lights and leaves me to my aloneness. There is nothing for me to do but be silent and let the tears leak from my tired eyes.

I will talk more about this particular incident later. But as you are about to see, my life has been defined mostly by my solitary journey through darkness to find light. I realized later on that my mission in life was to give light to those in the dark. I suppose you could also say my purpose has been to show people there is no fear in being alone or being in the dark. Simply put, there should be no fear. We are all alone in some way. You must not fear being alone. If you find yourself alone in the dark, you can listen carefully and find a way to the light.

I want to take you on a journey. My journey. It is somewhat scary, and often painful, but a grand adventure. I want you to see my darkness and my light so that you may live a better life. Come with me and let me show you my deepest darkest secrets. I am about to tell you everything I have never told. However, I think it is best we start at the very beginning, don't you? So, let us begin at the beginning.

I should have called the whole thing off and never came out. But, a fetus has little choice but to be born when it's time. The problems started before I even saw the light of the birthing room.

On one cold night in January during a blizzard, my mother went into labor and did her best to make her way to the hospital many miles from her home. There was a large suitable hospital close by, but my mother did not like the doctors there, so she had chosen a doctor in a hospital much farther away. Through the cold whipping wind and snow, my mom wobbled on the ice into the hospital entrance where she found out her regular doctor, she had counted on to deliver her baby, was not available. So, the doctor on call was employed.

The only indication that I had some intelligence and knowing of what I was about to come into, was the fact that I actually did NOT want to come out gracefully. I fought like hell to stay in the comfort of my mother's womb, far from the horrors of life. But while you can temporarily hide from life, you cannot hide forever, and eventually out I came. A freezing blizzard, hospital in a different state than where I actually lived, the wrong delivery doctor, and a pissed off mother who did not sign up to have a child in the first place. That was the setting for my beginning.

Oh yes, let us not forget the part beforehand. My mother had accidentally gotten pregnant with me at the end of high school, because she became overly infatuated with my father "who was hot, had a red car, and kind of liked her." Yep. That was the total extent of the intentions that brought me into the world. My mother was a highly intelligent, straight-laced, straight A student, who thought the trouble makers, party people, and fringe group types were hot. So, she was straight A Advanced Placement student by day, and dabbled in the leather jacket fringe group by night. My father by all accounts was even more horrified about the pregnancy than my mother was. OH... and I later learned that if my mother HAD to be stuck with a baby, she definitely had wished for a girl, not a boy like me.

So, it is safe to say that NOBODY got what they wanted in this deal, especially me who had to start this horrendous journey into a difficult lifetime, and even more difficult world.

Anyway, at some point in all this unfortunate chaos, my mother and father had gotten married. I am not sure if shotguns were present, but I have a feeling they could have been. There are no pictures I have seen of such a wedding, but I know it happened because there was a subsequent divorce in very short order.

I think my father wanted to keep enjoying his nice red car and freedom of youth. I only have a couple memories of him. I know there was a short time of visitation, in which he took me to his friend's house to party while I was left in a guest bedroom to sleep. My last memory of my father is him letting me (age three?) "drive" his car while sitting on his lap at the steering wheel. I admit it was fun and even now, I can remember that moment. He was probably a cool guy, but not so cool really. He shortly thereafter abandoned his responsibilities and vanished so that he could avoid paying any child support. I never saw him again. It all makes a small child wonder if they have any value, yes?

My mom on the other hand, was extremely responsible and took very good care of me. We were very poor, but I was always safe, clothed, fed, and a roof over my head. She never showed much affection toward me, but I know she loved me and was obviously just trying to keep the wheels on the bus from falling off, despite having my father abandon us and having little or no help from family.

My mom had grown up in a family where she was also abandoned by her father and was left under the responsible care of her mother, who showed her much less affection than I received. History tends to repeat it itself. In consideration of this, I'd say my mother did quite well to improve as a parent from the previous generation.

But anyway, it did not take long before I became even more of a problem for my mother. Regular doctor appointments determined there was a problem with some kind of valve or something in my bladder. To this day, I am not sure what the hell they did, but I have a huge scar along the top of my bladder to prove something significant happened. My mother tells a story of her, a single mother with no resources, family, or otherwise, having to bring me in for this major operation. She said she was terrified and cried all alone not knowing what would happen to me. Whatever operation or part they replaced must have worked out okay, because I am still alive and don't piss my paints. I am grateful for that at least.

A bit later on in my childhood around age five, the universe decided it was not done punishing my mother and me. It turned out I was developing asthma and had it really bad. It became so bad that I had to be admitted to a major hospital three hours from home for observation, testing, and treatment. My mother was working full time just to keep us fed and could not afford to take any time off from work. Thus, she had to drop me at this hospital, and then drive three hours back home to work for a few days. After a few days of eternity, she would drive back to the hospital to visit me. The separation was difficult for both of us. From what I understand, my mom was inconsolable just leaving her little boy in a faraway city alone; and I as a little 5-year-old boy was naturally terrified that I did not have my mommy, and I was very lonely.

I remember vividly being alone in this hospital for hours and days. I remember I did have a private room with a window view at least. But I would lay there in bed for hours and hours and days with no visitors except the occasional nurse which would come in to check my vitals and serve my food. I truly think it is this event that started the process of molding me into the independent, disconnected, brave, tough person I would become. I learned early on that I could cry for hours and days and it changed nothing. I could beg my mommy to please not go, and not leave me alone in that hospital and she would still have to go anyway. I would ask a nurse to please stay with me and yet they would ignore my pleas because they had other things to do. I remember moments when I just laid there silently with tears running down my little face, and I can still taste the tears running down my lips and into my mouth.

But it was not long before I got my revenge on one of the nurses. One night they brought my dinner. I cannot remember what it was exactly, but I know it included orange sweet potato. I politely told the nurse that I didn't like the orange stuff. The nurse insisted I had to eat it. I again insisted I HATED that orange crap and couldn't eat it. The nurse put some of the orange goo on the spoon and stuffed it into my mouth. In one fluid motion I immediately involuntarily projectile vomited all over her. I am not sure who was more surprised and horrified, her or me. I was distressed, sick, full of puke, and so was she. Suffice it to say I did not have to eat any more of the orange crap after that. To this day, I will not eat sweet potato or squash.

My asthma condition was eventually stabilized, and I was condemned to weekly shots at my doctor's office via a very long scary painful needle. Every Tuesday. For years. Isn't life great? Are we having fun yet? Not really. Little did I know all this was the easy part. We will get to much more later on.

Once I was getting close to enrolling in school for the first time, I was tested for my aptitude and readiness for starting into school. I remember the old mean looking lady with scary glasses asking me questions and telling me to do things. I just wanted to leave. After the evaluation, my mother was told that I was probably not ready for school because I could not use scissors properly. Perhaps I was not developed enough and would be too "slow," and would struggle and fail in school if forced to start too early. (In other words, your kid is an idiot and should wait.)

Thankfully my mother ignored the advice and started me into school anyway with the caveat that I needed extra attention to "catch up" with the rest of humanity, and all the totally brilliant 5 and 6 year olds who surrounded me, many of whom would later grow up to be morons.

I actually remember always feeling smarter on the inside than I appeared on the outside. I started to understand the concept of living separate lives. One on the inside, and one on the outside. My inside life was very clear and confident, but my outside life was one of frustration and persecution as everyone seemed to always doubt me in some way.

Other than the many difficult events previously endured, my childhood was pretty good. We lived in a rural area in the woods and were surrounded by trees, mountains, streams, deer, and peace. This environment is where I would have my first psychic encounter.

At the age of six I was outside wandering around in the woods myself. Yep, that's right, a six-year-old wandering off alone in the woods. I ended up a bit too far from home and became confused as to where I was. I was officially lost and certainly entitled to a major panic. But I did not. Instead, I just stood very still and quiet and looked around. In front of me walked a beautiful little deer, about my size. We looked at each other, wondering if one or the other of us should be afraid. While watching the deer, I thought in my mind, "Help I'm lost." The deer then pointed her head around in a certain direction. She turned and looked at me again. Then she turned her head and looked in that same direction again. Then she calmly walked away. I decided to walk in the direction the deer had twice pointed. A very short distance away, I found myself in my back yard where I had started. That was lesson #1 in being completely open, observant, and listening for signs from the Universe.

I did not say anything to my mother or anyone else about the incident. I was afraid my mother would be mad I got lost, and I knew she would dismiss my interaction with the deer. How many little kids experience such innocent psychic events, but never talk about them, or if they do, they are dismissed as silly? How many adults experience such things but never speak of them for fear of being mocked? I feel humans are capable of so much more if we open our senses, but our society has basically beaten it out of us. This conditioning begins early on when we dismiss our children's intuitive experiences.

In addition to nature, I loved my rural elementary school and my teachers. Contrary to the earlier belief that I was an idiot with scissors and should delay school, I actually excelled in school. I loved the sensation of learning, improving, growing, and succeeding. I was somewhat competitive and always wanted to do as well or better than my classmates. School became a very good structured life for me. However, I was about to have my next episode of heartbreak.

My mother had developed a relationship with a man named Brad. Brad was a military veteran and I think he may have had some emotional issues, but Brad was very nice. His hobby was car racing. He owned his own little green convertible race car that we would take to regional amateur racetrack events. He usually lost, but the one time he actually won, during his victory lap he saw me sitting atop the hill above the track watching. Much to my surprise, he waved at me during his victory lap. Due to his taking his hand off the steering wheel to do this, he lost control of the car and it started spinning and spinning and spinning. Somehow, he managed to not hit anything. He straightened it out and continued onward without missing a beat. Brad will never know how much that wave meant to me. It stayed in my heart forever and can still illicit a tear from deep inside my heart.

I felt Brad loved me. For the first time ever, I felt like I was in a real family with a mommy AND a daddy. But Brad was having problems. His car mechanic shop business was failing financially. Soon he had to close the shop, and he was unemployed. He spent months trying to find a job with no success. I think he began to feel like he had failed my mother and I and he grew very despondent and depressed.

One day my mom and I got home from town and Brad was not there as expected. There was only a note left on the kitchen table that said, "Be back tomorrow. Brad." But Brad never came back the next day. Or the next day. Or the next day. Every day for weeks I would pray that today was the day Brad would come back home. What could he possibly be doing? Each day that Fall, I got home with my mom from town and more leaves were on the ground, but still no Brad. My heart sunk more and more each day. I started to wonder if maybe Brad did not love us anymore? Did I do something wrong to upset him? Maybe he did not love me that much after all and found a better family to be with? Nothing but questions swirling in my worried little mind.

One night while I was sleeping, my mother received a knock on the door of our trailer home from a state trooper. He gave her devastating news. The next morning when I woke up, I found my mother and her closest friends sitting in the living room very solemn as if they were waiting for me to wake up. My mom took me to the living room couch and held me on her lap. She said to me "Brad is never coming back. Brad is gone." And my mom started crying. I asked, "What do you mean? Where is he?" My mom replied, "Brad is in heaven and can't come back." I only remember having an absolute total breakdown and crying uncontrollably for what could have been hours while my mom's best friends watched with horror.

Brad had apparently been found in the woods far away in the mountains. He had set up a tent and backed his car up to the tent so that the engine exhaust went directly into the tent. There was no further note, but it was obvious what had happened. And yes, it apparently took weeks before he was discovered and identified.

This was my first personal connection with death and suicide. I understood death, but suicide was more confusing to me. All I wanted all along was for Brad to come home. I did not care if he never got a job. I was angry that he left me just because he was frustrated with his life. But of course, I also did not understand the pain he must have been living with. That's the thing with suicide. Those left behind are angry that the person was selfish and left in such a manner. But people do not realize how much intense pain a suicidal person feels. It would not be until later in life that I truly understood both sides of the fence.

After Brad's death, I would hear my mom late at night in her room crying for an hour before she went to bed. I think she was holding his ashes because I know for the longest time, she kept his ashes next to her bed. I never went to my mom or said anything about it. I would just lie completely still in bed with eyes wide open listening to my mother cry and cry and hoping she would go to sleep soon.

In an effort to try and help me process Brad's death, my mother, bless her heart, put me into counseling. My counselor was this really nice lady who would put a toy in front of me that I had no interest in, and then would ask me probing questions about Brad's death. I knew what she was doing, and it felt pointless to me. I would say things like, "Yeah Brad is dead, what do you want to know?" She would ask things like, "But how do you feel about his death?" I would reply with things like, "Whatever." The truth is that I had processed Brad's death as part of my nightmare life and integrated it into who I was and moved on. I remember thinking how it was MY MOTHER who needed the counseling, not me. But I cannot fault my mom for doing the right thing and making sure I was okay. But I was okay. Actually, I wasn't okay.

But I was.

Also, as part of our emotional recovery, my mom started getting involved with our church. In an effort to get me involved, my mom enrolled me in the church choir. There was only one problem. I could not sing. I sounded like something resembling the cross between a frog and a distressed cat. But I soon learned that the children's choir consisted of the two kids who really could actually sing, plus several others who could carry a good tune, then the rest were those like me who could be buried into the crowd without causing too much damage.

I kind of enjoyed the choir actually. I was participating with one of my best friends at the time and it gave me something to do a couple times a week, and I kind of liked "performing." But one day on a very hot Palm Sunday, we were singing our performance in front of the entire church, and I started to feel crappy. I just kept singing, but then all of a sudden, I saw black snow in my eyes, and everything went black. Apparently, there was a very loud THUD when I fainted and dropped to the floor with nobody even attempting to break my fall. I woke up on the floor with people looking down at me. I quickly realized what had happened and I was more embarrassed and mortified than I had ever been in my life. They took me outside to get some air. I was sitting on the granite steps outside with my head between my knees and thinking I could never go back in there again. And I never did. So that was the end of the church choir for me.

Eventually my mom started dating again. She ended up dating a man named Dave. I think she very quickly fell for Dave and I could tell there was a romance blooming. I was not ready for this. I was still heartbroken about Brad deep down, and I had gotten used to it being just my mother and me. I had become the man of the house and I liked that. So now this new guy is going to waltz in here like he owns the place? I think not!

Do not get me wrong, Dave seemed like a nice guy. I had no problem with Dave personally. I was just having a reaction normal for a tween in my situation. But it did not take long for an incident to happen which doomed any chance of a good dynamic between Dave and I.

One night, Dave was leaving our home to go back to his mom's where he was staying since his divorce. My mom offered to give him one of her record albums she collected, as a nice gesture I am guessing. She happened to offer him one of my favorites at the time. I actually don't remember exactly which one it is, but I recall loving the album, and the album having special meaning to me. I immediately went into panic mode. That album meant a ton to me. I LOVED the music, and I identified that album and music with our time with Brad. Perhaps that album was my remaining link to Brad and that former life I missed. I interceded and insisted my mother not give away that album. My mom and Dave were both in complete shock that this obnoxious child would raise a hissy fit over my mom giving Dave a gift. Dave got super annoyed and refused to take the album. My mom got upset at me, I was upset at my mom, and Dave was annoyed at both of us. Dave left without the album. I assume he also left disliking me, and that would set the tone for years to come. My mom eventually married Dave and then I officially had a stepfather.

The situation with Dave was very unfortunate because it was an example of miscommunication. I did not dislike Dave, nor did I mind my mom giving him a gift. I just could not part with that specific item. Dave would have naturally felt I did not like him and was rejecting him. The entire situation could have been rectified if someone had asked me exactly what my problem was with this transaction. Nobody did.

By this time, I had grown into a tallish skinny weak string bean with a bowl haircut given by my mother to save money. We had established singing was not in my future, along with any chance at sports, which might require any strength or coordination, because I had neither. Being in fourth grade, we were encouraged at school to play an instrument. I decided on the trumpet. I sucked at it. Then I tried the guitar for an entire month and sucked at that too. After those fails, I took a break from extracurricular activities. But when I entered middle school, I decided to try out for the school play. The English teacher was in charge of the play and I think she was surprised I wanted to try out for it. She knew me as a shy quiet studious child who got top grades, but never wanted to participate in discussions. I was not the type of kid who would do well in a school play. So, at the time of auditions, she got to my turn and said to me in an amused condescending way, knowing there was no way I could do this acting stuff, she said to me "Act like an obnoxious spoiled brat." She and everyone present just froze and there was dead silence in the room as they were all waiting and wondering how shy little me was going to respond to this challenge. Despite not knowing what the audition would be, without hesitation, without thinking, I automatically fell to the floor in front of them all and started begging for candy. I acted as if they would not give me any candy. I then had the biggest damn hissy fit temper tantrum anyone in that school had ever seen. I was rolling around on the ground crying, begging, screaming, crying again, and causing total and complete mayhem. To this day, I have no idea where all that came from. But when I finished and cleared my eyes, I saw that half the people were laughing their asses off, and the other half had their mouths wide open in shock. I looked at the teacher and she had this look on her face as if she had just seen a two headed monster rising out of a fire like a phoenix. I got the part. I was the bratty child in "The Emperor Has No Clothes." A small part, but I was an underclassman and shy so that was fine. I LOVED performing in that play. A definite spark was lit. But after the play had done its final performance, my acting career was stuffed away in a box and would not come back out until many years later.

That one school play aside, I learned I needed to stick with academics. Academics were something I was great at. The kid who shouldn't start school on time because he was not developed enough and might be an idiot, was very soon getting straight A's. Somewhere during the process, I believe I may have set some sort of school record when I got straight A+'s without a single flaw for a full term. I graduated from 8th grade with the award for the "Highest Academic Average," and a second award, "Best Overall Student," or some such thing.

Academics were not the only thing I would be good at. Finally, after a very rough start, my stepfather Dave and I found our happy place together. Dave taught me how to hunt and fish. It turned out I loved outdoor sports and was a fast, eager learner. Hunting and fishing would soon become a major part of my life. All thanks to Dave.

One thing I was not good at was being a big brother. During middle school, Dave's son Richie moved in with us. Richie was a year younger than I was. Richie naturally had problems adjusting to the change. He was entering a family with an existing older dominant brother (me), and he was going to a new school where he had no friends. I remember Richie being alone at school at times, as well as acting out at home. Richie would get very competitive with me. I interpreted it as him being a snotty pain in the ass. But looking back, Richie just needed some attention and to find his place in his new world. I was ignorant to all this and his feelings at the time. So, as far as adapting to becoming a big brother, I give myself a failing grade. Sorry Richie.

With that said, I had grown into a young man who could hold his own in the outdoors, was unstoppable academically, and had my sights on becoming a medical doctor. By the time I had finished middle school, I had read the medical book *Grey's Anatomy*, and had memorized the name of every bone in the body. I had also shown aptitude for counseling. I was known as the "class counselor," as my fellow students would come to me for advice on all their personal problems. I quickly learned I could know everyone's secrets by being the class counselor, which made for some interesting entertainment because I was the only person who actually had the back-stories to all the classroom dramas.

I was a good kid. I was quiet, calm, very well mannered, kind, considerate, and I never broke a rule. I was a bit of a nerd, a prude, shy, but trustworthy, dependable, and smart. I often heard people comment to my mom at how lucky she was having an easy kid like me.

Girls did not like me much though. I was still too skinny, awkward, with a bowl haircut, and old clothes with pants that sometimes suggested a flood might be imminent. Some of the kids used to pick on me for how I looked, and this made me assume I was not terribly attractive.

I never had a girlfriend, and any attempts I made at chasing girls ended in failure. The *one* girlfriend I managed to procure ended up having her best friend call me and dump me. I was that kid everyone wanted for advice and friendship, but not for the fun stuff. This general trend would continue for much of my life.

CHAPTER TWO

High School

I entered high school with high confidence, infinite hopes, exciting anticipation, and total focus on achieving academically. In my mind, I was Pre-Med and was most certainly going to become a medical doctor. Even though I was only 14 years old, I was drop dead serious about it, and had been since I was a very young child. I was not looking to be social, not looking to party, and not looking for a girlfriend. Good thing, because I did none of those things my first couple years of high school.

I was taking all "Advanced Placement" classes, all available medical course electives, and I was getting straight A's across the board in everything. I was still overly skinny with a slightly less offensive bowl cut, but still out of fashion in both clothing and overall look. I recall it was my one and only ex-girlfriend from middle school (the one who had her friend dump me), that commented to me in 9th grade that I should start wearing the jeans that the cool kids were wearing. I did not consider her comment picking on me. I considered it a valid critique, which I totally ignored. I had grown up poor in the country and looks or fashion are not important in that culture. Perhaps in the city high school with tons of kids I should have placed more importance on looks and image? Correct hindsight answer is: Yes.

I wanted a well-rounded resume for college, so I joined the track team and cross country running team. This way I had a sport in the spring and one in the fall. Despite my asthma, I enjoyed running and embraced the two sports, committing to them for all four years. I would eventually "letter" in both sports, get my letter jacket, and would end up as a Team Captain in both sports.

The only other extracurricular activity I participated in was something called "The Leadership Project." It was a new pilot-program where a variety of kids from different social "cliques" were put together for workshops and social interaction. They looked for leaders within all the different cliques. Since I was a top student academically, student athlete, could still hang with the cool kids despite being a nerd, and also hung out with the nerds because I was one, I was an obvious choice, I guess. We had workshops on reaching out to kids from different backgrounds, and "at risk" kids. We were trained on how to tear down walls which divide us and extend a hand to those who might need it. They were basically trying to train an army of kids to step in and stop bullying, prevent suicide, curb school violence, and so on. We were to be kind of like a band of student counsellors. I loved the program and participated for as long as it was offered. It was in this program I fully realized that I truly enjoyed diversity of people and loved interacting with people of all types, colors, races, economic backgrounds, sexual orientations, and personalities. I realized my true "tribe" was actually those who could mix with anyone. The "interesting kids" were my tribe. It was not lost upon me that my mom had been the same way, in that she could hang with the smart kids, but also the fringe types. So perhaps I got that from her.

I loved my school and my teachers, and I think my teachers loved me. I was always present, had my assignments completed, was well prepared, always got an A on the test, and I started participating more in class. My prior extremely shy persona was changing to someone who was actually good at public speaking and presentations.

I used to give my Law and Debate teacher fits. I would argue with him about everything. You could say I took "Debate" too seriously, as I am sure he did not intend on me debating everything he said. But I loved pointing out mistakes he made or argue opposite sides of his argument just for fun. The Law and Debate classes truly came natural to me. I only had to be myself. I am sure he was glad to be rid of me, but I so deeply loved his classes and his patience in letting me stretch my mental legs in challenging him constantly. My mother always said I should have been a lawyer. She was probably right.

Mostly, I never got into trouble and was always quiet as a mouse in my other classes unless called upon. I was silent and intently paying attention in class because that was a crucial part of my learning process. I was never a reader. I did not like reading books, and therefore did not read books, including those required for class. This continued through all my years in high school. In fact, I think I only read about four books my entire four years of high school. Despite this, I still got straight A's. How did I do this? Well, I listened very carefully in class. Usually the teacher would talk about everything that would be on the test. Therefore, I listened and remembered every word. Before exams I would read the first and last page of each chapter. Then I would have a classmate give me a 3 minute debrief on the book. That's all I needed.

In return for classmates helping me in literature, I would help them in English writing class. Writing was always my strongest class. I would review their papers for errors before they turned them in. I was not very creative, so I was weak on fictional short stories, but great at essays, formal papers, and technical writing. However, I would certainly never even imagine or contemplate writing a book or being an author. For me, writing was just a form of communication in which you needed to be extremely clear and expressive.

During high school, my relationship with my stepbrother Richie remained detached as it had been. We were not as competitive and sniping at each other as we had been doing as younger kids, but I think it was still hard for Richie. Every kid wants to shine at something and gain the approval of their parents. It would have been difficult for him because I was one of the top students in the school and while Richie did fine at academics, it was not his gift. Richie was very into sports. He wanted to be a sports superstar. The only problem is that Richie was short and small. I think he tried basketball and did not make it, and that was devastating to him. I don't know for sure because I was too disengaged from him to be paying much attention. He also played Junior Varsity football, but again his size would limit his ability to thrive upward in that. Eventually Richie tried Track. This meant he was directly competing with me. I was older and more established on the team, but Richie took it seriously and worked hard. Eventually he ended up pretty equal to me, although in the track meet races, I would usually edge him out.

That is, until one day. On this particular day, I think our parents were able to make the track meet because it was a home meet. It was rare for one of our parents to make it to a track meet, so when they did it was special. I think this might have lit a fire under

Richie. During our race (one mile), Richie hung right behind me the entire time. But right toward the end, he started surging as hard as he could. I felt him coming up on me and I was not about to let him beat me. I had to keep him in his place, literally and figuratively, which I viewed as behind me. But Richie gave 110% while I was giving 100%. Our parents were watching, and he wanted it bad. He had something to prove. On the home stretch Richie and I were both running for our lives. It was a battle to the death. I was running as hard as I could. I just could not go any faster. Richie put in a final superhuman effort, and he was going past me. I was thinking... "Nooooooooooo." But there was no way to stop him, and he got me. He beat me. He won. My first instinct was to be pissed and embarrassed. I had never lost anything against him. But this time he beat me for sure. He was faster. He was better.

My parents did not say anything about it. Richie said nothing about it. Richie did not rub it in or anything. He won with dignity. You know what? I'm glad Richie won that race. He deserved it. He deserved to be better than me. He had finally proven it, and I'm glad he did. Richie and I never talked about this event, and I respect him for that, but I also respected him for beating me that day. Good for you Richie!! Cleary, I ended up being the one with the larger competitive issues, not Richie. And you know what else? Life would later serve Richie with greater success than me, and he deserved that as well.

In addition to my strong academics, I developed a strong work ethic outside of school as well. I had been spending my summers riding my bike five miles through the countryside, past dogs trying to bite me, all the way to my workplace, which was a natural garden center that sold various outdoor plants. My job was to do all the lawn mowing on the side of the hills. It was a really tough job. Just getting there was work, but then the lawn mowing and trimming on the side of a steep hill was not easy. My pay was $7/hour I believe.

However, my harshest work lesson would be dealt to me by Dave. Dave offered me an "opportunity" to make $20 if I would chop down the bee and snake infested jungle that was in front of our trailer home. $20 seemed enticing momentarily, and I agreed to do the job during those ten seconds of being momentarily enticed. I immediately regretted it. This job would take an entire day and I would have to face the snakes(garter), of which I was terrified. For this reason, I procrastinated doing the work. Dave checked with me a couple times, asking when I was going to do it. Then after even more time passed, Dave warned me that I better get to it. I still procrastinated. Finally, Dave lowered the hammer. He said not only would I do it now, but I would also do it for free. He cited that I agreed to do the job, and failed to do it as agreed, so that meant I would do it free of charge. Forcibly enslaved, I did the entire job that day. I did a great job also. He never paid me. I hated him for that. It must still sting because I remembered it, and put it in this book, right? That lesson would forever burn into my mind the importance and seriousness of work obligations. From then on, I took all my obligations in life seriously, sometimes to the extreme.

My first and only legitimate job would come mid high school. Yes, spoiler alert, this would be my only legitimate W-2 job I would ever hold in my entire life, up to this point today as I write this. It was at the local grocery store. Dave had his start in life by working at a grocery store when he was a kid, and had turned it into a successful career, working his way up the ladder. Dave started as a stock boy and ended up a Vice President within a major food wholesaler corporation. Thus, he encouraged me to try and get a job at this grocery store that he himself had worked at 100 years ago when dinosaurs roamed the earth.

So, I did. I was hired as a stock boy. Oh, how exciting. Not. The worst part of the job was the pay. It was minimum wage and a union shop. So, after taxes and union dues were taken out, there was barely enough money to pay for my cookies I bought at snack time. No joke. I literally spent my night's pay on my snack time there. I tried to make the best of it though. I had one of my friends from my nerd crowd working there with me, and we had lots of fun together. We would be like, "Oops, a bag of M&Ms "ripped" open, so I guess we need to eat the bag of M&Ms since it's garbage anyways." Yeah, we did that. Horrible, I know. It was boring work stocking shelves. They would pile cases and cases of product seven feet high on a dolly, and off you would go to enjoy hours of boredom stocking shelves.

Usually I worked slightly faster than a sloth. I figured as long as one of my arms was moving, it meant they were getting the value for which they were paying. Therefore, my arms moved slow and little, just like the pay. But one day the manager decided to make life interesting and have a contest. He set up a challenge to see which stock person in the store could stock the most cases of product in one hour. The prize was something stupid, but the challenge was intriguing to me. I loved a good challenge. I liked to prove I was the best. I wanted to be the best at everything, it did not matter what. With this particular challenge, I decided in my mind "GAME ON!" The staff loaded up my dolly along with everyone else's. The manager marked the time and yelled, "GO!" I took off with my dolly, as did the others. The sloth all of a sudden turned into a cheetah. I moved faster than anyone had ever seen me move. I had my mind working to organize which items went in which isles, and in what order to do which isles for the highest efficiency, and which items to stock first in each isle, and so forth. I had it all mapped out in my mind and my computer brain was processing constantly while my arms were moving in fast forward motion like a cheetah-octopus morphed into one. The hour went by fast and time was up. The manager was almost laughing because he could not believe I worked that fast. It turned out I did seventy-two cases in one hour, a store record. I would learn two years later that my store record was still standing, and the manager was still telling this story to those with the misfortune to work there years after me.

In case you are wondering, yes, the next day at work when there was no contest and life was back to normal, I immediately resumed sloth speed. I eventually got too bored and tired working, only to pay for my snack time, and I quit. Legitimate traditional jobs never suited me anyway. Adios.

In 10th grade, there would be a major shift in my life that would change most everything. We moved. My stepdad Dave had been doing great at his career and my parents were able to move us out of the trailer home in the woods, and into a middle-class house within an upper middle class neighborhood in the nicer town next door. I still went to the same high school, but it meant a new set of friends. Now I was more in the same fishpond as the cool kids and rich kids. I was still neither of those things, but I was now eligible to hang with them more freely, given where I lived. The department head of the high school athletic department actually lived in the house next door to us. In this neighborhood I would meet my best friend who would play a huge role in my life for years to come.

His name was Gary and he lived down the street. We had tons in common. He was a top student like me, a student athlete (but in baseball and football), and he loved hunting and fishing like me. He also had huge ambitions like me. These huge ambitions would bond us together. We spent endless hours hanging out, talking about our dreams, and all the things that best friends talk about.

Through my time and discussions with Gary, I started to feel my ambitions might be more money driven, or success driven. Maybe being a doctor was not what I really wanted. Maybe what I wanted was to get into business and become a wealthy kingpin in business. Real estate, naturally. It was all organic, and we talked each other into this ambition, career path, and life path. My other major concern regarding my path to becoming a medical doctor was that I did not see a way to get through medical school financially. My family did not have money, and the money for a top undergraduate school, then four more years of medical school, just seemed financially impossible. If I had known the money for medical school would have been there, I might have made a different choice, but at the time I saw no possible way forward.

Therefore, I formally changed my future plans and academic structure. No more medical classes, no more Latin. Instead, Gary and I both enrolled together into all the business and accounting classes. It was decided. We were both going to be successful, rich, and we were going to do it in real estate.

We started getting into motivational books and audio books. "Personal power" and "thinking positive" became our religion. We were training our young minds to only accept success. In this process, we were trying to reach out to very successful people for advice and mentorship. One of these efforts at making contacts would turn out to be interesting.

We wrote a letter to a man named Jack Canfield. We were asking for his advice on how to become successful. He ended up forwarding our letter to a man named Mark Victor Hansen. In case you have not heard of them, they both co-authored the "*Chicken Soup For the Soul*" series which ended up being one of the biggest selling book series of all time.

As it would have it, Mark Victor Hanson was going to be in our area an hour away, giving a paid motivational seminar at the corporate headquarters of a major real estate corporation. Mark Victor Hansen responded to our letter and was nice enough to invite us to his event where we could observe his seminar free of charge.

We obviously accepted the invitation with great gratitude and huge excitement. Gary and I put on our best suits and drove to the event in his old rusted out Toyota Corolla. We were graciously greeted by Mark Victor Hansen himself, who shook our hands, welcomed us, and spent a few minutes chatting with us before his presentation. He said he was impressed by the two of us and felt we would be successful if we stay determined and never gave up. We sat through his presentation wide-eyed and wide-eared, and it was amazing to us. We got a glimpse into a world of the ultra-successful and the attitudes that went with that. After the presentation, Mark Victor Hansen gave us, free of charge, a whole bag full of his audio books and regular books. We never saw or heard from him again, but I have to say, that was pretty generous of him, and it made a lasting impression on both me and Gary.

Gary and I were further motivated to focus and prepare for our futures. We decided our next step would be to take a real estate course so that we could end up with our real estate sales licenses. We enrolled in a local real estate course and went to this night class once each week. We never missed a class, and a couple months later we had completed it. We were now eligible to sit for the state real estate brokerage license. We were only 17, but there seemed to be no law preventing us from taking the state exam. We both sat for the state real estate exam, and both passed on our first try. I believe that made us the youngest to ever pass the exam at that time in our state.

All the while, we were both considering which University to attend. We had three criteria. First, we decided to go to the same University together since we planned on going into business together. Secondly, and the most important, it needed to be in an area where the hunting and fishing was excellent. Thirdly, and the least important of the three, it had to offer good business courses.

We settled on a state University in New England not too far from where we lived, but far enough that parents would not be popping in for visits often. Both of us were near the top of our class academically, with great well-rounded records. We were both easily accepted into "Early Decision" by the University. This meant the University accepted us before we even started our last semester of high school.

Due to this, we both slacked off our last semester of high school. I think I even got a C in Physics. A "C" for me was unheard of and blasphemous, but it no longer mattered. There were days I only stayed half the day and left. Other days I skipped all together. I was done. I was ready to move on in my life to the next step.

My last six months at home were really rough though. My relationship with my parents had deteriorated to "horrible." I would hide in my room whenever they were home and had zero contact with them unless it was totally necessary. The core issue was the fact my parents wanted me to join the military after graduation, and there was no way in hell I was going to do that. My parents viewed chasing a real estate fortune as stupid, foolhardy, and a waste of time and potential. They wanted me to follow a very traditional path; do at least four years in the military, get a free college education from that, and by the time I was 30, maybe get my first job in a cubicle someplace. Or, they also totally approved of me staying in the military for twenty years and collecting a pension. Either of those options worked for them.

I have to admit I actually brought part of this military problem onto myself. I had made the horrible mistake of taking the ASVAB exam. The ASVAB is an exam the military gives to test for aptitude. I only took the test because it was offered, I was bored, and I love a challenge. Huge mistake!!

I took the ASVAB and scored in the 98th percentile. They never told me my actual score, or I don't remember. But they told me I had scored higher than 98% of everyone who takes the exam. That's all I know. This exam result meant I had military recruiters calling my house on a weekly basis for months. My mother would take some of the calls, and I would take some of the calls. I tried to explain to the recruiters I had already been accepted into a University and was going into business as well. But then my mother would tell them I was still interested in the military. I had recruiters asking, begging, and asking again, what I wanted to do. Did I want to drive tanks? Fly jets? Fly helicopters? "Just name it kid." Ugh. I did not want any of that. They never gave up until I had totally left home for college.

This conflict regarding my future plans would get nasty between me and my parents. They started to threaten they would kick me out of the house if I did not secure a military future or get a traditional job. Some of what they said was actually confusing and conflicting, and I still don't understand some of their logic to this day. But they harassed me, tortured me, and if I am to be honest, they were emotionally abusive about it all. I started to become very depressed and upset. I seriously contemplated running away, but I could not reason through how I would do it, and where I would go. I obviously had to finish out my high school year and needed a place to sleep and food to eat.

To this day, I am very sympathetic to teens who suffer from any kind of emotional abuse, including threats by their parents to throw them out of the house. This does absolutely NOTHING to empower your child to make good choices. All it does is cause your child to hate you, give them major anxiety issues, and make them more likely to rebel or even seek solace in substance abuse. Parents, please stop doing this to your kids.

At any rate, I think my depression and attempts at always staying out of the house made them suspicious I was taking drugs. They actually accused me of smoking pot with Gary because one night I came home from the movies and they asked me what movie I saw. I told them I was not sure and forgot. What I meant by that answer was, "It's none of your business, leave me alone." But they interpreted my answer as me lying, and I was probably smoking pot or doing drugs instead of watching a movie. The truth is that I have never smoked pot. Ever. I have never done drugs. Ever. I never had alcohol, except for a few experimentations in middle school. To this day I have never smoked or done drugs of any kind, and I don't drink. But my parents were off the rails and really kind of mean in my view, during this time. To be fair, my parents have always been really good people and raised me with a very strong moral backbone, but them being parents at such a young age themselves, I think made them not entirely equipped to ride the fine line between love and discipline. Somehow, I survived the last six months though, and it would not be long before I would leave home for good.

Despite screwing off during my entire final semester, I still graduated near the top of my class, with Honors. I would also graduate as a virgin. Not only that, but I likely set some sort of record by the fact that in my entire four years of high school, I never once had a girlfriend. I never went to Prom. I was a total prude. I was 100% focused on school and my future success. My focus was like a powerful laser beam that could not be broken. My focus and persistence would be the secret to my success in the future though.

Due to my family problems, and Gary and I being excited to start our futures, we decided to leave home and move to our college town right after graduation. While my parents had finally indicated they would pay my college tuition and books, they would not pay for anything else. I would have to find a way to pay rent and food on my own. I had no plan for this, but having no plan never stops an eighteen-year-old. Thus, I was still set on moving out quickly.

But my parents surprised me. By the way, this behavior on my parent's part of detaching from me, leaving me for dead, but then jumping in to save the day, would continue my entire life as you will see. Anyway, one day my parents called me out of my room. I was naturally assuming they were going to yell at me or make me feel like crap for something again. Instead, they simply presented me with a check for I think $2,000 and said, "Good Luck." I was stunned. Finally, a show of support. Probably the first sign of support I had seen from them in over a year. Thank God! I needed that. So that $2,000 would get me up to my new town, my new home, my first apartment, and food.

The day came. I loaded up my old broken-down Chrysler that barely had any brakes. I stuffed all my needed things in large garbage bags and stuffed my car with as much as it would hold. I hugged my parents and said goodbye. I drove off in my deteriorating car full of garbage bags of personal treasures, and never lived at home again.

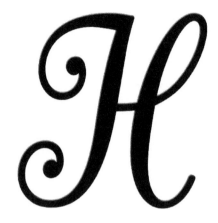

CHAPTER THREE
University Of Life

Gary and I left behind our childhood years, and each drove our cars up the highway into our adult years. After a few hours' drive, we arrived at our college town where we would start our new lives.

We rented a "student apartment" from a local attorney who was very reluctant to rent to us because he was afraid we would tear the place apart, being two young guys on our own for the first time. I think that is what "student apartments" are for, yes? Obviously, the attorney did not have a full appreciation for the fact that both Gary and I were top academic students who never partied or drank. This attorney read us the riot act as he gave us the keys, and I recall him looking down on us in a very skeptical condescending way. This same attorney would end up being one of many attorneys who would work for me in a few years, but let's not jump ahead.

We "moved into" our apartment with our garbage bags full of belongings. The apartment was a very old, empty, stripped down shell of a place that was held together solely by a fresh coat of paint. It was barely adequate. We laughed at the thought the lawyer-landlord was worried we might tear the place apart? Tear what apart? Tear the toilet seat off the toilet? There was nothing to tear apart.

We had no furniture, no beds, no nothing. Thus, we settled in within fifteen minutes. We had sleeping bags and a toaster. Our meals consisted of bread, marshmallow fluff, pizza, and McDonalds.

We also had a roommate. A huge scary spider. Rather than killing it, we made a joke of it. We named him (or her) Spidersei (pronounced Spider say). Spidersei would usually hang out in the bathroom but was seen outside the bathroom a few times as well. I am not sure why we did not just get rid of it because I am terrified of spiders, but I think we were so amazed that any creature could actually live inside this dwelling or would want to live in this dwelling. So, we felt a kinship with Spidersei and let him live. Incidentally, Spidersei ended up surviving our tenancy and was still there when we moved out of the apartment.

Fortunately, we were not in that place long. Gary's parents were fairly well off and had plans to buy a mobile home in a nice mobile home park for us to live in during our college years. So before long we were moving into a really nice two bedroom and two bath mobile home in a nice community. I was to pay $200/month rent, which was overly generous of Gary's parents, but they knew I was sort of on my own and did not have any money. We would spend all four college years in this mobile home.

After we were settled into our permanent home there, we needed to focus on starting our great adventurous careers of getting rich in real estate. We also needed to earn some money for food. We looked at the local real estate agencies and decided to approach the largest and most successful agency in the area, to see if they would accept us as sales agents. The owner of the real estate agency was Mr. Dawes. He was a very important and powerful businessperson in the community. For some reason Mr. Dawes agreed to a meeting with us. We once again put on our best suits (our only suits) and met with Mr. Dawes. Mr. Dawes was amazingly kind. He listened intently to our dreams and offered us an idea. He informed us that although we had passed the real estate exam in our home state, we would need to start over again in this new state. We would need to take the real estate course again, and then sit for that state's exam. But he said in the meantime, we could offer services to his existing agents. Perhaps we could take pictures of properties, do water tests, get copies of keys, and things like that, to make money while we worked to get our licenses in that state.

So that's what we did. We would show up to work at the agency every morning at 8AM and do errands for anyone who would ask. I recall getting copies of a key for $5, taking pictures of houses for $20, and things like that. So, at the end of the day we would be lucky to have a few bucks, and then me and Gary would have to split that between us. Basically, we were working for pennies and it was pointless. But it did not matter because the whole idea was for us to get our real estate licenses and start working at this agency as sales agents.

We enrolled in the very next real estate course available, and it was not long before we completed it, and then sat for the state exam. We both passed the state exam and were licensed real estate agents with Mr. Dawes agency.

Right about the same time, our classes at University started. Both Gary and I were Finance majors, but we had very different schedules. My schedule for most of those years was that

I would wake up at 5:00AM and go for my run around the mobile home park, trying to dodge the skunks that would still be out that early. I would then drive up to University for my first class at 8:00AM. I would have two or three classes, and then drive down to the real estate agency for lunch and for a couple hours of working. Then I would drive back up to University in the afternoon for two classes. At the end of the school day I would drive back to the real estate agency for a couple more hours of work. I would head home around 8:00PM, and then Gary and I would have dinner together and catch up on everything. I'd be sleeping before 10:00PM, and then do it all again the next day. Weekends we would both work at the agency all day, both days, together. The only time we ever took off was during deer hunting season when we would go hunting together on the weekends.

We slowly built our real estate sales business. Gary and I would get separate clients and work separately, but we supported each other and split the profits we each got. So, I would make a sale and give half to him, and he would make a sale and give half to me. It was a very slow and difficult process to build our sales business. We were new to the area, had no contacts, had no social connections, and many clients were nervous that we were too young. So basically, if you take all the things you want and need in a real estate salesperson, we had none of those things. Thus, we were not very successful and barely made enough to survive.

There was a pattern starting to emerge with my and Gary's talents though, that we would start to take advantage of. I was especially good at getting listings; meaning I would work with sellers. I was very professional, efficient, administrative in nature, focused, and could make a very good presentation. Gary on the other hand, was more of a people person. Gary, who was "Most Popular" and "Best Dressed" in high school, was more likeable than I was, and was great with people. Therefore, Gary was great at working with buyers. We started dividing the work that way, and it seemed to work better for us.

We worked and learned the business in this way for a few years, while also working to earn our college degrees. We ended up taking summer University classes in hopes we could graduate early. It worked. After only three and a half years, we both qualified for graduation and our degrees.

Did those three and a half years go by too quickly you think? Did you want to hear about all the college parties I went to? You wanted to hear about all the sexual conquests I had? You wanted to hear about all the fun I had? Well, I have nothing to write because none of those things ever happened. Go back to the paragraph of my daily schedule and imagine rinse and repeat for three and a half years. I had no "college experience." I sacrificed all that for my attempts at building my real estate empire.

So yes, I graduated from the University with my four-year degree in Business with my Major in Finance. Along the way, I also ended up taking some psychology courses because I was genuinely interested in that, and genuinely wanted to study psychology out of pure interest. So, I had unexpectedly worked toward a Minor in Psychology as well. And yes, after college graduation I was still a virgin. Yep.

It's not like I never had an opportunity. There was this one girl in one of my classes who I kind of liked. She was a bit loud for me, but she was pretty and seemed interested in me. We were working together on a group project and it was late and time to stop for the night. We had been having great conversation and were really getting along great. She asked if I would give her a ride home. I was a very nice polite naive young man, and I of course agreed to drive her home. So we drove the short distance to her apartment (which was easy walking distance for her), and there was this awkward moment in the car. I had stopped the car and put it in park. I was kind of waiting for her to say bye and get out. But she sat there for a moment. Then she kind of glanced down at my lap, then up at my face. I had a 1.7 second window to move in for a kiss I guess? But 1.7 seconds was not enough time for me to process what was going on. And the glance down at my lap??? I would not figure out what that was about until after I had gotten home and finally had the "ah ha" moment. Yep, I was that naive and pathetic. So, I missed my 1.7 second window and she was like, "Well, okay I guess I'll see you again," and she got out. Yeah. I know you are screaming at the page as you read this, and believe me, so am I. She never gave me another chance, and soon our class together ended.

Now that we no longer had University classes to contend with, Gary and I were ready to devote ourselves fully to real estate. One problem. It was not long before the General Manager of the real estate agency called a meeting with us and sat us down. The GM said our production was very low, and perhaps things were not working out for everyone. Were we being fired??? I asked him if Mr. Dawes was firing us. He hemmed and hawed and said not exactly, but that perhaps this was not the correct business for us, or the right agency, and maybe we should consider doing something else. Gary and I left the meeting not sure if we had just been fired or not.

Honestly, I think he fired us, but was hoping we would just pack our things and leave on our own, peacefully without official drama. Mr. Dawes was too nice a man, and I think took a liking to me, and therefore did not have the heart to outright fire us himself. I did not take the bait. I showed up for work the next day, same as always, and kept working as always. I pretended the entire conversation with the GM never happened. I remember the GM looking at me like "why are you still here," but I just ignored him and made sure I always looked super busy as if I was putting deals together. Pretty much I had been fired, but just refused to leave. For whatever reason, no further action was taken against us at that time.

Sales were indeed slow though, and therefore money was tight. Many times, I did not have my $200 in rent for Gary's parents and they let is slide. Let me just say for the record that Gary's parents were the nicest, most generous, accepting people to me. I was admittedly a drag on them, and they never complained or confronted me. They knew my relationship with my parents was not great, nor were my parents rich, and I was doing my best. They would certainly qualify as second parents to me from the last part of high school through college.

Regardless, the slow sales meant very little money for me. Gary had his parents helping him and always had plenty of food. I did not. For about a six-month period I ate nothing but oatmeal. I would buy those canisters of oatmeal and eat oatmeal mixed with brown sugar every meal. If I was lucky and had extra money, I might buy a pack of hotdogs for a treat, but that was rare.

Several months of only eating oatmeal took its toll on me. I think I was starting to not look very good or healthy. I was skinny, gaunt, and my eyes a bit dark and sunken. I recall my parents coming up for a rare visit and they saw me during this period. My mom made some comment that I was not looking that great. I told her I was eating nothing but oatmeal. Their reaction was something like "Oh that's too bad." My parents ended up leaving and going back home without doing anything about the situation they saw. The term "leaving me for dead" comes to mind. But you have to remember and understand, my parents whole deal all along was they felt pursuing this business idea was foolhardy, and I think they were still trying to have me suffer the consequences of my decision in regard to not taking their advice about going into the military. My parents have always been tough love people who believe in letting me "enjoy" the consequences of choices made. They were just repeating the patterns of how they were raised. Neither of them had it easy and also suffered on their own when they came of age.

With the real estate sales thing not making all our dreams come true, Gary and I decided to branch out and start doing our own real estate flipping. Don't laugh. Yes, we were penniless, but here is how we did it. We got a $4,000 loan from Gary's father. We purchased what appeared to be a useless vacant house lot on the side of a hill for that $4,000. It was a great deal though, because it was actually a legal buildable house lot. We sold the house lot for $15,000 by offering owner financing at a high interest rate. We then sold the mortgage note to another agent/investor in the office for $12,000, as a way of getting our cash out of the deal. For anyone not good at math, that left us with an $8,000 profit. We paid back the $4,000 loan to Gary's dad, and that left us with $4,000 in our pocket. Okay, please hold your laughter, but it's a start, okay?

For our next deal, we purchased an old, very rough mobile home inside a community outside of town, for $3,000. We fixed it up ourselves. We did all the painting, new flooring, and misc repairs ourselves. Gary was kind of handy, so Gary did the difficult stuff while I painted. We then sold the mobile home with owner financing for $13,500. We sold the installment note to the same investor as before, for $12,000. After about $1,000 in repair expenses, we were left with an $8,000 profit, free and clear. Pretty cool, yes? You might still be laughing, but that's okay.

Finally, we graduated up to a more civilized flipping deal. We went into partnership with that investor who had been buying our loan notes. The three of us bought a dumpy cottage, feet from the water at a nearby lake for $25,000. We all earned real estate commissions for buying it and put that money into the deal also.

The three of us did all the work to fix it up ourselves. Again, I was fairly useless, but was good for painting, helping, and cleaning. We sold the cottage a year later for $55,000. Much more respectable, yes?

Our next deal would be a more personal one. Gary and I convinced his parents to sell the mobile home we had been living in and invest in a duplex. So that's what we did. Gary and I moved into this huge duplex that we now all co-owned. Our unit had 9 rooms, 3 bedrooms, and a back office. It was really nice and very comfortable. We rented out the second unit upstairs, and it paid the mortgage.

However, as fate would have it, Gary ended up not living there with me. At the same time we were closing on this duplex, Gary had fallen in love with a woman he met at the real estate agency. He was very quickly living with her in her house. Poor Gary's parents had just made this purchase and their son was not even living there. That would be sorted out later of course. But Gary was in love and marriage was not far away. I would end up being his Best Man, and Gary was soon a married man with a life separate from mine.

All of this was fun and good, but one problem. Because we were spending so much time on our private deals and private lives, our real estate sales agent business was not doing any better. Our production with the agency had not increased. The General Manager of the agency called us in for another meeting. He gave us the same speech as before. This time he said, "So it looks like we will have to let you go." I took that to mean, "he might have to let us go *in the future*." So, I left that meeting simply ignoring him again. It worked last time, right? Well, it worked this time also. The GM had fired us for the second time, but again, I just refused to leave. If I am going to get fired, I will decide when I am getting fired and leaving, thank you very much. The GM ended up moving our desks to a very uncomfortable area out in the open as his way of trying to get rid of us. But it did not work because I just sat out in the open at my regular desk as always. He could have moved my desk out into the parking lot, and I would not have left until I was ready to leave.

The truth is that I was waiting for Mr. Dawes himself to fire me. If I was going to be fired, I wanted Mr. Dawes to look me in my young sweet chipmunk eyes and fire me himself. I wanted him to be looking me in the eyes while he stuck the knife into my chest. At that point, out of respect for him, I would have left immediately without protest. I respected Mr. Dawes so deeply. He was a kind man with true integrity. I considered him my mentor at that time, and a bit of a father figure because I looked up to him so much.

The harsh truth is that I sucked at sales. I should have been fired and needed to be fired. I learned a lot about sales. I learned that the top producers lie their asses off. They exaggerated everything, lied about some things, and were totally obnoxious about pursuing people. You literally had to be cringe worthy to be a top producer. No offense to top producers out there, but this is my story and I can speak truth as I see it. So, I knew I was not a salesperson. I was too honest, too polite, too idealistic, and really preferred the administrative end of things rather than hustling.

I had to do lots of thinking about what I wanted to do, and so did Gary. Gary was now married and did not like the instability of sales or operating a business with a fluctuating income. Gary wanted to go to work, get paid, and go home to his family. So, I knew both of us were starting to question where all this was heading, and I was pretty sure things were about to change.

It just so happened I had made a great contact with a development company. I was the listing sales agent for office space they were trying to lease. But instead of finding a tenant, they had just procured a buyer for their entire building complex. A huge bank was coming in and buying everything. The bank would also be hiring a ton of people to fill their new facility. My contact person with the development company was actually leaving the company to go to work for this bank in the newly acquired facility. I knew a position with this bank might be a perfect opportunity for Gary. I did not want to lose Gary as a business partner and see him go his own way, but I knew that is where it was headed anyway. Gary was my best friend and I cared for him and his welfare, so I decided to fall on my sword and hook him up with this banking connection. Immediately, Gary was hired by this bank. Gary had officially gone his own way and would go on to have an amazing career he still works at today. He would turn out to be amazingly successful, and lives in a mansion with his wife and kids, as we speak. I have no regrets. That was Gary's destiny, and I am happy for the small role I played in getting him on his way. Gary and I faded away from each other over time and we no longer stay in touch.

 Gary's departure left me on my own in a real estate sales job I was failing at. I felt Mr. Dawes was going to fire me soon, and I felt third time might be the charm for a successful firing. I did not want to give them the satisfaction; therefore, I made an epic decision that would impact my life forever. I decided to leave the agency and start my own real estate company.

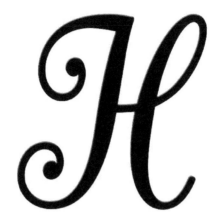

CHAPTER FOUR

Building An Empire

I had made my decision. I would leave Mr. Dawes agency. Through much contemplation and consideration, I figured out a niche for which I might be better suited. Property management. Property management was totally systematic, efficient, procedure driven, and administrative in nature. Those were all things I was good at. It fit my personality and comfort level much more closely than sales.

I decided to make my departure from the agency as beneficial as possible. I did not just simply leave. I made my announcement that I was leaving and let everyone know I would still be in the industry, and wanted to continue working with all of them, except in a property management capacity. Everyone was very supportive and happy for me, including Mr. Dawes. Well let's face it, Mr. Dawes was probably more relieved than anything else. He would finally get rid of me, but on good terms without having to stab me in the chest while looking into my young chipmunk eyes. The General Manager was happy and smug, but in his own way he was genuinely wishing me well.

I was hanging around the extra few weeks in an effort to drum up a base of business for my new enterprise. I wanted the other sales agents to turn over some of their multi-housing clients to me for management. It worked. I had several agents refer their multi-family clients over to me. Before I left the agency, I had a small handful of clients for my new business. Finally, on a Friday, I unceremoniously walked out of Mr. Dawes agency with my desk belongings. I left on my own terms, on the day of my choice, in the way I chose.

I set up shop in the backroom office of my duplex apartment. My big purchase was a small office photocopier. My other purchase was some specialized property management software. With that, I was off and running. But there was one other thing I needed before I got started.

I needed a cat. I had grown up with cats, and ever since I left for college, I could not have a cat because Gary was allergic to cats. But now with Gary gone, I could finally get a cat. YAY! Plus, I really needed a furry companion. Certainly, I was never going to have a girlfriend, Duh. I was also not a roommate kind of guy, other than Gary who had been my best friend, so another roommate to keep me company was not an option either. Thus, I needed a little friend to keep me company. I knew exactly what I wanted. I wanted a huge male grey Maine Coon cat. I loved huge cats, I loved how Maine Coon cats looked, and grey was my favorite color at the time. So, I searched the internet for my "made to order" cat. I got lucky and found a litter of grey Maine Coons that had just been born only one hour from me. I called the guy and immediately drove out to take a look at what he had.

What I saw in the big box he kept them in warmed my

heart. My eyes were immediately drawn to the biggest, fluffiest, most beautiful kitten in the box. He was sleeping with one of the other smaller kittens. I asked to hold the big one and I fell in love. I immediately decided he was my cat. He was way too young for me to take home yet, but I put down a deposit and sealed the deal.

Like any expectant father, I went out and bought everything I needed, such as a jumbo litter box, dishes, bowls, toys, food, and the whole nine yards. A few weeks later, I asked to come visit the little guy. It was still not time to take him home yet, but it was the weekend and I thought I would take a break and drive out and see my little baby. I arrived for my visit and saw my kitten had gotten much bigger. Oddly, he was still sleeping with the exact same smaller kitten as before. It seemed those two cats had bonded. The second one was a female and smaller, but very spunky and was trying to climb out of the box.

I was not looking for two cats, or a smaller female, but I had an idea. I called my mom. I told my mom how cute they both were together, and how cute the second kitten was. I somehow managed to hit the right button with my mom, and my mom agreed to take the second cat sight unseen. The two cats would be separated and not live together, but they could be reunited from time to time at our family gatherings.

When the time came, I picked up both kittens and brought them home. My cat, the male, was named Max. My mom's cat, the female, she named Graycee. My mom immediately came up and got Graycee. Now it was just me and Max. Best buddies. Max would become my companion and buddy for a good chunk of my life. He would grow up and mature into one of the most beautiful cats anyone had seen, with green eyes, amazing grey and white coloring, lynx tip ears, and the biggest, widest, fluffiest tail ever.

Now that I had my kitty, it was time to totally focus on my new business. The business became my life. I had nothing else. No friends, no family nearby, no social activities, no nothing, other than some hunting during hunting season. I was 100% completely focused on making my business a success. Not only was I depending on it to eat and survive, but it was my only hope at success. It was my big dream. This was my chance to build my own empire as I had always dreamed. I worked 7 days a week, from 8AM to 8PM. I did this every day, every week, every month, for a few years.

Whereas my progress at the sales agency went slow with little results, by new business was the exact opposite. I was getting new clients very quickly and building a very nice book of business. I had all kinds of properties I was managing, such as high-end single-family houses, duplexes, small apartment buildings, large apartment buildings, country homes, mobile homes, and mobile home parks. I was receiving a monthly fee for all these properties, but I was also receiving a lump sum fee for renting all the vacancies as needed.

Between the monthly fees, and the rental fees, I was earning more money than I ever had in my life. I was able to not only pay all my bills, but also buy extra things I wanted. I was living like a normal human for the first time ever. It was a good feeling. Pretty much everything went off without a hitch, except for one minor incident. Someone tried to murder me.

There was an apartment building I was taking over management on for an out of state owner. The building had been managed by some fly-by-night scam artist who had his daughter living in the building, and that is how he met the owners. The owners let the guy manage the building since it seemed like a good idea at the time. One problem. The guy was stealing all the rent money and allowing his daughter to live there for free. The owner was referred to me from a real estate agent in town who knew me from my work at Mr. Dawes agency. The owner of the building hired me to manage the building.

When I posted notices on all the tenant's doors that I was the new manager and all rent needed to come to me, I received an angry threatening call from this man, the former manager. He told me this was "his property" and I better back off. I could certainly understand why the man was upset. He had been taking all the rent money and his daughter had a free place to live. Obviously, the man did not want this sweet arrangement to end. I was firm and told the man he was terminated, and he could talk to the owner if he wanted.

There was a back and forth with this man for weeks. He was still trying to collect rent from tenants, his daughter was not paying rent, and he was being a nuisance. I continued to tighten my grip, had all tenants paying rent to me, and I issued an eviction for non-payment on the daughter who did not pay. The man somehow figured out where I lived. On several occasions I would wake up to find bags of trash spread all over my lawn. But it did not stop there. The man ended up calling and telling me that if I did not quit as manager of that building, he was going to "eliminate" me completely, and I would not be alive to manage any building at all.

At this point, it is safe to say he just threatened to kill me, yes? I started to become concerned and was a bit more paranoid and careful. One day I received a message from "a man," a "prospective renter," who wanted to see a very remote property I had available for rent. This property was located outside of town in the countryside. It had no immediate neighbors and was surrounded by woods, large bushes, and scrub brush. This person said they wanted to set up a time for me to show it to them.

I am not stupid, and I felt something was wrong. Plus, if you listened to the message carefully, it sounded like it could be the former manager man, as if he was holding a paper or something over the phone to distort his voice. I did not go on that showing. I would later hear a rumor from someone who knew the daughter, that the man had planned on meeting me there, shooting me with a handgun he had, then dumping my body in the woods where nobody would find me.

If you have never been in this situation, it's hard to explain how it makes you feel. But it's not really about fear. It's about anger and being violated, and no longer feeling free, because now you have to worry about being killed and can't live like a normal person. You are basically robbed of your freedom to live freely and relaxed. I reported this to the police, and they said without proof there was nothing they could do. I told them if the man were to come to my door, I was going to shoot him and kill him, and I just wanted it on the record that I was in this much danger. They told me to get a Protection Order so that if the man came to my door, I would have better legal coverage in case something happened. So, I did. I went to court and got a Protection Order. That night, I had bags of trash all over the lawn again. But that was the last I would ever hear of the man. Apparently, shortly after I won the Protection Order, he had fallen ill and either died or was too ill to be a factor. He was out of the picture. However, from then on, I was always a bit "aware" of things around me and always made security a consideration in my life. To this day, I don't readily disclose my whereabouts, travel plans, or personal information. People think I am paranoid and overly private. Yes, I am. But I call it being smart.

Besides that, one negative experience, most everything was going great. It was really hard work, but I was not afraid of hard work as long as there was a reward. It would not be long before I needed to expand my operations.

I had been subcontracting out all my maintenance work to various carpenters and contracting vendors. I had one of my independent carpenters, named Al, approach me and ask if I might consider hiring him full time. Al needed more solid consistent work and he thought if he got all my business, he would end up with more work, and I could also make money on the deal. I was scared. This would be the first employee I ever had in my life. What a huge responsibility. What if I did not have enough work for him? What if I lost money paying him? I agonized over the decision for a week, but ultimately accepted. We settled on an hourly wage for him and were off and running.

Turns out I had nothing to worry about. I had tons of work for Al. I kept Al very busy, and was able to bill out my maintenance services for far more than what I was paying Al. When I did not have enough maintenance work for him, I simply had him do the showings on the vacancies. My fledgling business was doing great, I already had one formal employee, and I was earning a nice income. But that was just the beginning.

Before too long, I would get my big breakthrough. Although I did all my own accounting for my business, I had a professional accountant do my taxes. I also had a friendship with my accountant, and we would contemplate doing real estate deals together while I often visited him at his office. My accountant had a close relationship with a small local bank. It turned out this local bank was going to be expanding. It was adding branches and was building a new large building for its corporate headquarters. The building was large enough for the bank, plus a couple of its investment affiliates, its primary law firm, and my accountant was invited to locate in the building as well.

My accountant was a smart guy and he had a couple things in mind. First, his operation was not big enough to take all the space the bank offered him. Secondly, he saw an opportunity for my company to do the management and maintenance of the building. He suggested that if I could get the management contract for the building that perhaps I could afford to locate my company offices in the bank and take the leftover space that was too big for him. I was nervous to obligate myself to a full-fledged professional office space with the rent that comes with it, but I kept open to it. I agreed to meet with the bank president about the prospect of my company providing services to his bank.

I went out and bought four custom made suits, new shirts, cuff links, ties, new shoes, and I transformed myself from a kid trying to start a business, to a man running a successful company. I would wear those nice suits and cuff links every day for years, from that day forward.

My accountant set up the meeting and I went to meet with the bank president, Mr. Bart. I was pretty nervous meeting with the bank president, but if I was going to have a big successful company of my own, I would have to get comfortable with such meetings. I went to the bank and met with Mr. Bart. It turned out Mr. Bart had already heard great things about me. We totally hit it off. He loved that I had the balls to start my own business at such a young age, that I busted my ass with endless hours every day, that I deer-hunted, that I was a straight shooter in conversation and presentation, and I was eager for bigger and better things. He told me he would be interested in giving my company a chance if I was willing to move into the new bank building to keep a closer eye on the bank's property. I gulped and agreed. This meeting and arrangement would turn out to be epic.

Not only did I get the management contract, but I also got the maintenance contract and the cleaning contract for the corporate headquarters. But that's not all. I also got the management, maintenance, and cleaning contracts for all their various branches as well. Not only that, but I received the management contract for their entire portfolio of bank owned foreclosure properties. This was amazing, but how was I going to do this with just myself and

Al?

I met with Al. Al was a real go-getter, and he was really smart. He was not just a carpenter. He was a smart guy who was presently stuck doing carpentry work. So, I rocked his world. I told him to go home and change into a suit because now he was Director of Operations of my company. I told him everything that was going on and that I needed to get fully staffed up. Fortunately, Al was more excited than scared.

We had some lead time before the big building was completed and before I had to start my contracts. I focused on preparing for the management, and I had AL prepare for the maintenance end of things. We both worked on the cleaning portion of the contracts together. We immediately started hiring people. I needed a couple maintenance people immediately just to replace Al. I was also still picking up new residential properties. I had to hire as fast as I could. Al was really efficient and great. It was not long before we had a lot of staff lined up.

I had done some structural changes to my "business" and turned it into a "company." I divided things into a Management Division, Maintenance Division, and Cleaning Division. I was the President of the company, Al was Director of Operations, and then we had a couple key right hand people for Al to lean on in running the maintenance and cleaning divisions.

The bank building opened, the bank moved in, and my company moved them in. We got the building running smoothly and the bank set up for opening. My company completed everything within deadline, and it was a great success. The bank president Mr. Bart was very impressed and amused I was able to put it all together without a hitch.

Around the same time, I moved my corporate offices into the bank with my accountant. I had to invest in all kinds of furniture and equipment, but it was not a problem. All I had to do was see the Vice President of the bank and I could secure any loan or funding I needed with just my signature. The bank was my income, and they knew it. Thus, they knew they had to give me what I needed to operate; and they knew I would pay them since they were paying me. It was a wonderful co-dependant symbiotic relationship.

My new corporate offices were really nice. I had designed the space myself, so it was built to my specifications. My personal office was huge. I had my giant cherry horseshoe desk at one end, a very nice long oval conference table in the middle of the room, and a huge entertainment center at the other end with a large TV, which always had CNBC running on it. I had windows lining the entire wall on one side, plenty of light, beautiful interior finishes, carpet, and woodwork. It was my dream office. Of course, I had other offices for Al, and a bookkeeper's office. I kept my maintenance division offices located at one of the rental properties we had because there were offices, garages, barns, and all the space I needed for the maintenance equipment and personnel we had.

All of a sudden, I was out of my backroom home office and driving into town at the bank for work every day. I made sure I was there early in the morning before Mr. Bart arrived, and would check the bank to be sure all was in order. I ran the place like it was my own home. I took pride in my job, and I loved my job.

My company continued to grow. I was picking up properties from other owners, investors, and even Mr. Dawes turned over some of his properties for me to manage and maintain. But my next big breakthrough would be when the bank expanded again. The bank ended up merging with another local bank that had lots of branches. I was lucky in that the other larger bank accepted to keep my company on with no changes. However, the change to me was that I now had twice as many bank branches to clean and maintain. I hired more staff to compensate.

However, I did have one bump in the road. Al had grown tired and unhappy in his job. It was very stressful and difficult, and he had other things he wanted to do in life. Al resigned. I was pretty shaken by this. I had grown to rely on him, and he had been with me since the beginning. He helped me build this company into what it was. But it's a free country and I had to wish Al well and wave goodbye. During his exit, we both decided to put his righthand man, Les into his job. Les was older and slower, but very solid, and a very nice man I loved dealing with. He had been with my company for a while and knew my systems and how I did things. So, I accepted Les as my second in command, and everyone moved up a notch below him. Les turned out to be very strong in making sure things got done, and at plugging holes, so he worked out great.

In all this chaos and success, I was able to indulge myself for the first time. My car at the time was an old car my parents had given me because my original car with no brakes had died. But this second car was also starting to have problems, so I decided to get a new vehicle. I simply drove to a local dealership, saw an expensive top of the line SUV I liked, took out my check-book, bought it, and drove away. Life was good. I had earned a reputation of being the youngest, most successful, self-made businessperson in the area.

Let's also not forget about the Cadbury Creme Egg incident. Back before something would make me fat just by looking at it, I used to have a fetish for those Cadbury Creme Eggs they sold only at Easter. So, I sent one of my people out to the local stores to buy up all the Cadbury eggs they could find. They returned with two giant boxes of eggs. I put them in my office closet, ate them, and gave them away whenever the occasion struck. The locals all wondered why our city had run out of Cadbury eggs. Well, mystery solved. Right here bitches! Those eggs lasted me a year by the way.

Business was not the only thing I would succeed at. One of my privileges was that I allowed myself plenty of time for deer hunting season. Before we discuss this, I ask that you indulge me. I know many are offended by hunting. But for me and others, it can be a very cultural thing when you grow up in a very rural area, in addition to a need for controlling the deer population. I do not want to put in spoilers, but my feelings about hunting would eventually change. So, for now, indulge me by hanging in there with my story.

With good management in place under me, I was able to take extended time off for hunting, which I loved. I would strike success many times by getting four different deer over the years that would end up in the state record books. My biggest one was listed at the time in the top twenty for the widest antler spread in the "Perfect" category. I became an accomplished hunter who let all the small ones go, and only took the biggest trophies (very mature deer). I would keep what meat I wanted and donate the rest to needy families.

I credit this extended time of hunting for my development in truly connecting to nature and learning to fully "tune in" and listen to nature. I would sit in the woods for many hours, motionless. I think once I actually sat for about eleven hours straight. I was able to develop a hypnotic state where I could close my eyes and still "see" everything around me. I would also listen for ANYTHING that might be a disturbance in the normal order of nature. Eventually, I was able to "feel" disturbances in the energy surrounding me and know something was coming. I learned to watch and listen to the birds, squirrels, and everything around me. It was an amazing experience and taught me to BECOME my environment. I still use all these skills today, even if my jungle is a concrete one.

Meanwhile, back at the office, my accountant and I were looking at buying some real estate together. We found a large mobile home park we wanted to buy. We marched down to the bank Vice President's office and secured our financing. We then were owners of a mobile home park. Rinse and repeat we bought a second one after that. The parks were great for me because not only was I part owner, but it also meant my company had the management and maintenance contracts.

My company continued to grow and expand even more. My maintenance division was starting to do small contracting jobs. We started building garages and doing full remodels. We were also starting to do huge renovation jobs on the bank's foreclosure properties.

One day, I saw the bank had given us a new foreclosure property to take care of. It was a huge house located right on the water, at the nicest most prestigious lake in the area. I was personally intrigued. Usually things like this never got my attention and I would just send my head maintenance guy to go look at it. But I was intrigued enough that I wanted to go look at it myself.

I took the drive, and what I found made me fall in love. It was a huge house, needing lots of renovations, on the best piece of land I had ever seen. The house was on a slight peninsula with lake views on three sides of the house. The owner, who the bank foreclosed on, was still moving things out. I was very nice to him and told him who I was, and why I was there. He said he just could not get his stuff out in time. I decided to be very nice and tell him I would give him more time and it was no problem. We chatted a bit. He explained that he had been into real estate big time doing development and contracting, but things went south, and he lost the support of his banks, and his whole company went bankrupt. He said he still owned the small cabin next door and would be living there with his son. I told him it was great he was still able to keep a place on this amazing spot. It was probably the friendliest foreclosure takeover in history because I left with him and me as friends.

I went into Mr. Bart's office and told him I personally looked at the property on the lake and I was in love. Mr. Bart said, "Then buy it." I told him I could never afford a property like that. He said, "Yes you can." I said, "No I can't." He said, "Yes you can." "And you will." "You are buying it." "Come see me tomorrow." I did not sleep much that night. I could never afford a property like that, but I loved it. It was my dream house.

I went back the next day to see Mr. Bart as he asked. Mr. Bart had drawn up paperwork selling me the house. He proposed a special financing deal to get me into it, along with funding for all the renovations. I looked at his deal and it indeed appeared doable. I shrugged and said to him, "You better not fire me after this." We laughed and signed the paperwork. I went back to my office and announced to everyone that the lake property was mine now and I had major renovations I needed done quickly. Jaws dropped.

I moved a crew of people over to my new house and had all kinds of work done. I turned it into a beautiful lake home. It had 3,500 square feet, 5 bedrooms, 3.5 baths, a glass room overlooking the lake, dining room, huge kitchen, sitting rooms, and an attached 4-car garage. I was in heaven. I had my dream house, all thanks to Mr. Bart, my official new mentor.

I was very relieved I had been so kind to the previous owner. He and his son, who was not much younger than me, were my neighbors and we got along great. His son Jo would become a great friend and many good times were going to be had.

I ended up selling the duplex for a large profit, thus getting Gary's parents out of that deal, and all their money back, plus some.

I soon bought a really nice ski speed boat, as well as the fastest customized Seadoo available. My modifications allowed me to dive under the water with it, and completely jump out of the water with it. I think the other inhabitants of the lake hated me, but I had a great time with it.

My house was a magnet. My parents started visiting more often. My relationship with my parents seemed to be fixed overnight with my success. They could no longer deny that I had made the correct decision. My stupid wasteful dream of building a real estate empire was maybe not so stupid and wasteful after all. I had a beautiful guest bedroom at the end of the house with the best view in the house always available and ready for them any time they wanted to visit. Not only were they invited, but all their friends were invited as well. We had many family gatherings and holidays there. I also got to see my stepbrother Richie more often since he would visit in the summer as well.

My house was also a chick magnet. In case you are still keeping score, yes, I was still a virgin at this point. I was all business and nothing else other than business. That's how I got to where I was at. But my neighbor and friend Jo certainly tried to change that. Jo would invite all kinds of friends and girls down to the house all the time. How it would work is Jo would invite people (everyone in town knew him), and they would start out at Jo's house next door. But then if they were cool, we might migrate to my house, play with my boats, have a campfire, or hang out in the glass room I had. Since I was still (and remain) a non-drinker, non-partier, we kept all their drinking and partying at Jo's house, and all the civilized fun at my house. I did not want my house trashed obviously, so only a select few would end up in my house.

We had an entire summer where I would get home from work and Jo would have all the plans laid out. He had certain people coming down for the evening, would start a campfire at his house, and then the festivities would begin. I would change my clothes, eat, and be ready for the evening. We might go out on my boat, hang out on my beach, or just stay at his house around the campfire. I think his thinking was that if there was a girl I liked, I could simply bring her back to my house alone, and no problems.

Jo tried everything. He tried all kinds of girls and situations and so forth. I can't explain why, but mostly I think I was worried about my reputation. I had a very dignified respected business reputation in the community, and I did not want to ruin it by seeming like a player, predator, whore, or user. Because of this, I always behaved myself. There were a couple girls I was attracted to. They were pretty, very nice, and easy for me to talk to. But when I mentioned to Jo that I was interested in them, he would start laughing and inform me they were lesbians. Sigh. This happened twice. I seemed to only be interested in the lesbians. What the hell is wrong with me?

So yeah. That summer would go by with me still being a virgin. And the next. And the next after that. I hope you are starting to feel sorry for me by now. But yeah, it was my own fault, as I was certainly marketable enough being wealthy, successful, having an amazing house, and with plenty of shiny toys, all at a very young age in my twenties.

One of the friends Jo would have down to the lake was a young guy who was the son of a local oil company empire. He and I became friends because we had Jo in common, but plus we had obvious common business interests. I ended up giving his family's oil company the heating oil contract for all my properties under management, including the banks. His company in turn, gave me the cleaning contract for all their offices in the state. It was the biggest growth spurt for my company since the bank's previous merger.

I obviously would spend winter in the house also. Winter was the complete opposite of the summer beach parties. During winter, I could go months without having any visitors. Most of the neighbors were seasonal and would be gone for the winter. Winter was a time of great isolation at the lake house. Sometimes I felt very vulnerable. Someone could break into my house and nobody would ever know it. Police or Fire could take an hour to respond if ever needed. For the most part I never had a problem. Until this one night.

It was the middle of winter, and very quiet and lonely. I went to bed early, as I usually did in the winter. Sometime in the middle of the night I was woken up by a noise. I had trained myself to wake up from the slightest noise in case anything weird ever happened. I opened my eyes and waited to hear another noise. What I heard was the sound of some banging downstairs. This was definitely something serious. I sat up in bed with the hair standing straight up on my neck. I heard more noises and a grunt. It sounded as if a person had crawled through a window and fell on the floor.

I was totally panicked inside. Frozen. I sat motionless unable to process what was actually happening. After several seconds, I got a grip and realized I needed to call 911. Just when I reached for the phone, I heard someone dialing my phone downstairs. I held off grabbing the phone because I did not want them to hear someone else on the line. Perhaps they thought nobody was home, and I wanted them to keep thinking that. I could then hear a man downstairs say, "Okay I got in." That was very alarming obviously. I presumed I was being robbed by someone very brazen.

While he was on the phone, I scooted over to my closet and grabbed my shotgun. I very quietly slid a couple shells inside the gun. While I knew he was standing next to the phone downstairs, I quietly crept down the upstairs hallway in my underway holding a loaded shotgun.

I decided I would stay upstairs and wait, but if he got to the bottom of the stairs, I would flip the light on and blow him away. I was freaked out that I was actually going to have to shoot someone, but I was totally ready to do it. I just needed him to step into the exact spot I had identified, and that's it. I turned the safety off and held the gun ready to shoot. Sure enough, he was walking over to the bottom of the stairs. When I saw his shadowy figure at the bottom of the stairs, I flipped the light on and screamed, "STOP!" I was just about to pull the trigger. But then I saw he was wearing the uniform of the heating company for my house.

I am pretty sure at this moment the man shat his pants, although I can't say for sure. He screamed. I immediately put my gun down and put the safety on. I told him it was okay, calm down, give me a minute, and I would be downstairs. I needed to go put my gun away and put something on other than just underwear. I glanced out the window that was previously out of reach and did indeed see his oil truck sitting outside. I laid the gun on the floor in my room and put some pants on.

I went downstairs and the man was hyperventilating. I was almost laughing. I told him I was not going to shoot him because I saw his uniform. But then I asked him why he broke into my house. The oil repairman explained that my heating unit alarm went off and informed them the heating unit had shut off. The man had driven 45 minutes to my house but had forgotten the key. Instead of driving all the way back for the key, he thought he would break in instead. They had thought I was not home because when they called, I did not answer. Well yeah, I had my ringer off at night.

The man fixed my heating unit, and I went back to bed. After that incident, the oil company always used that incident as a teaching moment in all their corporate training. Don't break into the customer's house.

However, the heating repairman would not be the only uninvited guest to join me in my home at night. My house was haunted. There were times I would smell an "old man smell," and could sense a presence. I was not too aware of my mediumship abilities at that point, but I naturally knew this was a spirit presence, and that I did not need to be afraid. I would ask the spirit to get out of my bedroom and stay out of my bedroom. I empathically made a deal with him that he could stay in the house if he stayed downstairs. Much to my surprise, he abided by our agreement. It was not long before I figured out who he was. One day Jo was showing me a picture of his grandfather, and I instantly knew that was the spirit I had been sensing. The energy pattern matched. His grandfather had built that house, and so it made sense he would still be there in spirit. After that, we always referred to that spirit as "Grampy."

Another incident at the lake house would leave me perplexed to this day. This incident also happened during the winter when I was completely isolated with no witnesses in the area.

As usual for wintertime there, I went to bed early, between 8:30PM and 9:00PM. I was feeling fine, was not ill, and nothing unusual was going on with me at the time. I think I must have fallen asleep fairly quickly. The next thing I remember, was waking up, opening my eyes, and seeing a huge bright flash of light outside my large picture window of my bedroom facing the lake. I had never seen a light like this before. It was huge and blinding. It was very momentary, and if I had opened my eyes a second later, I might have missed it.

Startled by the huge flash of light, I sat up and glanced at the clock. It was 10:02PM. I was expecting the clock to say 5:00AM or something like that. I felt like I had been sleeping all night. How could the clock be indicating I had only been sleeping for one hour? It was as if I was caught in some weird time warp. I sat in bed very confused. I was very disoriented, trying to figure out what the huge flash of light coming from the lake was, and why I felt like I had been sleeping all night, but had only been sleeping for one hour.

I ended up settling back down and falling asleep. I woke up at my normal time in the morning and went into the bathroom. When I got into the bathroom, I noticed something on my thumb. I took a closer look. There appeared to be a fresh puncture mark on the side of my thumb. It was on my right thumb, and it was a tiny needle puncture wound with no blood.

It was one of those situations where logically I knew nothing had happened, and I just brushed it aside. But intellectually, I knew something had happened. I had a puncture wound on my thumb, a very bright flash of light, and a weird time warp effect. Had I been abducted by aliens? Saying that sounds so ridiculous. All I can do is say what happened. That is what happened. You can draw your own conclusions. I obviously kept this incident private because I was a professional businessperson and did not want people to think I was crazy. Contrast that with now, where I don't care if everyone thinks I'm crazy, but let's not jump ahead.

Privately, I have always wondered what really happened. It was mind boggling. I am amazed at how this could have happened without me knowing anything. I can honestly say I had no negative effects and zero memory of anything. Whatever happened, it was done with amazing care and technology. I swept it all under the rug within my memory banks and went on with my normal life, focusing on my company.

There would be one more large growth spurt for my company, but it would be dicey. The bank was being bought out by a much larger bank yet again. This would be the second bank buyout I would endure. I was proactive and met with the bank president of the large bank buying out my current bank. They had heard of me and were willing to give me a chance. They kept me on and gave me the cleaning and maintenance contract for their bank branches and buildings, in addition to all I already had.

This meant I had properties all over the state. After absorbing all of those new properties, I had about 40 employees directly on my payroll, plus a bunch of independent contractors who worked for me. I had several attorneys working for me as well, including the one who rented Gary and me that first shithole when we arrived for college. I had a full-time bookkeeper/secretary working directly for me, plus my right hand Les, who had a couple right hand people under him. Then, all the maintenance and cleaning people, some of which I would never even meet.

It was a lot to keep track of, and I was starting to feel the weight of the world on my shoulders. I was very young for these responsibilities, and had not reached full emotional maturity, nor much experience or wisdom. I had become "too big to fail," in that if I did fail, my life would be ruined, everyone's life around me would be ruined, and it would be too destructive to imagine. For the most part, I kept up fine for a very long time. But once in a while, something would get past me.

I do remember one incident, where I was down in the bank lobby making a deposit and the bank branch manager came up to me smiling and whispered something in my ear. He whispered, "I am not concerned, but I just wanted to let you know that you are $50,000 overdrawn in one of your accounts." He told me he was not going to say anything, but since I was there in the lobby, he just wanted to give me a nudge. I was quite surprised by this news because I had no idea. Seriously. I was always so meticulous with my money and my accounts. I ran up to my office and looked at the situation on my computer. It turned out the bank Vice President was supposed to deposit some funds into my account for a real estate deal I was doing, but he deposited it into the wrong account. I marched back down to the lobby and immediately remedied the situation and told the branch manager I was no longer a deadbeat. He smiled and said, "Thanks."

I could pretty much get anything I wanted. My company had become well known and well respected, and thus I was well known and respected. My word was my bond, and I always met my obligations. I was iron clad with gold plating. I had gone from leaving home with a broken car full of trash bags of belongings, to building my own real estate empire as I had dreamed of in high school. I actually did it. I had arrived.

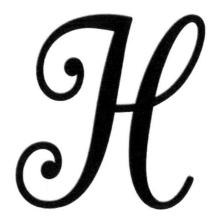

CHAPTER FIVE

She Rocks My World

In a relatively short period of time by the age of twenty-five, I had accomplished my life goal of building my own real estate company. I had my dream house, plenty of toys, and relative freedom to do what I wanted.

I know this sounds really great, but it actually created a problem. My situation pushed me into a "what now" mode of thinking. It was as if I had entered a mid-life crisis at the beginning of my life. I would sit at my huge desk in my beautiful office at the bank and stare at the walls as if I was bored. I would sit home in my house, stare out at the lake, and ask myself, "Is this it?" "Is this all there is?" "Do I just do this same thing for seventy more years, and then die?"

It began to feel a bit empty. Don't get me wrong, I was appreciative of my success, grateful, and I loved having money and all I had. But I had always been a person that strived for better, reaching for the next thing. My whole essence was about working toward goals. So, what goals would I work toward now? A bigger company? More clients? Another car or boat? None of that really impassioned me.

I kept going to work, doing my tasks, and going through the motions, but inside I was growing bored and scared that my life was over, and it would be Groundhog Day for all the many decades to come. So, I made a decision.

I decided to do something different and special to celebrate my success in life. I decided I would choose a place to travel to and stay there for the entire cold New England winter so I could contemplate life. I had good people who ran the day to day operations of my company. All of my work, which was mostly financial and phone-driven in nature, could be done from anywhere.

So where would I go? I quite randomly chose four locations to consider. The first was San Francisco because it had always fascinated me, I had never been, and the weather was mild. I considered Colorado because I had always been taken by the beautiful photos I had seen since I was a child; plus, Colorado has interesting weather where it gets snow, but lots of sun, and not as harsh as New England winters. Then there was Destin, Florida because my neighbor Jo was familiar with the area and said the beaches were amazing and I would love it. Finally, I considered Los Angeles because I had been there as a child and had fallen in love with it back then. In addition, LA had the attraction of being in the center of the Universe where literally anything is possible. (Yes, I know NYC people will disagree, so forgive me).

I did a good deal of research on each. I eliminated Colorado because this was supposed to be a warm weather vacation, so I wanted truly beautiful weather, not winter weather. I eliminated Florida because I was worried the area would not be big enough for me to really spread my wings, plus I hate humidity, which bothers my asthma. It came down to San Francisco or Los Angeles. I chose Los Angeles because it had better weather, as well as more appeal and possibilities to me. If I was going to take a leap and experience something new, I wanted to go big. It does not get much bigger than going from the woods of New England to Los Angeles.

In looking at Los Angeles, I had decided quickly and easily I wanted to be at the beach. I had remembered scenes from Bay Watch episodes, and that is what I wanted to see. I wanted to be there in those scenes with the beaches, life-guard shacks, roller skating paths, palm trees, and endless sunshine. So, I booked a hotel in a beautiful beach area south of the airport. I would stay in the hotel while I searched for a short-term rental for the entire winter.

During the process of researching LA, I used chat sites and bulletin boards to get people's opinions, thoughts, and information. On one of these chat groups I ended up conversing with a young woman who was also thinking of moving to LA. She was living in Minnesota, but wanted to move to LA. She was doing the same as me and trying to figure out exactly where she wanted to live in LA, or if she wanted to move there at all.

Her name was Luci (pronounced Lucy). She had recently gotten divorced from her first husband and was looking for a big change in her life. She worked in the medical field and already had an amazing job in Minnesota working at the Mayo Clinic. Having a great job was giving her doubts on moving, and she was on the fence as to what to do.

We totally hit it off and clicked immediately. She was so easy and fun to message with. It was not long before Luci wanted to move our conversations to the phone. I was nervous cause I had never really dated, and I was not sure how this all worked. Recall

I was pathetic and still a virgin. Luci and I started talking by phone; we got along great and had fun talking with each other. I started to work on her to try to convince her to go to LA at the same time I was going there. That way we could meet up and explore LA together, and it would be less scary and more fun. She agreed, and we coordinated our dates so that we would be there at the same time during my initial visit to find my rental for the winter.

I flew to LA and settled into my hotel not far from the beach. However, I actually had business to attend to. Believe it or not, I managed to find a way to turn this into a business trip, and I was interested in exploring opportunities to expand my business into LA. I thought I would love LA, and if I wanted to stay, I could justify staying by having a branch out in LA. So, I set up a meeting through a broker to meet with the owners of a huge real estate services company that were interested in selling off some of their service divisions. Buying one of these divisions might be the perfect way for me to get started in LA.

However, at the same time, I heard from Luci and she informed me she would be able to meet me (for the first time) on that same day. I could not cancel either of these engagements, so I felt I would have to manage somehow. I was not really sure what Luci's intentions were. Was she staying in a hotel nearby, or was she going to keep this a short visit and have to travel to a further part of LA where she was staying? What would we do for this first meeting? Questions, questions. I decided I would simply meet her and see what she said and go from there. Leave the ball in her court.

Luci called and told me she had arrived at my hotel. I went down to the lobby to greet her. I was very nervous, sweating, panting, shaking, and my stomach was in knots. She walked through the doors and I immediately knew it was her. I put my best calm smile on, and walked up to her and said, "Hello," and gave her a very awkward hug. She was smiling and full of sunshine, except I think her smile was real and not a nervous cover like mine.

I led her up to my room, which was room 345. It would have been super awkward since I had no idea what to talk about, except I had to inform her about my impending business meeting. So, I used my meeting as the icebreaker topic. I told her this was awkward, but I had to go to a meeting shortly and would be right back. I invited her to wait in my room and promised I would take her out for a proper date to include dinner after I got back.

I used the bathroom to change into my suit and told Luci to order any drinks or anything she wanted, and I would try to only be gone an hour. Okay, I realize this was stupid okay? It was rude for me to leave her there like that, and also to leave someone I had never met alone in my room with my luggage. She probably rooted through all my stuff to learn more about me. Fair enough.

I went to the meeting. After speaking with me, the owners were less interested in selling me only one division, and more interested in me buying into their entire company and becoming a full partner who would take over daily operations of their company since they were both aging and wanted to transition out. They only wanted $1 Million dollars from me to buy in. Oh, is that all? Are you sure that's all? Well, lucky for you I have my check-book with me today. Not. So, I tabled that discussion since clearly that was turning into a much bigger discussion than just an hour meeting. I scooted back to the hotel not much more than an hour later. Luci seemed comfortable and had made herself at home. She seemed relaxed and not annoyed. I told her I would change, and we could go out to eat.

I asked her what she wanted to eat. She asked me what I liked. I said anything, steak and Mexican is always good for me. Luci perked up and said "MEXICAN!" I said, "Perfect, Mexican is my favorite." So, we jumped into my black Mustang rental car, and I took her to a Mexican place I had seen right on the beach.

We found a comfortable booth to sit at and settled in. For the first time I actually had a chance to be fully "present," and really get a good look at Luci. The very first thing I noticed was her absolutely perfect teeth. Her teeth were not just perfectly white, but they were perfect in every way. She had a big smile to go with them as if to show them off. She had nice medium length hair that you could tell she had spent lots of time grooming. Her hair was auburn brown with some red tint mixed in. She had a nice olive skin tone. Luci was Hispanic. Her dad was Mexican and her mother Spanish. Oddly, she did not know how to speak Spanish or much about her culture though. She had been raised as "white" by her parents so that she would fit in better within her Chicago school system. Luci was short, but not fragile. You could tell she was in good shape and probably very strong for her size. She had a nice presence and was always ready to laugh. She was beautiful, glowing, and ready for prime time.

We enjoyed our dinner and talked as if we had always known each other. After dinner, we took a walk on the concrete walkway between the beach and the mansions. I remember she started taking my arm and my hand. I was quite shy and not sure how to act, but thankfully Luci sensed this and seemed to lead the way. It was getting late. The moon was shining, and the waves were gently crashing onto the shore. It was about as romantic as you could hope for. But we were getting tired and it was getting cool and brisk out, so we started walking back to the car. We slowly and reluctantly got back into the car, as we did not want the night to end, but knew it was time to go.

We returned to the hotel and back up to the room. I was not really sure what would happen next. Was Luci going to leave? Was she spending the night? There was one bed and we had barely met. We hadn't even kissed yet. Was she staying, but it was going to be a slumber party? Should I stay fully dressed? Should I stay way over on one side of the bed and make sure not to touch her so as to not seem aggressive? Again, questions, many questions. They were soon answered.

Luci was in the bathroom brushing her teeth and appeared to be getting ready for bed. Ummm, okay. So maybe I will go with the slumber party option. I decided to sleep in sweatpants, shirt, and behave myself on my side of the bed. Yes? Right? Yep, I was trying to be that nice "safe" guy, but this is why I was still a virgin though, right? Well it was decided anyway. I was going to remain pretty well dressed, and not touch her. I did not want to make her uncomfortable or overstep any boundaries.

She crawled into bed wearing her bedding wear, which consisted of some sort of silk top and shorts. She certainly was not naked, and definitely not showing much skin, so I felt I was pretty well on target with my assumption of a slumber party theory. I went into the bathroom and changed into my sweatpants and a big shirt. That should not scare her, right? I came out of the bathroom, she checked me out, and I wondered what she was thinking. I reluctantly and gently crawled into bed, being sure to not make any sudden movements which might alarm her. I stayed over on my side of the bed as much as possible without falling off.

We talked for a while with the TV on and it felt pretty normal and okay. Not too awkward really. But then she asked where the remote was, and I asked her if she wanted the TV off or a different channel. She said she wanted the TV off. I reached for the remote and turned the TV off. It was totally pitch dark in the room now. I laid on my back thinking there was zero chance of me actually falling asleep. For the first time in my life I was in bed with a girl and she seemed totally at ease with it. I obviously was not, but I did my best to play it cool.

I moved a few inches more to the middle just because being on the edge was uncomfortable. I was still just lying there on my back wondering if I would just stare at the ceiling all night. Luci then moved to the middle of the bed. She was now just a couple inches from me. After a few minutes, I felt a hand on my waist. Whose hand could that be?? It wasn't mine. Not only that, but the hand was moving. All around my waist and on top of my waist it was moving. It started to feel good. I just laid there motionless, partly as if frozen in terror, and partly as if I was getting a massage or something. Luci was obviously working on something, and she was making progress. Being a young guy in bed with a girl, nature started to work its magic quite quickly. A couple minutes later, Luci most certainly felt and noticed the sign, or green light she was looking for.

I may have been totally silent and motionless, but there are certain things a guy can't hide, and she had that firmly under her control in her hand. Before I could even decide what to do next, or whether I should take control now and do the "guy routine" as I figured it should go in my head, Luci was one step ahead of me. She somehow managed to do an amazing magic trick. She managed to take off all her clothes without me realizing it. At the same time, I noticed this, she flipped over on top of me in one fast fluid motion. She was like a lion mounting her prey. She was going to feast on me, and I had no control over it. I was clearly there for the ride. Oh, cancel that, it was actually *her* who was about to go for a ride. She pulled my sweatpants down swiftly and forcefully as if I was a tiny little weakling.

I then got to do the only masculine thing I had done during the whole process. I took my shirt off. Yes, I actually took the initiative to take my own shirt off without any prompting, and without Luci ripping it off, which I am sure was just about to happen.

A few seconds afterward, the powerful lion poised over her

prey, kind of took a moment as if she was deciding what part of me to devour first. Then she thrust herself on me and all the parts went exactly as they were intended to go without a hitch. And oh my God did it feel good. The powerful lion took her prey. She used her prey for everything she wanted. She squeezed out every bit of pleasure she wanted and used me in every way she chose. And like a hopeless prey being eaten by a lion, I just gave into it.

Eventually Luci flipped us both over so now I was on top of her. Was this woman a professional wrestler or something? I'm pretty sure she could have put me in any position she wanted, and done anything to me she wanted, and there would have been nothing I could have done about it. Not that I was complaining. I wasn't.

Now with me on top and totally worked up, finally male masculine nature took over for me without any over thinking necessary. With a tiny bit of assistance from Luci, everything went where it needed to be, and I went to work. Now it was my turn. My gauge of progress was based on her reactions and pleasure. I firmly gave her everything she seemed to love. I felt I was not going to last much longer because it was too intense. Thank goodness she seemed to explode in some sort of volcanic eruption, because three seconds later my eyes rolled back into my head so far I was not sure they would come back down; and my stomach and abs got so tight I felt they might permanently cramp. Over a decade of pent up virginity released in that one explosive moment.

Then it was over. I laid on top of her momentarily not sure what to do next. All I knew for sure is that I was exhausted and had done something that could not be undone. I rolled over on my side of the bed and no words were spoken. Luci got up and used the bathroom. While she did that, I attempted to retrieve my clothing which was partly crammed down at the foot of the bed under the covers, and the rest flung on the other side of the room. I managed to get my sweatpants back on before she came out of the bathroom. Not sure why that would matter, or why I would be embarrassed at that point, but it still seemed like the thing to do. I used the bathroom after her. When I came back out to the bed, Luci was sound asleep. I gently crawled back into bed and stared at the ceiling contemplating how I had not only lost my virginity, but Luci had ripped it from me like a savage beast. I was totally wiped out though, and it was not long before I also fell asleep.

We both woke up the next morning at the same time, the sun was bright, and it seemed so nice outside. Things were not awkward at all. It was amazing. It felt very natural. I took a shower, and then Luci took a shower. She did her makeup and hair, and we headed out for breakfast.

I was so relaxed with her that I turned the radio station onto Power 106, which is the best rap station in the world. I figured Luci would say something and I would have to shut it off, but why not try and see what happens. Luci surprised me and seemed to love the music. I asked her if she really liked rap, and she said, "Yeah I love it." That was it for me. That is the moment I was sold. I had this really pretty girl with perfect teeth, who was a savage lion in bed, who was totally cool, and loved rap music. SOLD.

Luci would turn out to have other positive points as well. She loved to cook for me, and I loved to eat. Luci and I loved to eat out, and we loved all the same restaurants and types of food. We also both loved to go shopping. That was Luci's moment when she said, "Do you really love shopping? Most guys hate it." I replied that I actually loved shopping. And that was true. I think that might have been her moment of "Wow this guy is cool, SOLD."

During this initial scouting trip, I was able to find a temporary rental for the winter. It was in the back end of a house owned by a nice middle-aged woman. I had my own guest suite and separate entrance, with parking. Perfect.

It was time to go back home though, and Luci and I had another fabulous evening before I went. I told her I would be back in a couple weeks to move into my new place. Luci agreed to do a bunch of shopping for me and buy sheets, towels, and basic things for my new place while I was back home in New England settling my affairs for the winter move. I thought that was super nice of her. I went back home glowing, and finally had my man card. I think most everyone back home felt I had changed, and something had happened.

After getting caught up with work and finalizing my winter trip, I was back in LA. Luci had also gotten a permanent place in LA, but in a different area. Mostly, I spent the nights at her place, then would drive back to my place in the morning, where I would spend the day working. Then I would drive back to her place in the evening.

It was a nice routine. Luci would cook us dinner, and then later we would go at it like rabbits. We would wake up in the morning and go our separate ways for the day. She had found a job and worked full time. Rinse and repeat this routine for three months.

At the end of my time in LA, I had decided I wanted to live there permanently. However, I also knew I had to go back home and resume my life and responsibilities. So, I put my things in storage and knew I could visit and stay at Luci's place when I wanted. But there was one thing I really did not want to leave behind. Luci. I had decided I did not want to go back to my lonely empty virgin-esque life, just running a company with nothing else in my life.

I decided to try and convince Luci to come back with me. I explained to her that she would not need to work. I had plenty of money to take care of her and any bills she would have. Luci, however, seemed reluctant to give up her job, her home, her car, and her own independent life. Who could blame her? But I had to try.

A few days later, I had an idea. I decided that I would buy her a "promise ring." It would not be a big expensive fancy engagement ring, but it would be a nice diamond ring to show her my eventual intentions. I had only known her a few months, so it seemed imprudent to get engaged, but I wanted to show her that with time, it could get there. I wanted to make her feel more comfortable about giving up her life and coming back with me. I explained to her that I could reorganize my affairs, and perhaps we would eventually move to LA, or go back and forth.

I got the ring and kept it in my pocket for the right moment. I was not sure when that right moment would be, but I knew I would recognize it when it arrived. That moment would arrive very quickly.

Pretty much the next day when I went back to Luci's for the evening, I brought the topic up of her moving back with me. Time was getting short. I had to go back in a week. The discussion turned into an argument. She seemed very resistant. She finally boiled over and for the first time since I met her, she showed me that hot spicy Hispanic Luci attitude that was apparently hidden from me up until now. She said she was not going to just give up her life because some guy did not want to be alone. She said she would only go if there was a commitment. I said I would give her a commitment. She then looked at me and screamed, "THEN WHERE IS MY FUCKING RING?" I paused, totally shocked at her, umm, attitude and language. But I had an ace up my sleeve, and I have always loved playing my aces. So, I replied, "It's in my pocket." She looked at me, amused by my response, but not believing me. I then slowly took the ring out of my pocket. I extended the ring to her and said, "Here is your fucking ring." She looked shocked.

But here is the thing. I had intended to give it to her as a "promise ring," right? But Luci took the ring as an "engagement ring." I had all kinds of things going through my head, but I was also partly scared of her now, and did not dare bring the "promise ring" thing up. I instead said, "I know it's not a fancy ring, but it's all I could come up with on such short notice." But the truth is that it was actually a very nice diamond ring anyway, I guess. And so, it became an engagement ring, just like that.

No date was set, but she had her commitment. I don't even think she said yes. But she took it and said, "Well okay, I'm going to be your problem now then." Holy shit, truer words have never been spoken, but the proof of that is coming up later in the story.

Luci quit her job, gave her car to her father in San Diego, threw out all her large belongings, and put the rest into storage with my stuff. I got another plane ticket, and off to my home back east we went.

During the plane ride, I saw a moment of panic on Luci's face. I think she finally realized what she had done and was not liking it. I calmed her and told her it would be fine. I had more aces up my sleeve, such as my beautiful home on the lake. How could she not like it? We landed at my home airport. I had one of my employees bring my car to the airport for me, so we just jumped into my vehicle and started the thirty-minute drive home.

On the way home, Luci had a request. She told me the only thing in the world she needed right now was a Starbucks. Could I please stop at a Starbucks and she promised she would be fine! Uh oh. What Luci did not know was that there was still no Starbucks in my mostly rural area. I tried to break it to her gently. I told her there was not a Starbucks, but I could get her a coffee somewhere else no problem. Yikes. I think her head started spinning and might fly off her shoulders. She screamed, "THERE IS NO STARBUCKS???"

"HOW CAN YOU FUCKING LIVE SOMEPLACE WITH NO STARBUCKS!"

She had a total and complete meltdown. I think in that moment she felt she had totally fucked up coming here, but obviously it was way too late.

She told me never mind about coffee. She would just get something at my house when we got home. I didn't dare tell her that I had no coffee or coffee maker at my house. I did not drink coffee, so yeah.

We arrived home, and fortunately the ace up my sleeve worked. She was so amazed by my house and its location that all her anger and desire for coffee went away. She was excited to have arrived. She looked around the kitchen and told me everything would have to be changed around. I told her that it was her kitchen now, and she could do whatever she wanted. This seemed to satisfy her.

We went to bed that night and slept well. We woke up in the morning at the same time. However, we were not alone. Standing on top of Luci, staring at her, was my cat Max. Max was just standing on her chest staring at her like "What are you, and why are you here in MY house?" It was pretty hilarious. To be honest, I don't think Max was pleased at first. But whatever. Everyone had adjusting to do, including Max.

Luci actually adjusted well over time. You will recall she had grown up in Chicago, and lived in Minnesota, so she was okay with cold weather, rural areas, and that environment. She appreciated the lake, the beauty, the setting, and the house.

Luci still got to be Luci, in that she would go into town and get her nails and hair done whenever she wanted. She also got to go shopping whenever she wanted. She would spend three hours doing her hair and makeup, and then forty-five minutes driving into town, get her nails done, and then drive forty-five minutes back home. To me this was, umm, ridiculous. But Luci seemed to like it, so it was good with me.

I introduced Luci to my various company employees and neighborhood friends. They were not sure about her. I think they felt maybe she was a bit bitchy and too "city." I subconsciously took it all in, but ignored it because I had chosen Luci, and that's the end of it. Over time everyone accepted her though, including my parents. My parents came up to meet her and seemed caught off guard, as if they were expecting someone else, or a different type, or something. Maybe my parents were also put off by the whole "city" vibe Luci put out. But my parents accepted her.

After Luci settled in, we started discussing a wedding date. We decided to be practical. We would have the wedding at our home on the lake and do it in the summer when the weather would have the best chance of being the nicest. Luci went into planning mode and we had plenty of time to put it together.

In the meantime, we ended up taking trips back to LA for visits which we enjoyed very much. I think we both had decided we wanted to live in LA for sure. Thankfully, Luci understood my business responsibilities and that it would take time and work for me to get to the point where I could actually live in LA full time.

During the wedding planning period, Luci and my mom started to develop a very close bond. Even though my mom seemed caught off guard at first, she seemed to have decided she not only liked Luci, but she loved Luci. They became mother/daughter. This would later become a problem for me, but at this point it seemed like a very positive thing and I encouraged it.

The wedding was drawing closer. Since Luci kind of got the short end of the stick with the engagement ring that was just supposed to be a promise ring, I told her to choose whatever wedding band she wanted, and to make it fabulous. She chose an amazingly beautiful wedding band studded with diamonds all the way around. I enthusiastically agree to it because it was truly stunning. I let her plan whatever she wanted for the wedding. Really, my only requirement was that I wanted the ceremony at my home, on the beach by the lake, and that I did not want a huge expensive honeymoon because of all the traveling we had already been doing. She was fine with both requirements.

We decided on a very relaxed, open celebration that would last three days. The first day would be a formal dinner at a nearby restaurant/Inn with the wedding party and closest family. The second day would be the actual ceremony and would include all extended family and good friends. The third day would be a very informal beach party with a DJ, catering, and everyone would be invited, including neighbors, company employees, and anyone who knew me.

Luci comprised her wedding party to include her favorite sister and a couple close friends. Mine would consist mainly of Gary as my Best Man, my stepbrother Richie, and my neighbor Jo. We chose a neighbor to perform the ceremony and marry us. I had become good friends with a lesbian couple who lived in my neighborhood. Some shunned away from them because of their "lifestyle," but I loved them. One of them had become an ordained minister and could legally perform marriage ceremonies. So, for me, this was a no brainer. We asked her to do the ceremony and she enthusiastically agreed. My mom and Luci worked on many of the plans together, such as the flowers, cake, and details of the ceremony.

The wedding ceremony day arrived. I was nervous as hell, I won't lie. I spent most of the day pacing inside my home office with my Best Man, Gary, who attempted to keep me calm. I was pretty calm I suppose, it's just that I was nervous. Finally, it was time to walk out. It turned out to be a perfectly beautiful day with a tiny light breeze. Everyone was seated in white chairs on our beach and dressed so lovely. I was touched to see all my favorite people who had arrived to share this with us. It put me at ease. The music started and Luci came marching down in her beautiful white wedding gown she had chosen. Totally beautiful. Such a nice sleek, classy, modern wedding gown. She looked her best and totally amazing. Luci was beautiful on any day, but with the professional hair and makeup person we brought in for her, she was way over the top amazing. I was totally at ease now. I made it through the vows and ceremony without crying, puking, passing out, or running away. It was all good. We were pronounced man and wife, and we kissed. The deal was sealed. And so was my fate.

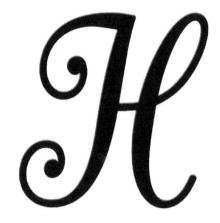

CHAPTER SIX

An Angel Is Born

After our wedding, Luci and I settled into normal married life. Our first priority was to get pregnant. Despite being a prudish nerd only focused on business, I had always wanted to have a child. I just did not see it happening before I met Luci, so I did not focus on it. But now that I was married, my dream came alive and I was totally excited about the prospect of being a father. I always felt awkward around kids, but I think I knew deep inside I would feel differently around a child of my own. Our efforts started in earnest, with no success.

While we were working on that, I had one important business task to complete. Mr. Bart, the bank president, had asked to meet with me. He explained to me that the bank was up for an audit by the regulators, and the loan he gave me to get me into the lake house might raise some questions. He said there was nothing illegal about it, but they might question whether the transaction was "arms-length," and the loan did not fit the criteria of the other bank mortgages in his portfolio. He asked me if I might be able to refinance the loan to get it out of their bank. My simple answer to him was, "Yes Sir."

Like Mr. Dawes, Mr. Bart was one of the few people I looked up to and respected like a mentor and father figure. He had done amazing things for me. He had pretty much made my company what it was, and he had delivered to me my dream house on a silver platter. I loved the man for all this and was fiercely loyal to him. Mr. Bart had a reputation in the bank as being grumpy, mean, and harsh. I remember one day I walked into his office and was chatting with him, and we both ended up laughing our asses off at something. When I walked out, the bank Vice President waved me into his office. He looked perplexed. Apparently, earlier that morning Mr. Bart had gone on a rampage in the office, destroying everyone in his path. The Vice President looked at me and said, "How the hell do you do it?" "How do you get him to laugh and be all happy in just five minutes?" I just shrugged and said it must be a magic touch. But the reality is that Mr. Bart liked me. I always did everything he said, and I did it with obedience and immediacy. Mr. Bart interpreted that as respect and professionalism, which is what he valued most.

Thus, I was intent on refinancing my house mortgage for Mr. Bart. I got right on it and within two months I had completed the transaction. I was able to refinance with a major national bank and was even able to pull some extra cash out to help pay for business equipment, and Luci's purses and shoes.

I went into Mr. Bart's office and informed him that his loan portfolio was free of my mortgage loan. He looked at me as if he was shocked I had actually done what he requested. He laughed and said, "Wow, that was fast." I replied, "You asked me to do it, so I did it; thank you for everything Sir." And I walked out. That was a typical scenario of how I always handled Mr. Bart, and probably why he liked me.

With that matter behind me, I was back focused on this baby making stuff. My mom was all over us about it, and it seemed like it was a top national priority. However, Luci was having trouble getting pregnant. Believe me, it was not for lack of trying. I was always good for morning, night, and whenever. Luci was fully cooperative herself. We ended up turning it into a science and monitoring her cycle and the optimum time for conception. During this four-day window we had figured out, we would go at it usually three times a day. After a few months, still no success.

It was December and my parents had invited us down to their home outside of Boston. My parents had bought tickets to the Boston Pops and invited us. Believe it or not, this rap boy was also into classical music, and especially the symphony. I enthusiastically wanted to go and Luci seemed to be into also. It was a perfect Christmas season activity. I blocked out my schedule, and we planned to drive the four hours to my parent's house, then we would all go into the city together for the concert the next day. We would return back home a day after that.

When we were one day from departure, Luci panicked and informed me that the timing of it all would put us on the road to my parent's house, and at the Boston Pops concert, right exactly at the peak of her ovulation and fertility cycle that month. Luci was seriously wondering if we should cancel so we could stay home and "take care of business." I most definitely wanted to go to the concert, and insisted we go. I told her we would figure something out and it would be fine. I think she was slightly annoyed, as if I was pushing her priorities to the side. But she agreed we would go.

The morning of departure, we half-heartedly "took care of

business," and then hit the road to my parent's house. It was a long trip, and we were exhausted that night, and just went to bed with no further action. The next morning, Luci went right downstairs for coffee with my mother, so there was no action that next morning either.

Soon it was time for us to get showered and dressed for the concert. We were in a hurry and had a deadline to leave by, or my stepfather would start blowing horns and having a fit. The thing about Dave is that when Dave says we are leaving at 11:00AM, what he really means is 10:45AM. Yes, he's one of those.

Luci and I had rushed to use the one guest bathroom and get dressed. She was in a nice dress, and I was in a suit. It was Boston Symphony Hall after all, and we were seeing the Boston Pops! So, when we were all dressed and about ready to depart our bedroom, Luci all of a sudden had a fit. She said we were missing our "window," we hadn't "done it" much, and this is why she did not want to come here, and we shouldn't have gone, and now we will never have a baby, and we will have to wait another month, or forever, or never, and. Ugh. You get my point.

In addition to this, my mother was rushing and asking if we were almost ready to go. My stepfather Dave was already pacing up and down near the door with his jacket in hand. I looked at Luci and said, "Let's do it quick." Luci replied, "I can't ruin my hair and my clothes." I said, "Get on the floor, it will be easier." "Let's go, quick, we don't have time to argue about this."

Luci actually got on the floor while doing her eye roll and being totally not into it (not helpful). We did not even take any clothes off. We just created the minimal access that was required. Neither of us were into it at all, we were on the floor of my parent's guest bedroom while my stepfather was yelling for us to hurry up. So, I did what he said. I hurried up. Somehow, I was able to conjure up my game and perform like a champion. Three minutes later we were done. We put ourselves back together in two minutes and went downstairs where they were ready for immediate departure, and so were we after our slight delay.

The Pops concert was amazing, and we left my parent's house and went back home to the lake house. We did not think much of our "efforts" this fertility cycle because it was kind of messed up, and we assumed it was a "no go," and we would be trying again next month. However, something weird happened. Luci started feeling very sick every morning. At first, we thought she had gotten sick from the crazy travel and public concert, restaurants, and so on. But after several days of her being sick in the morning, but fine in the afternoon, we kind of knew what it could be. I think we were afraid to get our hopes up though. We had been disappointed for several months in a row and were getting discouraged and losing hope.

As the days and a couple weeks went by, we were almost certain. Luci stopped having her daily glass of wine. It was almost Christmas, and my parents were coming up to our house for Christmas. We did a lot of talking about how we were going to handle this entire situation. We were fairly sure she was pregnant but had not done a pregnancy test yet. We decided to do this in a special way. We decided to buy a bunch of pregnancy tests and a special announcement card. What we would do is very early Christmas morning, we would wake up, and Luci would take her test. We would then find out for ourselves, or rather, confirm for sure, that she was pregnant. If so, we would then make our announcement in this card and put the card in the Christmas tree for my parents to open as their grand finale gift.

Christmas morning arrived. Luci and I woke up at 5:00AM because we were so excited for the test that we could not contain ourselves. Luci went into the bathroom and took the test. We waited the required time. She looked at the stick and seemed perplexed. I sighed. How hard can it be to read a stick? It's either two lines or it's not, come on. So, I went over, took the stick, and looked at it myself. The stick had one solid line and a second faint line. Hmmmmm. Now, I was just as perplexed as Luci. What the hell does this mean? Why is there a second line but it's faint and not solid like the other line? Ugh.

I told Luci to try another test. We had a pile of them, so let's try again. Luci went in again and tried again. This stick was the same as the last. The second line was faint. What does this mean? Is she pregnant or not? I considered myself a pretty smart person, but I could not read this fucking pregnancy stick.

I told Luci to try another one. She was getting annoyed and said she can't keep peeing forever. I told her she had to try because we had to get this right. I could not give my parents that card, and then find out Luci was not pregnant. We really had to get this right and it had to be done this morning! Now! So, Luci tried again. This time the second line seemed slightly more solid.

I took a breath. Deep breaths. Calm. Think. I did all the math. The morning sickness, and plus the fact she would have only been pregnant for two weeks, thus making the test sketchy maybe. I also considered the fact that the instructions said if there are two lines, it's positive. Well, yes, there were two lines. If it was negative, there would only be one line. Yes, the second line was faint, but it DEFINITELY was there. So as if I was judge and jury, I pronounced Luci pregnant. We did not have any kind of touching moment though, because we were both distressed from the multiple testing, vague results, Luci was tired of peeing on a stick, and I was terrified at the prospect I was wrong. Regardless, we decided to proceed, so we put the announcement card on the tree.

When all gifts had been opened, I said there was one more gift. I got the card from the tree. I handed it to my mom. In this moment, I think my parents knew. I know my mom and how she is, and I could tell she knew this was something special. Even Dave got all serious and moved close to my mom while she opened the card. The card said inside "We give you this Christmas the gift of a grandbaby." My mom immediately started crying and sobbing. Even my stepfather shed a few tears, which never happens. For sure, my mom was the most touched and happiest among all of us. Luci and I kind of already knew and processed it already, and had been so stressed over the testing, that we did not get our moment. But my mom had her moment in all its glory. I really believe it was the greatest Christmas present she had ever received.

After Christmas, Luci went to the doctor, and thankfully was indeed pregnant. I still wonder to this day, if doing it on the floor was the real trick, but I digress. Anyway, the pregnancy officially began. Luci was a real trooper. She put up with morning sickness, then she had to put up with her body distorting into something she did not consider attractive at all, but she handled all of it with strength and grace.

She had finally gotten far enough along that we could find out the gender of the baby. We both were totally stoked to find this out. I especially needed to know so that I could buy all the right stuff. I was not a person who wanted to buy green everything in case it was one or the other. I really had to know what it was so that I could go all blue or all pink.

We arrived for our doctor appointment and the doctor was looking on the screen to see what he could see. To me, it just looked like a bunch of garbled nonsense. How in the world can they actually see baby parts on that thing? Anyway, he told us that the baby appeared healthy and all was good. He then asked if we wanted to know the gender. We both answered in unison "YES." He then probed a bit more. I was expecting from him, "It's a boy," or "It's a girl." What he said was, "Oh there's a Labia."

I will confess that for one or two seconds I was confused. I thought we were having a baby, not a Labia. But by the third second, I got it, and so did Luci. Wow, it was a girl. For some weird reason I was expecting a boy, but I don't know why. I had no preference though, so I was not disappointed. Luci, however, seemed to really be expecting a boy because she looked a bit taken aback. We were both hit by the big news and were both processing it quietly in our own ways.

On the car ride home, I said to Luci, "Phew, for a minute there I thought we were having a boy and I was going to have my hands full." "Turns out you are having your daughter though, so good luck with that." "I'll be in my office if you need me." I was joking of course. I said this because I could tell Luci was totally freaking out and actually did feel a much heavier weight knowing this was a girl and would rely on her for everything. All I knew is that I would love this child with every bit of my being. I knew I was ultimately responsible for protecting this child and making sure she had everything she needed and was set up for a wonderful life. I took it very seriously and pledged myself to this child during that car ride home, while I was prodding and poking Luci for fun.

Time went by and Luci got bigger and bigger and bigger. I have to admit, she got bigger than I had ever imagined possible. She never drank a drop of wine ever. She would always leave an area if there was even the slightest whiff of cigarette smoke. She only ate good foods. Luci did everything anyone would want from an expectant mother.

We attended birthing classes together, and the time was getting close. We had bought everything we would possibly need, and often two of them just in case we needed a spare. We had a diaper lying on the changing table ready to go. She was due any day now. Luci was tired of being pregnant. I felt sorry for her. She was as big as a house, her body totally ruined, and she never complained.

She had taken perfect care of our baby.

Luci and I had discussed in great detail how we would handle the birth. Luci insisted that when the baby was born, I would follow the baby. I am not sure if she was afraid the baby would be switched, or lost, or what. But I kind of agreed with her thinking. So, our agreement was that baby would pop out, and then I would never remove my eyes from that baby. I would follow the baby to the nursery, and not take my eyes of her until she was all tagged, labeled, and in a certain cradle that I could identify. Then after I felt I had the identity of the baby firmly in control, I would come back to Luci.

After she became overdue, we set a date on which they would induce labor if Luci had not given birth by then. That date arrived. There was no way this baby was coming out on its own. We had our bags packed and totally prepared for birthing day. With car seat firmly in the back seat, we drove to the hospital early in the morning.

We got Luci checked in and were in our nice birthing room for a very long day. And it was indeed, a very long day. My mom had been informed and was driving up from Boston to arrive later that day. Luci was given the medication, but it was slow going. It was all starting to feel anticlimactic. We were so excited driving to the hospital, but now we were just bored and tired of waiting.

Finally, in the evening, things started happening. I think our doctor wanted to get this done so she was not stuck there all night, so they may have increased the meds or something. At any rate, things started happening. Luci was having real contractions and was fully dilated. Luci was in a lot of discomfort, I was starting to freak out inside, and really, we needed to do this now and get it done. The doctor was on the same page and suggested Luci try pushing and see what happens. Luci followed the doctor's instructions exactly, and was pushing, and breathing, and doing everything correctly. I have to say at this moment I thanked God I was born a male. Seriously. It's horrifying. So Luci was pushing and panting. I was standing there completely useless with my hand on Luci's leg, and trying to encourage her. Luci was working hard. It was going slow and not easy. The doctor said the baby was coming out slightly crooked, and that was causing it to be more difficult. Luci kept going. Soon I could see the top of the baby's head. Then more of the head. Then more. The doctor attached a needle into the baby's scalp, which was a monitor of some kind.

The baby seemed to be kind of stuck. Then Luci gave a massive push. A spatter of blood splashed out onto my hand that was still resting on Luci's leg. I felt the splatter land. I looked at it and saw what it was. I thought I was going to puke. Or maybe pass out. Or maybe both. I really had to get a grip on myself in that moment. I stopped looking at it and eventually subtly removed my hand and wiped it on my side and kept my hands-off Luci from then on but was still passionately encouraging her as much as possible.

The monitor that the doctor put into the baby's scalp kept falling off and the doctor kept re-inserting it. Every time the doctor stuck the needle back into my daughter's scalp, I swear I felt pain. Eventually when it fell out again, I said, "Please don't stick the baby with that again." The doctor complied with my request without acknowledging me. The doctor was doing a great job by the way, but it was a hard delivery and I was freaking out. I'm sure our doctor was used to this and took it in stride.

The doctor said, "Almost there." "One more huge push Luci." Luci then gave the biggest push anyone could imagine a human could give. The baby immediately popped out. More like flew out. Thank God the doctor was ready for this and literally caught the baby as it was flying out. I saw my daughter for the first time.

She was amazing. I had seen plenty of babies. Some are kind of ugly, but then grow into beautiful children. Some are normal looking babies. All babies are beautiful though right? But this baby. My baby. Was amazing. I am pretty sure the doctor and I gasped at the same time. The doctor was looking at her. Her head was perfect, eyes perfect, face perfect, everything perfect, and in perfect proportion. She literally looked like an angel. The doctor muttered under her breath so that only I could hear her, "Wow this baby is amazing, congratulations." She then added, "This is the second most beautiful baby I've ever seen." I asked her when was the most beautiful one, and she replied when her own baby was born. I laughed and agreed her answer was both complimentary and appropriate. Every mom knows their baby is the most beautiful in the world, and this female doctor was no different.

They let Luci hold the baby very briefly. The doctor then noticed Luci was bleeding and said the nurse had to take the baby so that she could sew Luci up. Apparently, she had torn in that final push. A nurse took the baby and I sprang into action and followed the baby, never taking my eyes off her. I scooted around to the nursery area and saw them cleaning up my daughter. I stood outside the window watching and never taking my eyes off her. They had her totally cleaned up, tagged, labeled, sleeping in one of those hospital new-born-cradles. I believe I had everything under control here, so I went back to Luci's room.

The doctor was just coming out and informed me that Luci had some bleeding she could not stop for a while, but finally managed to stop it. The doctor told me that she was actually scared for a few moments, but Luci was now fine, and all sewn up. I went in to be with Luci. Luci seemed to be fine. I told her the baby was all fine, all good, and all under control. I told Luci how great she did. Luci was totally spent. Nothing left.

I knew my mother was at the hospital in the waiting area. I wanted to do a special presentation to my mother. So, I asked the nurse when we could have the baby back in our room. The nurse said in a few minutes would be no problem. So, I got my mother and told her the baby was born and all was fine. I brought my mom into our room and she sat in the chair. The nurse came in with the baby and gave the baby to me. I then carried the baby over to my mom and said, "I present to you, Angel Grace." Grace is my mom's name. Immediately upon hearing the baby's middle name was named after her, my mom started crying and sobbing again like she did when opening the Christmas card. I asked my mom if she was okay to hold the baby. I did not want to give my baby to a hysterical woman. My mom nodded and I gave her the baby. My mom was in love. My mom finally had a little girl, which is what she had always wanted.

Soon it was time for the baby's first feeding. They brought the baby to Luci. I stayed out of the way. The nurse was coaching Luci on how to breastfeed. Luci was not taking to it well. For some reason, it was awkward for Luci. She was holding the baby kind of awkwardly and the baby would not feed. This went on for like an hour. The baby just would not breastfeed from Luci. Luci was growing frustrated and upset. Plus, the baby was getting fussy and obviously hungry.

The nurse suggested Luci try a bottle. The nurse went and got a bottle of formula. The nurse gave the bottle to Luci and Luci tried to feed the bottle to the baby. Same problem though. Luci could not seem to get a good natural comfortable position for the baby to feed. The baby was fussy and would not take the bottle. Luci grew tired and frustrated like she needed a break. The nurse asked if we should try giving dad the bottle. Luci agreed. The nurse gave me the baby and the bottle. I held Angel, looked into her eyes, smiled, and showed her the bottle. I slid the bottle nipple into Angel's mouth, and Angel started sucking from the bottle really well. It felt so natural and easy for me. I was relieved Angel was feeding and seemed satisfied.

To be honest, I was not thinking about how this might have made Luci feel. I want to be clear that maybe I could have been more aware of Luci's feelings. But truthfully, I was just 100% focused on the baby. Stuff needed to get done, and I needed to do it.

There were several further attempts at Luci breastfeeding the baby and it was not working out. Luci officially announced breastfeeding obviously was not working and would just bottle feed her. I did not protest. It was painful watching this situation. However, sometimes even the bottle feeding did not go well. Angel seemed to take a bottle from Luci sometimes, but other times would not.

Angel would always take a bottle from me though. So I ended up feeding Angel much of the time. It was just easier for everyone. I also changed Angel's diaper. I had learned to do it in birthing class, and again, it just felt natural to me. What was awkward and nerve wracking for Luci, seemed natural for me.

I held Angel on my lap most of the time. I was truly bonding with her. It was ironic because, when we found out the baby was a girl, I thought the baby would be "Luci's baby." But in reality, the baby was "my baby." She looked very similar to me, and when I looked into her eyes, I felt such a special bond. She always took a bottle from me, and it just really felt this was my baby. Which it was. But you know what I mean.

Before we left the hospital, the nurse wanted to make sure we would be able to cut Angel's nails. The nurse asked Luci if she wanted to try. Luci got all nervous and was afraid she might cut the baby's fingers and motioned that I could do it instead. I took Angel and calmly cut her nails. It was no problem. Angel was very cooperative for me. For someone who was always awkward around kids and did not think I would bond with a girl, the opposite was true. I was more deeply bonded than ever, and appeared I was actually really good at this parenting stuff.

    We finally got to leave and go home. I put the baby in the car seat, and we all went out to the vehicle. I secured Angel in the back, and we drove home. My mom was with us and stayed at the house for a week or so. My mom was very helpful.

    Even though I was the one mostly feeding and attending to Angel in the hospital, I really had to go back to work. So how was this going to work? My mom assisted Luci, and Luci got the hang of things. She never breastfed, but Luci became quite efficient at giving a bottle and changing diapers, and really Luci stepped up and was doing a wonderful job at being a mommy. Before long, Luci had taken on almost the full burden.

    The only thing Luci never did, and has never done, was cut Angel's nails. I literally was in charge of cutting Angel's nails from birth until she turned twelve and started doing her own nails.

    Things were not going too smoothly though. Angel was turning colicky. After a bottle, she would cry and scream for a long time, and sometimes even throw up. This went on for about four months. Luci was losing her mind. It was really difficult, but I knew to expect the first several months to be difficult.

    It was more than that for Luci. She was acting differently. She seemed depressed, pissed off, detached, hopeless, and erratic, all at the same time. I soon realized internally that I was likely dealing with a wife who had Postpartum Depression, and a baby who had colic or some issue.

    We went to the doctor, and the doctor suggested we try soy-based formula. This was the magical solution. It fixed Angel overnight. Why didn't someone suggest this sooner? Better late than never, I guess. Clearly Angel was lactose intolerant. Guess who else is lactose intolerant? Me. Eventually I would realize that Angel had all my wiring. Once I finally figured this out, life got much easier. Whenever Angel had an issue, I would just apply the problem to myself, and whatever solution worked for me, would work for Angel. It was like Angel was my twin. She was truly my mini me. I think maybe this annoyed Luci some and made Luci feel even more detached from her daughter.

We may have fixed Angel's issues, but Luci still had hers. I noticed Luci was getting worse. Luci started to have weird personality changes. Luci would have a crazy mean nasty meltdown one minute, then fifteen minutes later be totally fine as if nothing ever happened. It made getting along with Luci impossible. I was always afraid of setting Luci off, and there was no way to know what would set her off. It was getting bad. I was trying to run a company and had to focus on many things at once. Making sure my daughter was okay, running my company, and dealing with Luci, who was always unpredictable. Looking back, I should have given way more focus and attention to Luci. She was sinking and I was not really fully engaged with it.

One day, Luci got home and wanted to talk with me. Luci confessed that she had been intensely depressed. She said she even contemplated ending her life. She said she had a random thought of ramming her car into a tree with Angel in the back seat. It was the "with Angel in the back seat" part that got my attention. I asked her why she felt she wanted to maybe kill Angel. She kind of started to cry and said she did not know. Oh my God.

I suggested we go to the hospital immediately and talk to the doctor. Maybe they could give her something to make her feel better. We packed up Angel and we all drove to the hospital. They took Luci into a room and I waited with Angel. It took a long time. Finally, the doctor came out to see me and said he would like to talk to me alone first, then with Luci. I went into a room with the doctor while I held Angel. The doctor said he was prepared to diagnose Luci with Bi-Polar Disorder. Furthermore, he said Luci did not have Postpartum Depression. She had Postpartum

Psychosis, which is far more serious. He said she would need to be put on antidepressants, but they would take a while to kick in. He suggested that I might authorize them to admit Luci into the Psych Ward where they could watch her, and she would not hurt herself. He said it was my decision.

He then led me into the room with Luci. The doctor pretty much repeated to Luci what he had just said to me privately. I asked him for a moment, to talk with Luci alone, and the doctor left the room. I asked Luci how she felt about all this and what she wanted to do. Luci seemed very docile, sad, lonely, and scared about all this. Luci said she did not want me to leave her there at the hospital.

Epic decision. Hmmm. I heard all the doctor said. He said throw her in the padded room. Luci was begging for me to take her home. I was holding a baby which I would have to take care of myself AND run my company. Plus, I felt so horrible for Luci, and I loved her, and did not want to be separated from her. I decided to take Luci back home. I figured I would keep a very close eye on her and would not let her leave the house with Angel alone. I figured with this safety measure in place, it would be fine. Luci was given a prescription for antidepressants and we all went home.

Luci did okay at home and did not get worse. There was never another incident of her saying she wanted to kill our daughter. Soon, the antidepressants kicked in and seemed to stabilize her. However, Luci and I started to grow distant. Luci was still kind of depressed, or empty, or flat. I was horrified deep down that she had contemplated killing our daughter, and I think it psychologically traumatized me. By this time, I had completely and deeply bonded with my mini me. This is horrible to say, but I have to be honest and take full responsibility for my part in all this. My love for Angel was more intense than my love for Luci, and

Angel was my top priority. It was always Angel first for me. Always was, still is, always will be. So, I want to admit that I could have, and should have, been more loving and engaging toward Luci. Luci needed lots of help and extra attention. Although I was an attentive husband, I should have given more and done more. So, let's just say here and now that I was a crappy husband in this regard.

In addition to me and Luci feeling distant from each other, the antidepressants had taken away her sex drive. So, we also were not having sex anymore, and this was just increasing our distance. Our relationship as we had known it lay in ruins.

I think Luci eventually reasoned that the lack of sex was killing her marriage and she decided she was going to stop taking the antidepressants. Of course, for me it was not just about sex. It was about her crazy behavior. But Luci was determined to try what she could to repair the damage and distance in our relationship. Against the doctor's advice, and against my advice, she stopped the antidepressants. She did regain her sex drive, so that was good. But she started to become erratic again. We started fighting often. Luci would start fights about stupid things. She would grow frustrated with Angel easily as well. It was getting to the point where I dreaded being around Luci. It was always scary, and you would never know what mood she would be in, or what might set her off. I felt our marriage was dying. Certainly, my feelings for her were.

Bipolar disorder, Postpartum Psychosis, and Postpartum Depression are serious illnesses. Women do not ask to be afflicted by them, and women deserve support in dealing with it. It is not their fault. If you or someone you know are suffering from any of these, please seek medical or emotional help. When I was faced with this issue, I was ignorant of the facts and did not have a full understanding of what Luci was facing, or the issues at hand. It is important to clearly identify such issues, show the afflicted person support, and help them seek help. Although Luci was ultimately uncooperative and did not wish to have adequate treatment, in addition to some other personality issues involved, I still should have been more assertive and supportive of Luci with this challenge. Learn from my experiences.

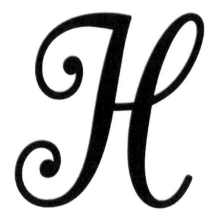

CHAPTER SEVEN

That's Show Business

With my marriage to Luci crumbling, I was desperate to do something to improve things. Even though Luci was no longer pleasant to be around, I still cared about her, and if I could do something to help her I would. Luci was dealing with Postpartum Psychosis, Bi-Polar Disorder, a new baby, and a harsh, dark, cold winter was hitting. It's no wonder she was unhappy. I had the idea that maybe if we moved to LA, it might pull her out of the abyss and give our marriage new life. Both Luci and I loved LA and I was certainly not against the idea of living there, full time. My only concern was what would happen with my business if I was never present. But with my marriage dying and Luci deteriorating, it seemed like moving was a risk I had to take.

I announced to Luci I was ready to do the move and asked her if she thought it was a good idea. Luci was enthusiastically all for it. She literally perked up that very moment. I might have even gotten sex that night. So, my decision felt good, and onward we went. My plan was to move us back to the beach town where we had spent all our time previously. I would go out there ahead of Luci and Angel for the purpose of finding and renting an apartment. After I had a home secured and set up from things we had in storage, Luci and Angel would come out.

    I left for LA one cold winter day and immediately started my apartment search. After a couple misses, I found one I was able to secure. It was a nice two bedroom within a block of the beach. You could hear the waves crashing in the morning if you left the bedroom window open. The second bedroom would have to serve as both my office, and a section for Angel's sleeping area. I got the place set up with the basics and told Luci to come on out.

    My mom had come up from Boston to stay with Luci and Angel at the house while I was gone. I did not really want Luci alone with Angel, plus Luci might need help preparing for the move. I would end up going back and forth between LA and New England for business reasons, but for Luci, this move was permanent, and she would not be going back east much.

    My mom claims Luci was so excited to get the hell out of there, that she left skid marks on the way out the door to get to the airport. My mom said Luci did not even make the beds or anything. She just wanted to leave and get to LA. And she did. Luci and Angel arrived, and I took them to our new home at the beach. Luci totally approved of the place and started nesting. I was really hoping this move would bring back the old Luci.

    I spent most of my days doing my business work in the second bedroom home office. Angel would come in often and I would let her sit on my lap, and she would "help" me work. I had decided to once again look at expanding my business to LA. I wanted to explore the prospects of getting some kind of property management contract for the studios in Hollywood. I did some thinking and research and somehow came across an administrative Producer working at a major Hollywood studio, named Carla. I sent her a note asking if she would meet with me about any opportunities that might be available to me in working with a studio. To this day, I am not sure why the hell she agreed to this meeting, but she did.

We set a meeting date and Carla had arranged for a studio pass for me since she worked on the actual studio movie lot. The idea of going to the lot was kind of exciting for me since I had no contact with the Hollywood world before, and now I could see it from the inside. I drove an hour up to Hollywood and found the correct gate. Security had me on the visitor list and gave me instructions on where to drive and park on the lot. I found one empty spot next to this big fancy Rolls or Bentley, or whatever it was. I went to the door as instructed by Carla and she let me in. We did our introductions and she seemed super nice. She seemed super busy but told me to sit down. She asked me why I was there. I explained I had this real estate company back east and I wanted to see if there were opportunities for me here. She paused and said she did not handle any of that. Then she asked me if we could try something. I said, "Okay."

She went over to the trash and pulled out some kind of script of a TV series that I would later see on TV a few months later. She asked me to read it with her. I was confused and had never read a script before. She slowed her roll and explained a little slower. I got it and we started to read. It was horrible. She gave me some instruction, and then we tried again. I was better this time. She gave me more instruction and said to try it again. I was even better the next time. This went on for maybe 45 minutes. I admit I was starting to have fun with it.

Carla then said she had a meeting soon, but she felt I would be perfect in front of the camera. She said I had the right look and presence. She suggested I take some acting classes, get some headshots, and jump in. She offered to coach me once a week. I automatically accepted without thinking about what had just happened. I thanked her and started to leave. On my way out, someone asked me if that was my SUV parked outside. I said yes, very nervously. They said to be careful as I leave because I was parked next to George Clooney's car, and there would be hell to pay if I dented it. I replied yes okay. But in my mind, I felt like I was in some alternate reality or dream. I assume his car was that fancy thing I had initially parked next to, but no way to be sure.

 I went home and told Luci what had happened. Luci seemed wary, confused, and maybe even a little disappointed. I am not sure what Luci was expecting, since I myself did not know what to expect from that meeting. I told her I was going to go for it, and explore what Carla threw at me. My naive thinking was that if a producer for a major studio says I would be good in front of the camera, then maybe it means I would be good in front of the camera. I had zero experience other than that middle school play I was in.

 I enrolled in an acting class in Beverly Hills and continued with my coaching sessions with Carla at the studio lot. During my second meeting with Carla, she explained to me that this business runs on a "secret understanding." She said she would teach me what this was, and that I would do fine. She said talent is only a small part. It is more about who you know and your "look." She actually seemed more interested in building my image than in my acting ability. We discussed at length what kind of headshots to get and how to present myself to others. I took it all in.

 I arranged to have my headshots done with a recommended photographer in Beverly Hills. It would be my first photo shoot ever. I arrived with all kinds of clothes and no idea what I was doing. It was a female photographer; one of the few female photographers I would ever work with. She was very nice and guided me on what to wear, and through all the shots. I told her what Carla was looking for and she immediately understood what I needed.

We got the shots and I took them back to Carla. Carla looked at them and picked out the perfect shot. She loved it. She told me to have 100 copies printed. She then asked me a question. She asked if I would consider being on a gay themed show. I asked her what she meant, like what kind of gay themed show. My mind was obviously racing and wondering and confused. She asked if I was familiar with "Queer As Folk," or "Skins." I said I did not watch them, but I was familiar with them, yes. She asked if I could do a show like those. I indicated I could. She then said she might have an opportunity for me if I could prove my acting abilities. I said I was still taking classes and would continue.

I enthusiastically continued my classes. They were fun actually. I looked forward to my acting classes every Tuesday and had fun doing them. There was a new me emerging. Instead of being all closed and business-like, I had to open myself up completely emotionally, and be in the present for acting. I loved the fact this allowed me to be the opposite of what I had been for many previous years through college and my business days. I was progressing quickly and doing well in class. I went from being totally clueless in the first class, to having no problems carrying a scene in front of the class with someone else.

But then Carla threw me a curve ball. When I was confirming my next session with her, she asked if it would be okay to meet at her house in the evening. My first reaction was that I was bummed because I loved going to the studio lot. For me, that was part of the experience of it all. But then my second reaction was wondering what she was up to. I asked why. Carla said, "You remember when I told you about the "secret understanding?" I said yes. She said, "Well I will show you what that is when we meet at my house." Ahhhhhhhh! Right. Got it now. Ugh.

So, I had a dilemma. Do I go forward with this and deal with whatever happens so that I can maybe get some amazing opportunities? Or do I be a good married boy and decline? I had never cheated on Luci. Even though Luci and I were no longer getting along, or even having sex much, I still had never cheated on her and did not want to. But if I turned Carla down, I'm probably done, and there would be no more Carla, movie lot visits, opportunities, or parking next to George Clooney. I decided to gently decline the "session," and asked if we could reschedule for next week at the studio lot as usual. I never heard from Carla again. Ever.

So, I had blown that opportunity, but I learned a lot from Carla and had gotten my start. I continued with my acting classes. It was not long before I was to get my first interesting opportunity. My acting teacher knew someone who was working on a movie starring Corbin Bernsen, who used to be a star on a show called "LA Law" many years ago. I was offered a very tiny part where I might have one line or no lines. I very excitedly accepted.

This would be my first time on a live set. I was nervous and excited. I was given a ridiculous wardrobe to wear and pretty much just had to stand around and occasionally nod. There is one shot of me shaking Corbin's hand and that's it. Total loser nothing part. But I loved it. I learned tons. I learned about "blocking" (how and where to move during a scene, while hitting your marks), and learned how a set runs, and a scene runs. It's more complicated than it seems. You have to truly pay attention and be exactly where you need to be at the exact correct moment. If you are two inches off your mark, or two seconds late, you may have ruined the shot. Plus, the giant camera is right in your face sometimes, and you can't EVER look at it, no matter how tempting or natural it feels. It was a wonderful experience. I could not get enough.

I continued to get better and started auditioning for student films. I finally nailed my first lead role in a student film. This was my first taste of what it was like to be the center of attention on a set. I loved it. It made me even more enthusiastic about my performances, and I did great. I would go on auditions regularly for student films and got cast in a long line of lead roles. Of course, you would never see any of these since the student films are only shown at the film schools. I had a great time doing them though and learned tons.

I would go on to get other tiny parts in bigger films as well. I appeared in films or TV shows with people such as Chelsea Handler, Tom Sizemore, Faye Dunaway, Andy Dick, and many more. I also appeared in much bigger productions, but we will get to that later.

Acting was not the only thing I would dive into. I would also get into modeling, really by accident. I have never considered myself modeling material. You will recall I was that skinny string bean awkward kid with a bowl haircut. But with time, I guess I grew into myself. With Luci's influence, I had cleaned and groomed myself up. I was also running and working out, so the string bean was gone. In the process of doing my headshots, then doing shirtless shots, it was suggested I try modeling.

I had some photographers who liked my "rated G" headshots and wanted to do shoots with me. The only catch is that I needed to be open to taking most of my clothes off. I decided to give it a try and did some underwear modeling and things like that. My pictures were really good, and nobody was more surprised than myself. It's amazing what a great photographer can do, and how great they can make you look. It was not long before I was in demand by Class B and Class C photographers. I did shoots with a couple A class photographers, but I'll be honest and say mostly I was entirely in the B and C crowd. So, don't expect to find me in old Calvin Klein ads. You won't find me.

However, if you look hard enough, you will find me in art pieces that were sold around the world. Don't ask me if I was wearing any clothes. You already know the answer to that, right? So yeah, I did a lot of shirtless, underwear, art nude, body paint, special art pieces, and such.

Mostly, my experiences were very positive. When modeling, you have to expect and accept you are a piece of meat, or manikin, that will be touched, poked, and prodded. You have to change your clothes out in the open on set and have no issues with this. I have even had a photographer reach into my underpants without warning and arrange things how he wanted. It's part of the deal. Again, this is not shooting a multi-million-dollar ad campaign for Calvin Klein. The stuff I was doing was more for small underwear or clothing companies, or fetish type houses who put out certain types of photos that involve young men.

It is what it is. Some might have been too embarrassed or ashamed to admit they do it, but if I'm to be honest with you, I'd have to say I had fun doing it and looked forward to the jobs. It was much more informal than acting on a tight set, and there is satisfaction in seeing photos that make you look better than you actually look. So do not feel sorry for me, because I really enjoyed the weird awkward modeling stuff, and I could take care of myself just fine if it got too inappropriate or uncomfortable. Of course, the only downside to all of the acting and modeling up to now was that it was no pay or low pay. I was not in the acting union (SAG), so I received the equivalent of minimum wage or less.

I was not the only family member who would enter the Hollywood industry. When Angel turned three, I decided to get some photos done of her and send them to some agents for feedback. Feedback was immediate and positive. Angel was very quickly signed by a management company and a top children's agent in Beverly Hills. She was very beautiful with a nice calm presence.

I know I am a biased father gushing here, but Angel really did stop traffic. People would often comment on her, and how amazing she looked. People would often say "You need to get her an agent." We would just laugh, rather than tell them she already had an agent.

Even when she was a baby in a stroller, people would comment on her. Poor Luci had to endure a couple instances where people would stop her in our beach community and compliment Angel, but then ask Luci how long she has been the nanny for Angel. Remember, Luci was Hispanic. Angel on the other hand, was exactly like me. Angel was white as snow and looked exactly like me. So there really was no resemblance between Luci and Angel. Therefore, people naturally assumed Luci was just the nanny, since most nannies in our neighborhood were Hispanic. I thought this was endlessly entertaining and hilarious, but Luci would say she does not share in the humor. It's still funny even today. Sorry Luci.

Luci was also stuck taking Angel to all her auditions. It was lots of work and time consuming. It was always funny to watch this process though. In Luci's mind, Luci was always the star. Before one of Angel's auditions, Luci would spend hours getting herself ready. Then Luci would spend five minutes getting Angel ready for the audition, even though the audition was actually for Angel. I was always amused by this.

It was not always fun and games though. I recall one audition where Luci had to drive Angel an hour north for an audition in bad traffic. Angel would almost always fall asleep in the car. When

Luci arrived, she would have to wake Angel up. Angel would always wake up crabby, and Luci would have to get her calmed down and happy before taking her inside for the audition. On this occasion, Luci got all the way up to the audition location in bad traffic, woke Angel up, and Angel puked all over herself. Luci had to just go back home in the same horrible traffic. Useless, pointless trip. Poor Luci. Poor Angel.

It was not long before Angel started getting cast in small roles. She was in a few TV commercials and music videos. Her prized appearance would have to be the time she was in a music video with Grammy Award winner Kelly Clarkson.

I remember being very excited when she auditioned for that role. However, at the time, our agent told us Angel was second choice. So, Angel did not get the part, but we were on notice that she was the substitute if anything happened to the girl who got the part.

Well wouldn't you know it, we got the call. The girl they had chosen was being a huge problem, crying and carrying on, and they had to replace her. They asked if Angel was available. Guess where we were? We had flown back east to spend a couple weeks at the lake house. I thought about it and decided this was super important. We told Angel's agent we could be available in two days. I put Luci and Angel on a plane the next day and sent them back to LA. I stayed back east because I had some business things to do.

Luci and Angel made it to the set of the Kelly Clarkson music video as scheduled. Kelly Clarkson introduced herself to them and made sure Angel would be comfortable with her. Angel loved her and it looked like it would work out fine. They shot all day and Angel did great. Kelly would let Angel sit on her lap during some of the down time, which was sweet and helped Angel bond with her.

Luci said everyone on the set was very nice and they even took Angel in the limo to get an ice cream during the break. When shooting was over, Kelly said she was in love with Angel. Kelly started taking off her gold necklace she had been wearing and was going to give it to Angel. Unfortunately, the Director yelled at Kelly that they were not done shooting and needed her to keep all the same wardrobe and jewelry for consistency. Damn it. Yes, Angel was that close to getting Kelly Clarkson's necklace. Even so, it was an amazing experience for which I am forever grateful. The day the video was released, and I saw Kelly Clarkson with my little girl in the video, I had tears running down my face, and I had never been so proud in my life. Since then, I've continued to be proud of Angel in ways I can't even express.

I would have to say the move to LA was mostly successful in many areas except two. Luci and I were still having problems, and my business was showing signs of stress as well. I had a feeling the fun and games might be coming to an end soon.

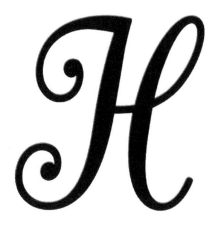

CHAPTER EIGHT

Watch Those Dominoes Fall

Whether it is a house of cards or a row of dominoes, it only takes one piece to unravel the whole thing. In my case, I had a war on two fronts: my business and Luci. I suppose it was only a matter of time before one or both of those might fall. But when both fell at the same time in some twisted interconnected perfect storm, it was too much to handle.

The major domino to fall on the business front was that Mr. Bart was fired as the bank president. This in itself was not inconceivable. Mr. Bart had been the president of a small community bank. That bank more than doubled in size with the first merger, and he survived that. But when the much larger bank bought out Mr. Bart's now medium sized bank, I guess his days were numbered. I remember Mr. Bart saying to me "They are coming for me, and eventually they will get me." "And after they get me, they will come after you."

I was young and inexperienced. I mostly had only known success. With time and hard work, I had always been successful at all I did. I heard Mr. Bart's words, but I think deep down I always felt I would somehow overcome and prevail any obstacle. Wrong.

Soon after Mr. Bart was replaced, I received notice that the bank was reviewing my contracts and would be putting them all out to bid. I had been very loyal to that bank. They were always the #1 priority with me. I personally would see to the smallest details with the greatest of attention. Never was I ungrateful, or did I ever take the bank for granted. Nobody there could say they received less than over the top service from my company. But there were two factors my naive mind did not consider at the time.

Firstly, they were paying me a fortune. I was a major expense item on their financial statement. Because they were now a large corporate bank, they did not care about service or loyalty. They only cared about saving a dollar to justify executive bonus structures. So, if they could save $5 on my services, they would fire me without hesitation. The second factor was that I caught wind of the fact that one of the upper managers had a buddy who had a real estate services company like mine, and he was trying to help his buddy get my contracts.

Without Mr. Bart protecting me, I never had a chance. All the contracts were awarded to various companies other than mine. I was out of the bank. Instantly, I had lost 50% of my company's business.

I obviously had to let go of all my cleaning people associated with those properties, and some of my maintenance people. However, there was no way to fully compensate for losing half my company's revenue. Like a deer in the headlights, I was not sure what to do. I found it hard to believe that I was looking at certain death. I had always been successful and could overcome anything. Certainly, something will fall out of the sky and save me, right?

I had an idea to try and follow Mr. Bart. I was thinking if he landed at a new bank, I could just sweep in behind him and have new contracts with a different bank. However, Mr. Bart ended up at a small bank out of the area, so that idea was useless.

It was not long before I started having financial problems. I started paying things late. Then really late. Before too long I was way behind on my oil bills to the big oil company I did business with. You will recall I had the contract to take care of all of their buildings in return for giving them all my oil business. This was solidified by the fact I was "friends" with the son of the owners.

Due to the fact I had lost the bank properties, and thus the oil company lost all the bank properties as well, and the fact I was late on my oil bills, the oil company terminated their relationship with me. Not only did they stop delivering oil to my properties because I was paying late, but they stopped paying me for all my cleaning and maintenance services to their properties. In an impassioned appeal to them, I wrote letters to my "friend," and to his parents (the owners). I explained to them my situation and asked them to please give me more time and work with me. I needed their help to keep my company afloat and I was willing to open up to them and make sure they got paid.

I was working on selling the mobile home parks I owned with my accountant in order to bail out my situation. I only needed time to do this, and everyone would have been taken care of and made whole. My letters to the oil company owners and friend went unanswered. They just ignored me and sat back while I sank. After losing the oil company, I was down to about 30% of my peak size. Soon after my relationship with the oil company terminated, the mobile home parks sold, and I was able to pay the oil company in full. It made no difference and changed nothing. I had lost that business relationship.

Now enter Luci. Despite having moved to LA, Luci did not

improve. Her depression seemed to fade, but in its place came a dark bitterness, anger, and narcissism. She wasn't just a depressed victim of Postpartum Psychosis or Bi-Polar anymore. She became a mean person. A nasty person. She would pick fights over the smallest things and have tantrums without warning. She would throw things, scream, yell obscenities in public, and just be mean in general.

Luci was even mean to Angel. I remember one incident, which my mother also witnessed, in which Luci had spent some time getting dressed, doing her hair and makeup, and came downstairs to the living room. Angel was just a little girl and ran over to her mommy and tried to sit on Luci's lap. Luci reacted by immediately pushing Angel over onto the ground in a pretty harsh way. She didn't want any little kid on her I guess. Angel was devastated and was crying. Luci just ignored Angel. That incident kind of symbolized what Luci had become. Luci had become a self-centered narcissistic person who only cared about herself, and believed the entire world revolved around her. Some might say Sociopathic in nature.

Many times, Angel would be upset about something and crying, and Luci would scream at me, "GO DEAL WITH YOUR DAUGHTER, I CAN'T DEAL WITH HER!" It was heartbreaking to see Luci being so mean and detached toward Angel, and it was also painful to see her so full of hate toward me. Luci started calling me a loser for my business failing. I am not sure what she expected me to do. Although I was the guy who kept Luci a housewife with fresh nails, new shoes, and purses; I was a loser all of a sudden because I was struggling and sinking. I needed Luci's love and support, but I received neither.

Luci had written a letter to my mother which I intercepted. My mother never received it. The letter was blaming my mother for me being totally inadequate and not able to maintain good relationships. The narcissist in her was not only blaming me for all the world's problems, but now blaming my mother as well for not raising me properly. The letter went on to say that my mother failed to raise me correctly because my mother also had nothing but dysfunctional relationships. It was pretty brutal, and even though I have had every right to be critical of my mother regarding my own issues with her, the letter was overly harsh and I disagreed with all of Luci's accusations and shortcomings she tried to paint on my mom. Everything was always everyone's fault except Luci's. Luci was perfect in her own mind. Luci could do no wrong. These are the traits we find in classic narcissists. I'm sure many of you reading this know people like this and have been victimized by them as well.

There were many times I would try and talk to Luci. I explained how every day she was chipping away at our marriage, and eventually it would just be a pile of dust. I was being sincere. I was genuinely depressed my marriage was failing. Luci's response was always to scream at me and blame me for everything. Remember, nothing is ever Luci's fault. Luci never once has ever apologized for anything she has ever done. Why? Because in her mind, she has never done anything wrong.

On a few occasions I begged Luci to go back on antidepressants or try counseling. I tried to have an honest and frank conversation with her about Bi-Polar Disorder and how antidepressants could help her and help us both. I told her I would rather lose my sex life with her than lose her and my marriage. I always tried to be very calm and sincere. Luci's response would always be one of anger, nasty hatred, and she would say the problem was not her, but it was me. Luci was always the one person in the world who was totally okay, and it was actually every human surrounding her that was wrong.

One epic example that was burned into my brain forever is

when we attended a wedding of some friends of ours. After a very nice wedding event, we were being taken back home in a stretch limo. Upon exiting the limo at home, Luci realized a minute later she had left her purse in the limo. She immediately had a total tantrum meltdown. I tried to calm her and tell her we would call the limo company and get her purse. She instead turned on me and said it was my fault she left the purse in the limo. She said I should have noticed she left it, or I should have checked for her purse before exiting. She really felt it was my fault she forgot her purse. I defended myself and told her that SHE had made a mistake and forgot her purse, but we would get it back. This response made her enraged. She took a box of donuts I had in my hand, went into the middle of the street, threw the donuts on the street, jumped up and down on the donuts, and screamed obscenities at me which the entire town must have heard. It was a full psychotic meltdown episode. I was genuinely scared of her. She was fucking crazy. As you would expect, we were able to get her purse back later that night without any issue.

On a couple occasions, Luci would walk out on me, and threaten to leave me for good. I would always panic and try to reconcile. But eventually, I asked myself why I was trying to keep her. She was a total nightmare. I came to the realization that I actually did not want her anymore. We were fighting constantly in front of Angel, and that was not good. I wanted to keep Angel in my household, but I did not want Angel growing up in a mean hateful environment. I had to accept that Luci and I were headed for divorce. It was just a matter of time. I decided in my mind that the next time Luci walked out on me, I would just let her go and not let her back in.

That day came. Luci and I had been fighting for days, and not even speaking for days after that. I was leaving for a trip back east to deal with my crumbling business. I left our beach apartment without even saying goodbye to Luci. When I was at the lake house, Luci called me and calmly said she felt it was best if she moved out. I did not argue. I was shaking, I felt sick, scared, but I also felt empty. I had made a deal with myself that the next time Luci "walked out on me," I would let her go. So, I let her go. I said to her, "Fine."

Luci's plan was to stay with my parents for a short while and then decide what to do next. Luci was very close to my mother and lord knows what Luci had been telling my mother. My mother clearly was willing to support Luci in all this drama and had invited her to stay with them. This would be the start of a rift between me and my parents that still has remnants remaining today.

Luci and Angel stayed with my parents for a short while. To be honest, I was relieved and loving my time alone. I no longer had to be victim to Luci's constant abuse, tantrums, and psychotic behavior. It confirmed for me that Luci and I splitting up was the correct thing to do. However, Luci ended up talking to me and wanting to reconcile. I kept the deal with myself to not let her back in, and I refused.

Luci ended up coming back to LA, but she had a plan to move out immediately. Luci decided to move out of the beach apartment permanently and stay with some friends of ours. They only lived fifteen minutes away, and my visitation with Angel would be no problem.

Of course, Luci made sure to make her final departure from the apartment as dramatic and damaging as possible. I am not sure what she told Angel, but Angel believed she would never see me again. Angel was crying hysterically as Luci was making her final exit in a nasty huff. It was all I could do to keep myself together. My heart was breaking because Angel was my world and I did not want her living outside my household. But Angel was very young, and I felt a very young child needed her mother. I also had many business problems and had to travel often. I felt letting Angel stay with her mother at this point was the correct thing to do.

In talking with Angel when she was older, I determined I screwed up. Angel to this day is still traumatized by that moment of departure. I suspect her mother may have vindictively told Angel she would not see me again, but I can't say that for sure. I honestly don't know. What I do know, is that Angel has since told me that she truly believed she would never see me again. Additionally, it was irresponsible of me to allow my daughter to be taken by a parent who behaved in a mean psychotic manner and could be emotionally abusive.

I have many regrets about how I handled things. Could I have been more understanding and supportive of Luci? Could I have done more to help her? Could I have somehow convinced Luci to get treatment and counseling? Should I have fought to keep my daughter from the very beginning? The answer to all of the above might likely be yes. But it is what it is, and I made choices based on my circumstances and conditions at the time. I am open to judgment.

I did not miss Luci at all. How sad is that? Apparently, I had gradually lost all feelings for Luci over time, and if anything, I was relieved she was gone. However, I was bereft at the loss of my daughter. Very often I would look at my daughter's toys in my living room and start crying. I missed Angel so deeply. I was so connected to her, and not having her in my home was very painful. This is a pain I would always carry with me through today.

With a divorce looming, Luci was starting to position herself for what she wanted. Luci knew my business was failing. She knew I had no money. But Luci was still hoping to come out of the marriage debt free, and maybe with some monthly payments. However, Luci's hate has always overcome common sense. Rather than leaving me in peace to try and salvage my business and finances, Luci did whatever she could to totally destroy me.

Luci called me with what she thought were some huge allegations of some sort. Luci said she found out I was talking to young guys on social media. I suppose she thought I was doing inappropriate things? Or?

Luci was actually correct about one thing. I was indeed talking with young guys on social media. Totally true. With Luci's departure, I started mentoring young adults on social media as a way of dealing with my own depression and sadness over the situation with Luci and Angel. Some of the young people were women, but most were guys. All were adults and mostly college age. Some were straight and some were gay. Most of them had many issues, and some were suicidal. I enjoyed reaching out and trying to help. It was very therapeutic for me. It's in my DNA. I would sometimes joke around with them about their relationships or sexual conquests to build a strong rapport with them. Other times I had very serious conversations, talking some down from suicidal thoughts and intentions. I did not meet them in person or even talk with them on the phone. All of my mentoring and counseling was over social media posts. So, I am not sure if Luci thought I was doing something wrong, or cheating on her with young guys, or what she was thinking exactly.

She took her accusations and talked to a friend she had back east who lived near the lake house. I am horrified to imagine what she told this person, because this person was horrified enough to start spreading rumors around town. She worked as a bartender at a local bar and decided to spread rumors about me to customers. Some of those customers were clients of my company. Those clients then terminated their relationship with my company because they must have not liked the rumors they heard.

Thus, I lost even more business. I had even less income, and less money. Aside from the fact that whatever was being said was untrue, it was also very destructive to my reputation and business. Luci had not only managed to make weird misguided accusations, but she managed to spread those accusations, starting rumors, and further destroying my business. All of this, of course, would mean less of a chance that I could help Luci financially. She was trying to chop off the hand that fed her.

Between all of Luci's hate, terrorizing Angel, terrorizing me, doing what she could do to destroy my business, working to turn my own mother against me, insulting me with obscenities constantly, breaking me down whenever she could by calling me a loser and other things, I had the epic realization way too late, of why her name was Luci. Luci was not Luci. Perhaps Luci must have been short for her full name, Lucifer.

At the same time all this was going on, I was having problems with my mother. My mother had taken Luci's side in the divorce. My mother criticized me for not leaving the beach apartment. My mom felt it should be Luci's home and I should just go out on the street. I explained to my mom many times that it was Luci who decided to leave. I never asked or told Luci to leave. Luci wanted to leave and decided to leave and left under her own power. Luci and Angel had a safe place to stay with our friends. Yet, my mother always felt I was totally in the wrong for not immediately moving out. My mother also sympathized with Luci regarding her various claims against me, including the rumors I suppose. My mother would always buy into everything Luci said. This would continue for years. I am not certain, but perhaps my mother identified with Luci in some ways, or maybe this went back to her preference for a daughter rather than a son. I am not sure, but Luci had been very successful at roping my mother into her fold and kept her there for years.

Luci was fine. She would actually land on her feet. She and

Angel stayed with our friends in a guest room for about a month. After that, Luci found an opportunity as a "nanny" for our friend's brother. The friend's brother was someone we had both met before. He seemed like a nice guy to me. Luci was not that into him at the time, so I thought. The brother had recently moved to LA after his divorce and needed help with his three kids. The brother offered to have Luci and Angel move into his home, and Luci would be his nanny for his three kids.

Luci and Angel moved into his home, located in a nice exclusive area near Anaheim. The school district was one of the best in the state, so I was satisfied that at least Angel would have good schooling. The drive was longer for my visitations, but they were located near Disneyland and in a nice area. I had no choice in the matter anyway.

I accepted the situation under the condition that Luci would keep taking Angel to her auditions and gigs. It was very important to me that Angel stay in the acting/modeling business because I deeply believed big things would happen. Angel recently had an audition with ABC for a soap opera that was airing at that time, and the casting director was very interested in incorporating Angel into the show at some point. I felt that, and many other things, were on the horizon for Angel.

However, as would become the prevailing trend with Luci, she lied. After moving to the new area, she informed me she was no longer going to work with Angel's career. She was done. She told me she had informed Angel's manager that she was no longer available. I was obviously very upset about this. But it never matters, because Luci will only do what's best for Luci. So right there, Angel's Hollywood career was over.

Luci settled into her new life. What I did not know at the time, is that from all appearances, Luci started sleeping with her "boss" almost immediately. It was not long before Luci announced to me that she and her "nanny boss" were in a relationship.

I found myself in a very dark abyss all alone. My business had been all but destroyed. My marriage had failed. My daughter had moved out of my household and lived over an hour away from me. My mother had defected in support of Luci. My reputation had been trashed. My income was destroyed. I had very little money. I was left with no friends I trusted. I was left with no support. I was left all alone. I was left with nearly nothing.

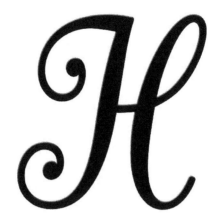

CHAPTER NINE

Meet The Illuminati

With my marriage to Luci effectively over, my business in gradual free-fall, and no longer having my daughter in my household, I was definitely up against the ropes, depressed, and feeling lonely and isolated. Believe it or not, this period would turn out to be the calm before the storm, as you will see later on. However, at the time, this "calm" felt like an all-out panic and awful moment in my life. I had spent my entire life prevailing over obstacles and succeeding. This time looked different and I was horrified. It put me in a particularly vulnerable state of mind. I think I desperately needed help and guidance from someone, or something, or somewhere, or all of the above.

So right on cue, enter stage left, Chaz. Chaz first approached me on social media. He was very forward and confident as if he already knew me. It was very strange. I was very standoffish and nervous at first. Everything was going wrong for me in my life and

I was growing paranoid. I resisted his contact at first, thinking he was just some crazy person on social media. However, even in very short messaging conversations, he seemed so intelligent and interesting, that I was very intrigued. It was like a mystery, and I wanted to know more. I was lonely, scared, sad, depressed, and seeking some kind of guidance, help, or comfort. Why not talk to Chaz. What could be the harm in that? What could possibly go wrong? Well, it was not long at all before Chaz said he much preferred to talk on the phone, so he knew whom he was really dealing with. He asked if it was okay if he called me. I was again very nervous and hesitated. But his confidence and seeming intelligence was so intriguing, I could not help myself. So, I agreed.

Ten minutes later my phone rings and it is a very nice, normal sounding young man on the phone. He was so at ease, it was kind of contagious, and I very quickly felt at ease myself. He asked me all kinds of questions. In retrospect, most people would have advised not to give any personal info away to a stranger. But I sang like a bird. I told him about where I lived, my business back east, how I was struggling, and so on. Totally crazy. He was clearly interviewing or interrogating me, and I was fully cooperating. He was so nice, and I think I was loving the attention and attentive interaction. Most of all though, I was blown away by his unusually high level of intelligence. He was so well spoken and seemed to always know exactly what to say, and he knew something about every topic that would come up. I had never really come across this before and I found it odd and refreshing. We clicked immediately and got along amazingly well. I felt connected and comfortable with him in minutes. Was this guy even human?

These phone conversations went on every day for a few weeks. I loved talking to him. He was such good company and I soon realized he appreciated my company as well. Somehow, I was able to learn a couple things about him as well, but not much. I learned he was gay. He did not *sound* gay at all, but he mentioned how he was usually attracted to young guys and did not interact with women well. It is important to note here that I was significantly older than Chaz, so I would not have been a "younger guy" that he would have preferred in that way. Also, I would later on remind him that I was "straight," and his immediate reply was, "Oh, you will be much more than that."

He had a brother who seemed to be a huge part of his life since every other sentence included "Martin this" and "Martin that." He had done lots of traveling and had been all over the world. He loved watching TV documentaries about any subject, but especially history and the paranormal. He was especially fascinated with spiritual powers, psychic ability, and ghosts. One thing I would have assumed he would be interested in, but he actually felt uncomfortable discussing, was anything to do with alien life and UFO's.

He shared with me that his family felt he was highly psychic, and they often called him "the alien," because he always knew everything and acted differently than most humans. He told stories about how he could predict what people were thinking and what actions people would take. He told stories about his brother taking him to casinos, and he would correctly choose numbers on the roulette reel. Chaz then asked me if I had ever been to a casino. I nervously told him that I had not, and that I was not really a fan of gambling. He asked me why, and I replied that I felt it was a waste of money since everyone loses eventually. He replied to that by saying that not *everyone* loses, and it takes risk and money to make money. I didn't argue further.

I found Chaz's comments on religion particularly interesting. Chaz said he was not religious, and actually resented the control that religion played in people's lives. But at the same time, he was intensely spiritual. He spoke many times of how close he felt to God. I could tell he had a very personal and valued relationship with God. Chaz had done in-depth research on Jesus from an archaeological and historical perspective. He had explained to me how he felt the real birth of Jesus would have been in the spring.

Chaz also seemed to be very well versed in Greek Mythology. He was fascinated with Atlantis, the Bermuda Triangle, and many such things. The topic of aliens would come up during the discussion of Atlantis, and although he clearly believed in them, he seemed uncomfortable talking about them, as I said. I think maybe it hit too close to home since his family and friends were constantly accusing him of being one.

One interesting conversation we had though, was him telling me about a time he had to go to a secret "installation" with his father. He said they kept things there that nobody thinks exist, and that nobody has any idea what is really going on in this world. He also said it was located in a place that would surprise me. At the time, I interpreted the topic involving "aliens" in nature, but it could have been military based, or technology based. I really have no idea. He did say that he, Chaz, had invented something once that solved a problem they were having, but he did not say anymore. He said it is always the simple solutions that work best, meaning what he did was so simple, that others there were embarrassed they did not come up with first. Mostly when talking to Chaz, I just listened in silence, wonderment, and confusion.

We also talked about the fact I loved hunting. I excitedly told him how I loved hunting season every year and had been successful at getting some nice trophies. This information did not go over well, though. He shared with me how he could not stand the thought of killing an animal. A person maybe, but an animal, never. I laughed nervously and changed the subject.

It did not take long for me to feel a bit intimidated, and I was always afraid he would ask me something I knew nothing about. At the risk of sounding overly arrogant, this was the first time I had extended interactions with someone so completely more intelligent than I was. I was way over my head with Chaz. It was obvious to me he was a certified Genius. Thus, when he started talking about a topic, I would typically keep my mouth shut and just listen, unless he asked me a question.

However, he did seem very interested in my thoughts and in me. He asked me many questions every conversation. There was one time he turned the tables on me and said, "So you were pre-med in school, own a business, have extensive knowledge of law, banking, and you do all your own accounting work?" I said, "Yes I guess that's right." There was a pause as if he was actually impressed for half a moment. Then he said, "You know my dad always said that a family needs three things: a great doctor, a great lawyer, and a great accountant." I laughed and reminded him I was not *actually* a medical doctor or lawyer. He said, "Yes I know, but you have extensive knowledge in all three areas; you know how rare that is for someone as young as you?" I did not reply, we changed subject, but I could tell he was interested, intrigued, and maybe 10% impressed.

Finally, one day, my curiosity got the better of me and I touched the third rail and asked if he wanted to meet up in person sometime. I could tell immediately from his reaction that I had just asked him to turn into a pretzel and crawl 20 miles through mud. I immediately backed off my request because I did not want to scare him away or alienate him, since I really valued our conversations and did not want him to vanish.

However, a couple days later he brought up the subject himself. He asked if I still wanted to meet him in person. I said, "Yes absolutely." He paused. I even think he put me on hold for a moment. He came back and asked if I would come to Santa Monica. I said yes no problem. He then said he would let me know in the next few days when and where exactly. Being used to his vague cryptic answers by now, I said yes, no problem. A day or so later he gave me the time and place and asked me to make sure it was only me coming, and that I did not tell anyone my business of where and when I was meeting people. I said yeah of course.

So finally, the day came. I was so nervous; you would think I was back in time on my wedding day. Why was I so nervous? I was only going to meet a casual friend, and I knew him really well by now so there should be no awkwardness. But something deep inside me knew it would be significant and epic.

I arrived at the specified location, which was a more remote than normal parking lot at the beach. I was in my freshly washed, old deteriorating white Jeep Grand Cherokee, dressed in white jeans, casual T-shirt, wearing some old $50 Sketchers sneakers. Nobody was there except for several stray empty cars. I looked all around to see if I could see something or someone of note. Nothing. I waited. After ten minutes I started to get a sinking feeling that I had been stood up like an idiot. Just when I was starting to become annoyed, I noticed some interesting movement. I saw a big black shiny SUV drive in the lot followed by three cars, which all looked like those undercover cop cars. They pulled off to the side of the parking lot near me. I just watched, not knowing what was going on. Certainly, it was not for me. Except it was. Two men in the first car behind the SUV got out first and approached the SUV. Then two more men from the other cars got out but stood by their cars. The men, who approached the SUV opened the door to the SUV. Out slid who I knew immediately was Chaz. I had never seen a picture of Chaz, but I immediately sensed it was him. I could feel it in every bone in my body. I was totally shaking in my Sketchers at this point.

Out slid this young-looking guy with dark, perfect, short, specially styled hair, $1,000 sunglasses, some kind of $10,000 jacket, and shoes that must have been worth thousands to match. He was like a movie star combined with a royal prince. As he started walking toward me, the first two men came with him. As he grew closer, I got a closer look at him. He was a "10" on the looks scale, and the value of his sunglasses, clothes, and shoes doubled in value. I was frozen like a deer in front of 1,000 spotlights. Thank God he spoke first. He said, "Hi Brian," and he shook my hand and gave me a hug. I said, "Oh my god, Hi." Chaz responded by saying, "My name is not Oh My God, it's Chaz." I actually said "sorry" because I was not sure if he was being funny or if he had been insulted. To this day I am still not sure. The two men looked inside my vehicle parked behind me, and they looked at me as if I was a possible terrorist, then they looked at Chaz, and Chaz nodded his head, and the men walked away back to their car and just stood there. I could not see how many people were in the SUV that carried Chaz, and nobody else ever came out.

I did not know what to do, so I let Chaz lead everything, including the conversation and where we would stand and talk. Chaz guided us a short distance closer to the beach so that we were not awkwardly talking in the parking lot. He said to me, "So are you nervous Brian?" I said "Yes, but it's okay, I'm fine." He then said, "Are you surprised?" I said yes. I told him he never said anything on the phone about "*this*", pointing to the security caravan. Chaz asked, "What is "*this?*" I again was not sure if he was insulted or not, and I said that I meant the security people and all that. Chaz said, "Don't worry about them; just talk to me like we do on the phone." So, I did. I talked to him normally from that moment on and never looked back. We talked for about an hour just like we had been doing on the phone for weeks. I began to feel totally at ease.

Eventually what I knew was coming, came. Chaz said he had to go. He said, "Well I better get going back to Malibu or my dad will kill me; he does not know I am here." Of course, I was thinking in my head, "how can nobody know where you are with a battalion of security following you." I was smart enough to keep my mouth shut on such thoughts. Chaz gave me a hug and said, "You know Brian, I knew I would like you; but I like you even more now after meeting you in person." I melted. I did not know what this "acquaintance", "friendship", "relationship", or whatever, was, but I naturally melted anyway. All of a sudden, I did not want him to leave. I do not know how, but he somehow knew something, because he stopped, walked back to me, hugged me again, and smiled. He then walked back to the SUV. Security opened the door for him, he slid inside, and his caravan of four vehicles drove away. I stood there in the parking lot for maybe ten minutes stunned. I did not want what just happened to end, so I stood there thinking that as long as I stayed there, I would still be in the moment. I finally broke out of my daze, got back into my old Jeep, and drove home on autopilot.

Chaz and I resumed our regular daily phone conversations that would sometimes last hours. I think we both felt more comfortable, and safe with each other, therefore, we both opened up more. He was very funny. Sometimes his humor could be dark and devilish, but always good natured toward me. I would ask him things like, "Do you always travel with that many security guards?", and he would laugh and say, "Of course not silly; I usually have twice that many, especially when I am with my family." He would go on to say that when the entire family travels out to dinner or any function together, they would usually have at least twelve "officers" and many cars.

I knew early on not to ask too many prying questions, but as time went on, I was able to gracefully, in the right times and circumstances, ask him certain things. Over time I would learn that his stepdad was a very important person high in the government. His mom worked for a very famous movie producer which I won't mention. They lived between two homes in Malibu and San Francisco. He told me they could travel back and forth between the homes with no suitcase, and not even a toothbrush, because they had two of everything. Each house was totally equipped with everything they needed, including in their bathrooms and bedrooms.

Their "second home" was the Malibu house, which was a huge fancy beach house. His brother Martin apparently had a brand new, white Lamborghini in the garage, which had plastic wrap around it to keep it safe; meaning he never drove it. Chaz told me when he was a kid, they used to have a tiger in their back yard, but eventually the tiger got too big, and they donated him to a zoo. He still went to visit the tiger from time to time.

Their primary home was in San Francisco in some ultra-exclusive gated neighborhood. The house sounded like some gigantic huge monstrosity of a mansion. Frankly, I had trouble even comprehending the level of wealth.

Chaz made it a point to discuss some of the practical and security measures they had. I think I was vetted enough at this point that he was being more open regarding such things. I kind of got the feeling that I was being groomed and prepared to deal with their "situation." He would explain how they had a lockdown procedure at night where there would be "last call." "Last call" would be when you could go to the kitchen and get any drinks or food you wanted, before you had to be locked up in your room for the night. After last call and lockdown, you were stuck in your room. I am guessing they had motion detectors and such things in the hallways and stairways, and that is why nobody could leave their rooms. I asked what would happen if I accidentally left my room and he said, "You might get shot." Then he laughed. Again, I was not sure if he was joking or not. They had "officers," which I would learn were a special type of FBI officers, similar to Secret Service Agents, but not technically Secret Service. They were stationed in the driveway and grounds all night. If anything odd was picked up on the sensors, the officers would go inside the house to check things (thus why I might be shot). Add to all this, two Doberman Pincher dogs which were basically set on "kill" mode, and you had to know the "secret word" to get the dogs to stand down.

Chaz and I discussed everything during our weeks and months of phone conversations that seemed to last longer as time went on. It got to the point that I was on the phone with him for like half the day. I realized that my "function" at that time was to keep him company. He was actually quite lonely and isolated because he rarely went out and did things, due to all the security measures and his family's limitations on him. He spent most of his time reading and researching things. He was a tested and certified genius and was always studying every subject known to man. Chaz could answer any question you had about anything. Go ahead, try him. Whether it was about cooking, Hollywood, cars, computers, history, world issues, (insert list of all items on Wikipedia here).

I took advantage of this knowledge daily. I went to Chaz about all my business and financial questions, asking him all kinds of things and for advice. He provided me with good guidance I used daily. I came to totally depend on him. I depended on him for my emotional contact, my business advice, and hope for the future. Chaz in turn would tell me very personal things about him, and deep thoughts he had. Our conversations could be very random. One minute he would talk about cooking, and the next minute he would joke, he hoped he died young and beautiful in some fantastic fiery crash or something. One thing that always stuck with me is when he said to me, "You have had to work very hard for everything you have achieved, and have not had an easy life; it's time for that to change." The conversations would go back and forth similar to this on both sides. We had become very close. Very, very close. I had only seen him in person once, but I totally admired and loved him. He became a mentor, friend, advisor, companion, and perhaps more than that.

Eventually, our conversations turned a little. They went away from random everyday things, to Chaz's ambitions and ideas. Chaz said he wanted to travel the world for a year. He wanted to go to all places, everywhere. He asked me what I thought about that, and if I would like to do something like that. I was a bit stunned as usual, but at the same moment I felt a pit in my stomach. I knew immediately that I could never take such a trip. I could never leave my daughter for that long. Yes, my daughter lived with her mother, but Angel was the center of my universe, and I hers, and there was no way I could leave her. Impossible. Plus, I had business responsibilities and mounting problems. Chaz was suggesting something amazing, but there was no way I could practically do it.

I lightly explained to Chaz I could not leave my daughter. He was a bit let down, but he totally understood. He asked me how long I *could* leave her. After much back and forth, I suggested that MAYBE I could do a six-month trip thing IF I could fly back home from wherever we were, monthly, to see my daughter. I could tell this was a stickler for him, but he was so kind, he just tabled the discussion while you could tell he was working on the problem in his mind.

This idea of me traveling with him also brought up my business situation. After long conversations, Chaz said he thought the thing to do was to close my business. He said my business was barely surviving and it was not worth the effort. He joked he earned in one hour's interest more than what my entire business was generating. He said he would rather just pay me that amount, instead of me spending all my effort on a dying non-producing business. I reminded him that my business was all I had. I was not wealthy like him. Chaz asked how much it would take for me to give up the business. He said, "What if I buy you out?" I asked him what he would do with the business if he bought me out. He said it would close immediately. This really did not sit well with me at the time. My business was my life's work and I was obligated to clients and myself in fixing it. He asked me for a number. I told him at one time my business was worth about $1Million, but now I would be lucky to get $300,000, and that would just go to paying off debts. He paused for maybe three seconds and said, "Then I will buy you out for $300,000." Once again, I did not know if he was serious or joking. It was so awkward I stayed silent. We changed the subject.

On another occasion, he asked what I wanted for my birthday, which was coming up in several months. I told him I did not need anything from him except his companionship. He said that was sweet, but really, what did I want. I was so uncomfortable with this. I genuinely really liked, *loved*, him. I did not want him to think I was using him or taking advantage of him, so I kept a very wide berth around any subject of asking him for anything at all. He asked what my biggest problem in my life was now. I sighed. I said "Everything." He said, "Like what?" I went down the list; my business failing, my bitch Ex Luci, the fact my daughter did not live in my household, and that my Jeep was dying. He said, "Oh yes your jeep." He then asked what kind of car I would want to replace it. I said I did not know. He said, "No, really, what car would you buy?" I told him I might buy the same thing, another Jeep Grand Cherokee Limited, because I loved the vehicle. Almost as if he was getting frustrated, he said, "Yes but what is your dream car?" I thought for a moment, and said to him, "Well I have always wanted a Ferrari or Lamborghini since I was a kid." I went into details of this fantasy, and color choices and such. He sounded satisfied with my answer and he said, "Well, hmmm." He said, "You DO realize if I got you a Ferrari, I would probably need to keep it in my name, but it would be your car, and only yours to drive." I of course immediately said, "YES, YES, that would be totally fine, of course, obviously." He indicated he would make some phone calls and look around. I did not bring it up again.

About a week later, I *did* receive a gift. It was not a car, but it was something just as special. I had a box in the mail from him and I opened it. Inside was a silver ring on a silver necklace. The ring did not look new and I was perplexed. In fact, it looked quite "used." I called him up and said I had received his package, and there was a ring necklace inside. He immediately said, "I know the ring is not fancy or expensive, but it means the world to me and I want you to have it." When someone like Chaz with all his money says something is very special to him, it means something. So, my thoughts immediately moved to how this must be very significant. He told me to wear it when I wanted, and not lose it. He said if I did not want it, he wanted it back. I wore it every moment with honor, pride, and love. I never got a chance to ask him more about the ring necklace, or what it meant.

As you can imagine, I was starting to yearn for another in-person meeting. One day I sheepishly asked him when he thought we could see each other again. I could tell he thought it was really sweet that I was requesting this. I confess I was melting (again). Clearly, I had fallen for whatever "this situation" was. He really had become very significant to me. His response was that he had been thinking of flying me up to their house in San Francisco for Thanksgiving. He said he had to get his dad's approval and it was complicated. I totally understood. You see, Chaz had not yet told me the actual name/identity of his dad. What Chaz did not know is that I already knew who his stepdad was. Chaz, as smart as he was, had made one tiny slip up weeks ago about something. I, not exactly being an idiot, caught it. I did my own research and figured out who his stepdad was. His stepdad was indeed a very important government official. I won't say.

I could not tell Chaz I had been stalking around and figured this out. I told Chaz I understood the complications, but that I would absolutely love to go up there for Thanksgiving. He asked how long I would want to stay, and I answered, "As long as you let me." We both laughed.

During following conversations, we talked about me coming to his house for Thanksgiving many times. Chaz also said he wanted to bring me up to their home in Whistler, Canada for Christmas (yes, another home). I told him that sounded great, even though once again I had a pit in my stomach, knowing I had plans to go to my parents with my daughter that Christmas.

Chaz warned me that if I came to their house, I would have to face his dad and his brother, and it would not be easy. I nervously asked why. He said his dad would for sure interrogate me in his office. Chaz warned me to always be honest in all my answers to his dad, because his dad would only ask me questions to which he already knew the answers. He said his brother Martin would likely make it his mission to have me feel as uncomfortable as possible, as a way of testing me, and initiation. Frankly, Chaz made a visit up there sound horrible. But I had so many stars in my eyes about seeing Chaz again and being inside his world that I was not scared away, and I made sure he knew it.

Chaz said he felt he almost had approval for my Thanksgiving trip, but that first he had decided he was going to wire me some money on a certain date as a first installment to buyout my business, and get me out from underneath it. He said he might have some papers he would need me to sign, and I of course told him that was fine. I was surprised, as I had not brought this up, but deep inside I was very relieved help was on the way. I immediately calculated how I would apply his funds to my finances, payroll, and bills. I asked him if the date of the wire transfer was certain, and he said yes. He warned me that his brother Martin would have to know about the entire arrangement and be involved and was that okay with me. I replied that I understood. I figured out early on that Chaz did absolutely nothing without his brother's knowledge. His brother Martin was clearly his protector, and Martin took his role beyond seriously.

Chaz then went on to tell me he would be taking a trip. I asked where. He said he had convinced his family to let him go to Oktoberfest in Germany. I asked how that works with his security. He said there would be no security, but he would be going with three of his closest friends (one of which I had heard about in detail already). He said his parents were very hesitant to let him go, but that he insisted and really wanted to do this. He asked me if it was okay that he was doing this trip, since we would not be able to talk much while he was away. I was a bit surprised he was asking for my permission. I asked how long he would be gone, and he replied a week or two. He said we would not be able to talk every day, but that he would call me every three days for sure. I then told him I would go to my New England lake house and have some time at my house there. So, I booked my trip for back east. Chaz was to leave for Germany before my trip back east. We had a long final phone call before his trip. I remember distinctly him saying at the end of the call, "Love you."

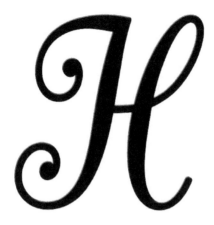

CHAPTER TEN

The Walk-In

I arrived back east at my New England lake house. Chaz was in Germany and I did not expect to hear from him for a few days. It was the beginning of October and the weather was perfect at the lake. I was so happy to be back "home" where I truly felt at home, even though I was completely living in LA.

I spent my first few days doing tasks around the house and going for my run in the afternoons. I felt so much better about everything. Yes, I had business problems and an ongoing divorce, but I had such a wonderful daughter out of the marriage, I had my beautiful dream house on the lake, I was living in wonderful sunny Los Angeles at the beach, and I had this wonderful amazing "friendship/relationship" with Chaz. I was also in peak physical condition; my health was near perfection, and all I could smell was fresh air and the lake breeze. Although I missed my constant daily conversations with Chaz, I was totally enjoying my solo time at the lake. Things were about as good as they could get under the difficult circumstances. Life was good, and it looked like everything was going to be okay, and maybe even great.

I had been back east for three days and I had not heard from Chaz. Thus, I knew I would hear from him the next day for sure, since he promised to call me every three days. That fourth day came and there was no call. My bliss turned to agitation. I started to wonder, what is going on? Is he so busy and having so much fun that he forgot I exist? Is he someplace where there is no cell service? Did his phone break? Does he hate me, and this was his plan on how to ditch me? You know how it goes. The longer one has time to think, the worse it is, and more crazy theories run through your head.

On the fifth day I started to become angry, scared, annoyed, and desperate. I called his phone and got voice mail. I left a soft but serious message that I was worried, and could he please just let me know he was okay even if he did not want to talk. Nothing.

On the sixth day, I had a horrible feeling in my stomach that something horrible had happened. I truly trusted Chaz and I knew he would not be this way. I knew something must be wrong. Was he sick? I knew it was something, and I officially became distraught and left another voice mail where I started to cry at the end, explaining how worried I was. Now in addition to being terrified and desperate, I was also embarrassed that I had gotten so emotional and dramatic, and I had clearly gone off the rails. It was also very unusual for me to get dramatic to the point of crying. It was as if I was truly certain something catastrophic had happened, but I could not explain how I knew this. My "vacation" was ruined at this point.

On the seventh day, I was in a solemn depression. I no longer felt like running or doing anything. I just moped around the house wondering what to do. Sometime around mid-morning, I walked into my home office to check my email. I saw an email from someone I did not know, but a name I recognized. It was the name of a person Chaz had described to me as "his best friend from childhood." His name was Jackson.

I very frantically opened the email. The email read, "*Brian, this is Jackson, Chaz's friend. Martin has asked me to email you. It is with great sadness I have to tell you that Chaz was in a car accident in Germany and has passed away. I am very sorry to tell you this way, but I don't have your phone number. Feel free to email me if you want.*"

As I read it at first, time stopped. I think I was struck with lightning. I actually did not believe what I was seeing. I read it a second time. The second time, I felt my heart explode into thousands of pieces and drop into my stomach. Still in confusion, I read it a third time. The third time, I started exclaiming, "NO, NO, NO, NO, NO," and gradually got louder with each one. Then I said some other things similar to No, which I do not remember what they were. As I was doing this, I felt a strong painful tingle in my arms, chest, and up through my head. I think I was likely wailing in some fashion, as if impaled by a huge metal rod. Feeling nothing but strong painful tingles, I saw black, and dropped to the floor. Out.

I don't know how long I was out for. When I came to, I was on the floor next to my desk with my face and eyes completely covered with a coating of dried tears. I remember I could not breathe very well; it was very labored and difficult. I immediately remembered why I was on the floor. I stayed on the floor motionless for a few minutes. It was as if I was paralyzed. Then I got up on my knees. I glanced at my computer and saw the email. I did not bother reading it again. I knew what it said. I stood up and had trouble keeping my balance at first. The tingling in my arms and chest was gone, but there was still some light tingling in my head. I felt like my heart had been removed. What I mean by this is that I felt dead inside. Actually, I felt dead period, like a zombie. My breathing continued to be very labored. All I could do is stand, or take some steps, then stop. My thoughts were very limited. I remember having to actually think and decide which direction I would walk in, as if it was a big decision and task. It also felt as if I had to actually *think* in order to breath. It was as if I had to *decide* to breathe and think through each breath in order for it to happen.

I remember the first task I did was to go get my ring necklace he gave me, which I had left on the table while I was doing work around the house. I got the ring necklace and clutched it as if it was my last and only link to Chaz. I placed it around my neck as if I was placing a gold medal or security blanket around my neck. It felt better to have the necklace on. I never took it off for a long time after putting it on in that moment.

Honestly, it is hard for me to write my account of what happened at this point because I frankly do not remember much. I was in some kind of zombie daze and was completely brain dead and heart dead. Only my labored breathing kept me alive, and that felt it could quit at any moment. I remember that I was very concerned at how I was going to get back home to LA. I literally did not feel capable of driving to the airport; talking to ticket agents, navigating airports, and driving back home once in LA. The thought of it all that was so overwhelming, it really seemed impossible to me. But I knew I had to somehow get home.

Let me just say now, there must have been some crying fits, and I threw some things around in my office during the couple days I remained at the lake house before going back to LA. I only know this because when I would return to the lake house many months later, there was evidence of damage and distress within my office.

I must have somehow got myself to the airport. I remember sitting on the airplane clutching and looking down at my necklace for strength and feeling like a zombie. I also remember my labored breathing. My breathing is forever burned into my memory, as taking all my effort and concentration to continue breathing.

I managed to make it back home to LA. I felt dead. I felt like a zombie. I was lost. I was sick. I did not think I could even feed myself. I was also worried about my visitation with my daughter. I could not let Luci know what happened, or that I was possibly not capable of visitation. I had to act normal with her and my daughter, and I was wondering how that would be possible. Fortunately, there were several more days to go before my next visitation.

What happened next is even more confusing to me than what I already detailed. I think it was the next morning after arriving back home, and I was sitting in my office at my desk, where I would always have all my conversations with Chaz. I started to cry uncontrollably. I am not sure if maybe it was because I was finally safe and secure back home, that maybe I felt I could "lose it." Well I lost it. I had an on-and-off crying fit for a good couple of hours. I only stopped eventually because I could not breathe anymore and was going to have a medical emergency if I kept it up.

The next moment, there was a sudden feeling of comfort out of nowhere. Well, actually it's not true it was coming from nowhere. It was coming from my right. I felt a "presence", as if "it" was sitting next to me on my right, next to me behind my desk. I looked over to my right and saw something. It was like a light energy force. It was not a "ghost." It was more like normal air, except thicker. I recognized the energy as feeling like Chaz, like how he is, his energy, the feeling I get when talking to him or standing next to him. A couple seconds after that, I started getting messages (silent voices) in my head. The voice or message in my head was "yes it's me I'm here." I felt so calm and comfortable in that moment. I started to cry again, but it was a different cry. This was not a wailing out of control stuck pig cry. This was a gentle cry of gratitude. I was so grateful and happy I was having this connection with Chaz. It was as if he was watching me cry and waiting. I mentally said to him, "I'm so relieved you are here, I missed you." For some reason, my next thoughts to him were "What's it like?" The voice in my head answered, "It was scary at first, but once I pushed off from my body, it did not hurt anymore." In my mind I was about to ask, "What's it like to be dead," but before I could even develop the entire thought and verbalize it in my head, the voice said "I can't taste, smell, or feel anything; but I can go anywhere just by thinking it." Then I said, "I don't want you to leave." The voice in my head replied, "I can live on inside you if you want." I immediately said, "Yes, yes, yes," and I cried a little. The voice said, "Are you sure?" I said, "Yes absolutely, please, please, please," through my tears. Then it hit! I felt a very strong and strange sensation go through me that made me shiver; the hair on my arms and neck stood up, and I had goose bumps. I felt a cool sensation, then a warm sensation. I think I almost passed out, but I know I did not. Then the energy that had been next to me on my right was gone. It was replaced by the sensation of a certain "presence" (or entity?) inside me. I went from feeling completely dead and empty inside, to having an actual life or presence inside me. The voice stopped speaking inside my head, and now I could *feel* the voice even though it was not speaking. I did not feel alone. I felt some "intelligence," or thing, or energy, actually inside my head. I became very tired as if the days of crying and pain had caught up to me finally, and I was going to faint. I went to bed.

    I slept for maybe 16 hours. When I woke up, I felt very sick and foggy. I felt like there was literally a fog covering my eyes that I had trouble seeing through. I felt very tired. One thing I noticed is that I seemed to be breathing much better. But the improved breathing was replaced by an overwhelming tiredness.

Days went by, one by one, where it was the same routine. I would sleep all night. In the morning, I would wake up and use all my effort to get out of bed. I would use the bathroom, check my email, walk out to the dining area and look outside, and then I would feel very tired and need to go back to bed. I would lie in bed. Sometimes I would sleep, and sometimes I would just lay there. Then I might get up and use the bathroom, and rinse and repeat. I would say there was a very long sleep each night, then a series of six or so naps during the day, while the rest of the day was filled with sitting or resting.

Not too many days went by until I was starting to run out of cans of vegetable soup I had been eating. Vegetable soup and toast was all that I was eating. I had already lost some weight that I did not need to lose. I decided it was time to try and go outside and walk down to my usual take out restaurants and get a good lunch. I usually alternated my lunches between pizza and Mexican.

I got myself dressed in sweatpants and t-shirt. I know my hair was a horrible mess, so I wiped water on it. I walked down my exterior apartment stairs looking like I had been sleeping for days. Well, I had been sleeping for days, so okay. I walked down the sidewalk, I recall being careful to place my feet and steps one in front of the other, because I felt it was possible I could fall. When I got down the street a bit where there were lots of other people, I started to experience some weird sensations. I noticed every time I looked at someone walking by me, I could sense what they were thinking and feeling. I was picking up on all kinds of random meaningless thoughts of each person walking past me. It was actually disconcerting for me. It was like constant noise coming at me that would not stop.

The second thing I noticed is that nobody was looking at me. I was looking at everyone, but everyone was looking straight ahead as if I was not there. I began to feel like I was not there. I felt invisible. I started to get scared. I wondered, "Was I dead?" Maybe I died when I collapsed back east, and now I have been a ghost all this time? I thought it through, and other than the airport, I did not have any contact with people, and certainly no people who actually knew me personally. So I started to test the theory, and I remember waving and saying Hi to some lady walking by me. She ignored me as if I was not even there. I went into the takeout restaurant; nervous they would not see me and give me my food. I stood in line, still invisible, and feeling invisible, but when I got to the front of the line, they seemed to recognize that I was a person, and they gave me my food. I was very relieved. I went home as quickly as I could while still hearing all the thoughts of people passing by me. I got inside my apartment and was so glad to be back home inside and gratified to have real food. I ate like I had not eaten in a month. I should have ordered three of those Mexican lunches.

I asked the inner voice if I was dead. There was no reply. I asked why I could sense what people are thinking. I did get a reply to that. It said, "There are many things you can do which you don't realize yet." My existing psychic abilities, which I had shown evidence of since a young boy, had just increased exponentially.

That was not all. I noticed I knew things I did not know before. I felt smarter in a way. It was a weird sensation, because I felt retarded in terms of thought function due to the "fog," but I felt I had volumes of data and information in my head that I did not have before. I was in a situation where I had to think carefully how I would take the garbage out, but if you asked me a question about anything, I would have the information to answer it.

Most disconcerting is that I also noticed my personality seemed different. I felt more laid back, relaxed, and funny. I felt like I was more interested in people than money and business. I was more interested in the journey than the destination. I had lost all interest in hunting, and just the thought of killing an animal, was alarming to me. I found myself with a new interest in history and viewing documentaries to learn new things. There were so many things where I felt I was a different person. Maybe the old Brian DID actually die?

One of the biggest changes for me was an overwhelming intense sense of spirituality. Previously, I had never had any interest in religion or spirituality. But now, I had very clear and intense feelings on the subject. I felt a disdain for organized religion, but a very strong closeness to God. I had never felt so close to God before in my life. I felt God could whisper in my ear and I could hear the messages. Over time, I would develop my own definite notions of what "God" was, and how it all worked. To this day, I feel I personally understand Jesus, and listen to God, while not subscribing to any formal religion.

Even more significant than my new sense of spirituality, was a feeling that I was now separate or detached from humans in general. I started seeing "humans" as different from myself. What does that make me? Not human? I do not know. I do not feel I come from an alien planet called Hectar, or CB41, or anything like that. I do not have grey skin, and I am not short or have huge eyes. But part of me does not feel of this world. It is very hard to fully describe this because there are no words for it. I feel "different" and "detached," as if I have one foot in each world. I also feel I have one foot on earth and one foot in the spirit world (in death?). Am I an alien? I can honestly tell you that I do not shape shift into a reptile at night though.

I realized I could ask the voice in my head questions, and I would sometimes get answers. I could ask, "Do I turn right here or left," and I would get an answer saying, "Left," and the "left" would be the correct answer. There were many examples of this.

I also found I could draw upon many different "sources," and not just the one "entity." I found myself very connected to "Source," as we say in Psychic Land. "Source," being Universal energy, "God," or Spirit.

I became a different person. But at the same time, I still had the essence and memories of the old person inside me. I became a new person that consisted of the old and the new, mixed together.

As far as my psychic abilities at the time, I felt I had three major abilities. I could sense what others were feeling and thinking sometimes; I could talk to these voices coming from "Source" (the Universe); and I had a tremendous amount of knowledge available to me that I never had before. There would be much more to come as far as abilities, but those were the major abilities I noticed immediately at the time.

I spent weeks and months in this dual universe of feeling powerful and smart, but also being completely mentally damaged and non-functional. I felt mentally disabled because I could not cognitively handle more than one task at a time. Just driving to the grocery store had to be planned out step by step. But on the other hand, I had these amazing abilities and abstract thoughts hiding in the back of my head. I knew I was not a genius, but I felt like one in a weird way sometimes.

My new abilities and repressed brainpower were very limited though, because I had a tremendous sadness and depression that lived with me always. I was very subdued. I had not opened my mail in many weeks and kept a huge pile of unopened mail sitting on the floor in my office. However, I managed to function enough to fool Luci into thinking I was okay. Luci would drop Angel off at my door, and I could act totally normal for a couple minutes. I was able to interact with Angel totally fine and watch her responsibly, although I confess, I would need rests, and I would set her up with her toys and TV shows so I could take a break. At the end of my visitation, I would bring Angel back to her mother and was able to do the exchange without anyone noticing that I was off.

The truth is that something was very off. Although I was now able to function at minimal levels, my sadness and depression seemed to be escalating. I was really messed up. I had gone through many losses, I had suffered some sort of paranormal mental trauma, I felt like part of me died, I was a totally different person inside, and I really could not cope with everything at once. I had Luci always ready to harass me and put me down, and I could not see my daughter as often as I wanted. I increasingly felt like I did not want to keep feeling all this and living all this. I really did not want to live anymore.

The depression was becoming so strong, it was the only feeling I had. But I think what was putting me over the edge was that I was living in this depression in a person that did not feel like me. I felt really lost with the feeling that the "old me" had died. I had no anchor in life, or reference point of existence. All I knew is that my old life was dead, I was totally mired in sadness and depression, and I saw no hope of things changing or getting better. I did not feel insane or controlled by the depression. Deep inside I felt sharper than I had ever felt in my life. But on the outside, I was very slow functioning in some ways. Draped over that contradiction was a depression as black and thick as any molasses you could find.

I found myself for the first time in my life contemplating suicide. I was very thoughtful about it. I did not feel I was being impulsive or insane about it. I was thinking through it, deciding if it was a good option for me, as if it were a business decision. On one hand, I definitely did not want to live anymore, but on the other hand, I had my daughter and could not leave her alone with her mother, Lucifer.

I thought about suicide for big chunks of the day every day. I knew I probably needed help and a doctor. I needed a doctor for many reasons. Firstly, I wanted to kill myself. But secondly, why did I go from being a very efficient person who could multi-task, to a mentally damaged person who could barely get to the grocery store. I once said to myself, "so this is what it feels like to be stupid." I always had top grades at the top of my class and knew all the business answers and so on. And now I had to think through how I was going to find my car, drive to the store, and then find my car again to come back home and so on. I had Albert Einstein in the back of my head trying to explain a Universal principle to me, but then I would literally forget where I parked my car. Sometimes I would be in the grocery store and for a few moments, not know where in the store I was, or why I was there. I would look at a list of ten items, and a few moments later not remember one of them.

I started to try and think how I would see a doctor. But like everything else, it became too complicated. I did not know which hospital to go to, or where, or if I was covered by insurance, and how I would even find the hospital and get there. I concluded I needed someone to actually do this for me and take me there, but there was nobody there to do this. The only person I knew near me was Luci, and obviously I could not involve her in this. Thus, I determined I could not see a doctor. I gave up on that and just kept living what I was living.

After contemplating how I was feeling, and my desire for suicide, I made a deal with myself. I said to myself that I would wait a bit and see if I got better with more time. I decided that if I were not better by my birthday three months away, then I would give myself permission to kill myself the day after my birthday. So, I officially had a date certain. This actually gave me a feeling of relief and comfort believe it or not. Firstly, I knew I would not do something crazy and kill myself randomly or impulsively, and secondly, that suicide was indeed an option for me eventually if I really needed and wanted it.

Since I had a suicide date set, I then spent much of my time trying to figure out how to do it, should the day after my birthday arrive without any improvement. My potential plan involved leaving my door unlocked so I could be easily found, then laying in my bed face up looking into the sun through my window, cutting myself, and just letting myself float away while basking in the sunlight. I thought about perhaps overdosing on sleeping pills at the same time. The only detail I had not figured out is that I needed to make sure I did it correctly so it would definitely work, and I was concerned about leaving a mess, so I was wondering about putting plastic on the bed. I did not want to be any trouble to the landlord, or anyone else for that matter. I took the step of going to the store and buying the plastic that I would put over the mattress so it would be easier for everything to be cleaned up. I continued to contemplate the details and work everything through in my mind. I wanted my effort to be final, giving me a peaceful exit, but also limiting the inconvenience to those who would find me.

Meanwhile, while I was waiting for my "death date" to arrive, life went on and my struggle continued. But exactly one month after Chaz's death, something strange happened. Another interesting person approached me on social media. I had been engaging on social media daily as a way of having contact with the world, while I was holed up inside, depressed in my home 95% of the time. Some seemingly younger guy from Brazil had sent me a message just saying, "Hi." I looked at his profile and there was something about him that made me want to reply. I can't explain it. I was compelled to reply. I said, "Hi" back. He later replied asking how I was doing. I told him I was not doing very well because I had lost someone close to me and had many other issues going on.

He introduced himself saying his name was Gez and that he lived in Brazil. I told him I was Brian, and that I could see he was in Brazil, and that I had never been to Brazil. He changed the conversation back to me. He asked if I was too sad. He could speak English, but it was not very good, so sometimes I had to strain to understand what he was writing. Being bored and lonely, I kept conversing with him. Our conversations became daily, just back and forth messages. I started to open up and explain more details of what happened to me. But left out all the weird paranormal stuff. It always felt odd to me because he seemed to be extra sensitive and compassionate toward me, even though he did not know me or fully understand my situation. I told him I was getting so sad that I did not even want to live anymore. He told me it would be okay. He had a very weird way about him. He was kind of weird actually, straight up. He had broken English and was too young to understand much about life and complex problems. But at the same time, he seemed to have an all-knowing angelic sense about him. He always knew what to say to provide comfort and support. He did not freak out at my suicide talk, and instead was comforting, and was always repeating that I would be fine.

After much back and forth with Gez for a good month or two, I started to really wonder about some things. Like, who is this person really? How did he find me? Why did he find me? Why does he seem so knowing? So, I started asking questions. I asked him how he found me and why he wrote me. His reply was something like, "Because I felt I should." What kind of answer is that? Hmmm. At one point, I got suspicious and said, "Did Chaz's people send you?" He replied, "Maybe." I could not get any more out of him. Then he started talking as if he was this way with many people, and he said his friends called him "Angel of Light." Gez would continue to be a mystery for a long time in the future as you will see.

With all that said, Gez's companionship was very welcomed and needed. We began a close dialogue and began to grow closer. He became my primary comfort and companion. His English also started improving gradually and dramatically the more we conversed.

In addition to the comforting companionship of Gez, I was to receive even more relief. Exactly three months after Chaz's death, and only two weeks before my birthday and suicide date, I felt a change in my "condition." One morning I woke up and the "fog" was gone. Just like that. I could think clearly. It was dramatically obvious. I noticed it immediately. My vision and thinking felt clear again. I could think again! I could entertain multiple thoughts. I could easily see how I would get to the grocery store, or any store. I could process complex thoughts again. The sun was streaming through my bedroom window. It was a nice bright day, and I could think again. Everything was so clear all of a sudden for no apparent reason. I couldn't believe it. I had gotten used to feeling like I was mentally retarded in some way. But now it was gone. This raised my spirits dramatically. I felt like a functional person again. A couple days later, I decided to cancel the suicide date. I justified my decision by the fact I simply could not leave my daughter no matter how bad I felt. I loved her too much, and she was my responsibility, plus I worried what my death might do to her psychologically. But realistically, it was the fog lifting that made me cancel the suicide date. For example, just look at how I easily, swiftly, and obviously, reasoned through how I can't leave my daughter. The fact is that now I had my marbles back, I could think clearly, and knew suicide was not a good valid option. I had healed enough and beat my death deadline by two weeks. Thank God for that yes? To this day, I think about what a difference two weeks can make. I was only two weeks from my death deadline before I got better and called it off. Good thing I did not have a deadline scheduled sooner. I am afraid I might have actually done it. I'm glad I didn't.

It does get better with time, if you give yourself enough time. Don't give yourself two weeks too little time like I could have done. Give yourself enough time for things to get better and they will. For those of you reading this that have thoughts of suicide, please wait. Give yourself more time. Also keep reading my story. I understand you. I wrote this book partly for you. I want you to see that things can get very bad, but you can survive it. One of the reasons I decided to release this book is so that you may decide to give yourself more time and live. I want you to survive. I want you to live.

Before I close out this hideous and scary chapter of my story, it is important for me to insert here the technical concept of a "walk-in." A "walk-in" is what I am convinced happened to me. A "walk-in," in the psychic sense, is thought by many to be the phenomenon of a foreign soul entering a body, existing there, or even totally replacing the current soul. This phenomenon most often happens in near death experiences, severe trauma, illness, or extreme depression and suicidal episodes. After the walk-in, the person usually exhibits a different personality and traits. The person can also have cognitive problems where they find it difficult to function in everyday life. That is the quick definition. I clearly had all the symptoms. I also did something which all experts would say to never do. I INVITED an entity inside me. The "entity" even asked me if I was sure, and I clearly consented.

There is also room for debate and discussion as to why the walk-in happened. Some would say that Chaz was some sort of

Illuminati "Reptilian Shape Shifter," who was seeking an adequate "host," and thus he found me acceptable, and used me for that purpose. It can't be denied that my entire time with Chaz seemed very much like an interview and evaluation. He constantly posed hypothetical questions to me in an effort to profile my psychology, morals, values, and thinking processes. He also seemed interested in my existing intellectual abilities and potential. Chaz also spoke on various occasions how he would die young, so perhaps he knew he needed a host.

Others might say that "aliens" are involved. Many close to Chaz joked that he was actually an alien. He had very odd behaviors, and a very unique intellect. I can attest to the fact that although he appeared very human, he was extremely unusual. Nobody could say that Chaz behaved like a normal human. He did not. He behaved like a "higher being." I also must confess that since the walk-in, I also have felt like an alien in the sense that I no longer relate on a "human" level very well, as well as other things. Add to this, the fact that I was possibly abducted much earlier in time at the lake house. Perhaps my earlier abduction was me being evaluated for something to happen in the future? Perhaps I am now alien or part alien? I could not tell you if I was.

Or perhaps it really is what is seems. I was very psychically open, Chaz's spirit asked to enter, and I consented. Or perhaps I simply had a stroke or hallucination and am batshit crazy. But that would not explain all my abilities, personality changes, and such.

I leave it to each person's own views and interpretations of what happened to me. Whether a stroke, hallucination, psychic walk-in, Reptilian Shape Shifter host, alien, or a mixture of some, or all of these; I am just here telling my story the way it happened. You can judge me and speculate to your heart's content.

CHRISTMAS MOURNING

This is a poem I wrote some months after the "walk-in" event. Although the subject matter may be seasonal, the poem illustrates my state of mind and thinking at the time.

It's that time of year. The most wonderful time of year.
I listen to the music. It reminds me of Christmases past.
The music reminds me of my childhood filled with hopes and dreams.
The music reminds me of how a child's dreams can come true on that one morning.

I see the children this time of year.
So full of excitement and hope.
Everything in front of them.
Only good things to come.

I see families this time of year.
Joyous and invigorated.
Warm feelings of being together.
Comforting they have each other.

I see couples this time of year.
Lost in each other.
Could not be happier.
Nothing but love and joy.

A wonderful time of year.

And yet here I sit.
My childhood feelings a lost memory.
My dreams taken.

My hope void.
Excitement turned to pain.
Joy is turned to tears.
Togetherness turned to loneliness.

My loss remains.

I am left to watch the world from outside in the cold.
I see the warmth inside.
But I am not inside.
I remember it for it was once mine.
I know how good it is because I once felt it.

Now it is gone.

I wonder why it had to happen.
What did I do to deserve such punishment.
Why was I handed this sentence of pain and loneliness.
The pain of being outside and watching the warmth inside
And remembering how wonderful it was
My dreams won't be coming true this special morning.
There is no hope of that.

I dedicate this to all those who are lost outside. To those who feel nothing but loss or grief. To those who wonder why. Why them. Let us be grateful for those who are blessed and still inside. We wish no pain on anyone. And let us remember those who are not as blessed, or those who are in difficulty. For some this is a season of joy, and for others it is not. For those of you who are blessed, I ask you to notice those who are in pain and reach out to them. But to those of you who are on the outside, please feel the warmth from within you. It is there, however dim it might seem. And you are important to this world. You are not forgotten. I send you my understanding and my love.

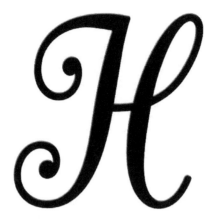

CHAPTER ELEVEN

The Party I Never Had

The good news is that my three months of sleep coma and being mentally useless was over. The better news is that I did not kill myself as planned. The bad news is a MAJOR Depression had descended upon me like the total sum of bricks and rubble from a falling skyscraper. It was heavy and hopeless. I was functional again and could do everything a normal person could do, but I was doing it with constant sadness and depression. It was always there. I cried a lot. It was not necessarily tears over just Chaz's death. It was tears because I was just sad and hopeless in general and in totality. I had set aside suicide as an option, and now was stuck in this horrible shitty sad hopeless life, for which I saw no good ending or future.

My business was in trouble, I no longer had Chaz's bailout, I no longer had Chaz, I had to deal with Luci's jabs and insults on everything, and I was missing my daughter during the week when

I did not have her with me. Most of all, I was chronically and seriously mentally ill with this severe depression.

Depression is a heavy insidious evil condition. It is a monster that moves into your head and tries to kill you. It whispers things in your ear that it hopes will cause you suffering, pain, and death. It steals your ability to function, and any chance of enjoyment or happiness. To this day, my work with clients who suffer from depression is mostly based upon my own experiences during this time. Suffering in this pit of Hell for years, I figured out what coping methods worked best for me. I kept a very structured schedule, led a task-driven lifestyle with daily lists of tasks to complete, and I exercised (ran) a lot, which got me outside. It is my personal belief those are the best methods for dealing with depression.

I did the best I could to cope and keep functioning. I was talking to Gez daily and he was a huge support. He never wavered in being there for me, providing endless comfort and companionship. I frankly don't know how or why he had the patience to deal with me. I would complain about the same things over and over, and repeat things, and I would never improve. He never lost patience in dealing with me. I came to the conclusion that he was indeed an angel. I did not even question it anymore. Why look a gift horse in the mouth? I accepted he was sent to me by Chaz's people, or by God, and it did not matter to me which, or either, or neither. I was grateful to have the support and needed it.

But someone else came forward also. Now that I had my marbles back, I began to have questions about Chaz's death and wanted more information. I contacted his friend Jackson who had originally given me the horrible news. Jackson was very willing to talk with me. Jackson and I actually hit it off really well and started conversing daily.

I think talking to Jackson gave me a link to Chaz. Jackson had known Chaz since they were kids. I was able to learn more about Chaz that I did not know before. I asked Jackson for some more information on Chaz's death. Jackson agreed to tell me what he knew.

Jackson said that Chaz was in a car with three of his friends. Chaz was in the back seat. There was some question as to whether he was wearing a seatbelt. From what the investigators could conclude, they rounded a corner and were hit head-on by a drunk driver. Their car started tumbling down a ravine and caught on fire. Chaz ended up being thrown from the vehicle and was killed instantly. All four guys in the car died, and the drunk driver was also killed.

When Chaz's family was notified of his death, Martin immediately took a private jet to Germany to identify Chaz's body. Jackson said Martin held Chaz's body for hours before he was ready to leave the morgue. Chaz's mother was too distraught to even leave the house, and Chaz's stepdad was, well, busy being whatever he is. The entire family went into mourning and silence, and cut off contact with almost everyone, including Jackson for a while.

I asked if there had been a funeral for Chaz, and if there was a place where I could go to visit his grave. Jackson said Chaz was cremated and his remains spread by helicopter on top of the cliffs at Zion National Park in Utah.

Jackson said that they had found Chaz's cell phone at the crash site, and even though it was charred, Martin was able to get the voice messages off of it, and had heard my desperate dramatic voice messages, and that is why Martin wanted to make sure I was fully notified.

Jackson and I ended up striking up a friendship and conversed for many months thereafter. I learned a lot about Jackson and

Chaz. Jackson and I were kind of a comfort to each other, as Jackson had also been very upset and not doing well with Chaz's death. We were able to provide each other with some comfort and companionship, I think.

Jackson told me many stories about Chaz, but he told me some information that was touching to me. Jackson said Chaz had spoken a lot about me and thought the world of me. Jackson said that he and the other friends were actually a little jealous of how Chaz was affectionate toward me more than they had seen with others. Jackson said Chaz had recently asked him to help plan a surprise birthday party for me. The party was supposed to consist of me being picked up by limo and taken to the airport. Chaz would be waiting on a private plane, and we would fly to NY where he had a venue picked out. All of Chaz's friends were invited, and Chaz was hoping it would be the method of officially introducing me to his friends. Jackson said there was going to be a tiny box wrapped for me, and inside the box were keys to a you know what. A red one. But Jackson said Chaz had not actually found the car yet before he left for Germany.

Jackson asked me if I still had the ring necklace. I was a little surprised he knew about that, but clearly Jackson was Chaz's best friend and he told Jackson everything. I said, "Yes of course I do, I wear it all the time." Jackson then shared with me some information I did not know. Jackson said that Martin had the matching ring necklace to mine, and he treasured it enormously. To this day, I have no idea of the significance of the ring necklace. I still have it obviously.

As Jackson and I became friendlier, I started to open up about all my problems with the business and such. I explained to him what Chaz's plan was. I was actually afraid Jackson would think I was a gold digger or trying to scam or something, but Jackson actually said straight out that yes, Chaz had told him everything I just said about helping with the business. In this case, I was very relieved Chaz shared everything with Jackson, so Jackson knew I was telling the truth.

I talked to Jackson about how the loss of Chaz was bad enough, but the first installment for my business buy-out never being received, put me in a horrible situation because I had actually done some expenditures based on receiving that money. Jackson asked how much it was and some details. He said he would talk to Martin about it.

Jackson got back to me and said Martin told him that he did not have any paperwork for such an arrangement, and that there was no provision in Chaz's will for me (obviously). In other words, Martin was saying "no." Okay fine. I was not expecting anyone to say yes and help me anyway.

However, I would later get into a bind with rent a couple times, and I did receive two separate payments of $2,000 each for my rent. Both payments came from an account labeled "Chaz (last name) Memorial Fund." I was very appreciative of these payments. Those would be the only funds I ever received from Chaz or his family. Chaz was gone, Martin was lacking any compassion for me, and I had not been fully introduced to the family before the passing, so basically, I was screwed. Some people do not realize that when you lose a loved one, you have the actual loss of the person, then you have the depression involved which means you can't work or function, then you have financial problems because of that. The honest truth is that I did not care about the money. Money only became a factor after his death when I went into my "mental coma" for three months. It is what it is. I had to let it go and blame myself for depending on someone else for my own problems.

The other thing I figured out is that I had disability insurance through my business, but of course many months had passed now, and I was feeling better. I was a bit pissed at myself for not taking advantage of that when the loss happened. But I never thought of it because I was too "stupid" (literally) to think of it when I was mentally not functioning. Plus, I would have had to go to a doctor for a formal diagnosis, and I could not go to a doctor, and never went to a doctor. This is one reason I was never sure if I had a minor stroke or similar medical event that could have caused my mental condition.

Jackson maintained our friendship and dialogue for a couple years, before drifting apart. Eventually I never heard from him again. I have never had any contact with him or anyone from Chaz's family since. Besides Gez's messenger companionship, my only other stabilizing force was my daughter.

Now that I was feeling a bit better and able to cognitively do anything I wanted, I decided I needed to change these pathetic visitations of having my daughter play with her toys in front of the TV. She was five by now and was easier to work with in the sense she was going to the bathroom by herself and was generally lower maintenance. I had the idea that maybe I would try to take her to Disneyland as a way of making up for being such a boring useless dad for so many months. Therefore, I surprised her one weekend by taking her to Disneyland. This would turn out to be one of the most monumental things I ever did.

My little Disney buddy and I had such an amazing time at Disneyland together, that from then on, I took her to Disneyland EVERY weekend, other than those rare occasions I had to travel. In all, we went to Disneyland pretty much every weekend from when she was age five to age twelve. I am willing to bet that for a time she had the Disneyland record for the most visits by a young child. It became our second home and our special place. It became the foundation of our close relationship that exists today. I actually got us a brick in front of the Disney gates with our names on it. Personally, I think they should give my daughter an honorary key to the place, but I digress.

My weekend visitations and trips to Disney with my daughter became the anchor for my existence. I would pick her up Saturday morning and we would have our Disney day. I would be in heaven this day. I would actually be happy and not sad. It was the one and only day I would not be totally depressed. She would spend Saturday night with me, we would watch Disney channel together on Sunday, and then I would take her home Sunday afternoon. What she never knew is that immediately after dropping her off at her mom's, I would cry, and even had to pull over down the street many times until I could clear my eyes and drive again. Once I dropped her off on Sunday night, I would be immediately back to my lonely horrible depressing life. I would get back home and see the leftover mess from her playing and have to clean it immediately so that I would stop being so despondent. I would be heavily depressed Mondays and Tuesdays, also depressed Wednesdays and Thursdays, then on Friday I would get excited for the weekend. Rinse and repeat this countless times for all those years of her childhood.

The other item of interest that had been going on during these many months is Luci's new relationship, and her wanting to finalize our divorce. You see, when I was occupied with Chaz, and then being in a waking coma unable to think, Luci was positioning herself for post-divorce life.

Luci's relationship with her nanny boss had progressed. Luci showed me a ring he had given her. I congratulated her while shaking my head inside my mind. Eventually, they apparently wanted to get married, so Luci was pushing hard to finalize our divorce. I had no problem doing this. The only reason I had not been pushing the divorce or working on it, was because I had been busy being brain dead and depressed. So, with Luci leading the charge and organizing all of it, I fully cooperated with the divorce. Three days after the divorce was final, and ON my birthday, Luci married her nanny boss and third husband. Classy Luci!!

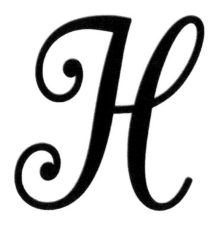

CHAPTER TWELVE

Brazil

It was about nine months after the "walk-in event," and I was feeling very functional. I was still very depressed, but I was capable of complex thought, doing tasks, going places, and being a responsible human. Gez suggested that I come to Brazil and visit him. I had never thought of going to Brazil, and I was hesitant as to whether this was a good idea. After all, I did not actually know Gez in person, and was I really going to travel to a strange foreign land far away, where they don't speak English? But Gez was convincing. He would be my interpreter, companion, and Rio sounded very exotic. I thought maybe a crazy illogical trip was perhaps exactly what I needed to help me heal.

Fortunately, I still had a tiny bit of income flowing in on autopilot from my faltering business, so I thought why not go while I still could. Therefore, I threw caution to the wind and booked the two-week trip to Rio. On Gez's recommendation, I booked a hotel room right near the beach in Copacabana.

I climbed into my cramped coach seat on a July day with excitement, as well as a nervous knot in my stomach. Many thoughts such as, "What the hell am I doing?" crossed my mind several times. After the long overnight flight was over, I landed at Rio airport, and out the window I could see old remnants of the Brazilian Air Force, which consisted of a few rusted out old airplanes, including some with no doors. I thought, holy crap, what the hell am I doing here. I deplaned, luckily found my luggage, and then went straight for an ATM machine to get local cash. I was immediately approached by a man asking if I needed a taxi. Now, anyone who travels to Brazil knows to never accept a ride from such a person, and to instead go to an official taxi stand instead. Well, I was stupid and not aware of this at the time, so I said, "yes I need a ride." I followed the man as he took me to his car, which of course was not a taxi car. I gave him the address of my hotel and we started on the trip. We drove through endless ghettos until finally we arrived at my hotel. He then requested some horrible ridiculous amount of money. I was shocked and confused. He gave me a price list, and sure enough, the amount he requested matched the price on his list for Copacabana. I was scared and sweating and just wanted to get inside my room, so I paid him what he asked, which amounted to all the cash I had taken from the ATM. I had been in Brazil less than two hours and had already been scammed. Yes, I was naive. Anyway, I checked into my room, and thankfully the hotel and room was totally legit and acceptable, so I considered things okay.

I texted Gez to let him know I was at the hotel and asked if he was on his way. He said he would be there shortly. Please remember, I had never actually seen Gez yet. I only had an idea of what he looked like from horrible vague photos he had on his social media. I knew he was young, skinny, and not a monster, but that is about it. I had never really seen a clear full picture. I assumed he was very shy or private.

After I had settled in, there was a knock on my door. I opened the door and what did I see? I saw what appeared to be a very scared 15-year-old looking boy who was shaking, and skinny looking, as if he had not eaten in a week, carrying a little old suitcase. I am certain Gez must have seen the total shock on my face.

It was Gez, the person who had been so kind and ever-present for me all these months, plus I knew he had traveled a long distance to arrive at the hotel. There was nothing I could do other than let him in obviously. I immediately tried to make him feel at ease, as he appeared to be terrified. I tried to act like nothing was wrong, and I was totally relaxed in my auto pilot business swagger that kicks in immediately when I am thrown into terrifying situations where I don't want the other person to see I am uncomfortable. I shook his hand, gave him a hug, and said it was nice to finally meet him in person. He acted relieved that I let him in, as if he was afraid of what would happen when I met him in person. Therefore, he relaxed a little and looked slightly less terrified, although still very awkward and uncomfortable. However, he seriously looked like he had not eaten in a week. I asked him if he would like to go down to the hotel lobby and get something to eat. He said, "Yes, yes."

We walked down to the hotel restaurant, which happened to be empty, yet over staffed by many bus boys, water tenders, and waiters. It was a bit uncomfortable because they were all standing around, watching and whispering to each other. I can only imagine what the hell they were saying to each other, as the possibilities were endless, with an American tourist there with a needy and young-looking boy who looked like he never ate.

I told Gez to get anything he wanted on the menu. He seemed

nervous about everything. We ordered, and he ate as if it was the first high quality meal he had in a long time. We were talking and his English was pretty good now that he was no longer totally terrified. In fact, his English was amazingly good considering his youth and resources. He told me his English became good from messaging with me all these last months.

After we ate, we went back up to the room. I nervously had a question for him that just could not be avoided any longer. I was so nervous about it, and I just could not avoid it any longer. So, I gently asked him, "Gez, wow you look really young." "Are you really nineteen like you told me before?" He laughed and said, "Yes," like he was expecting this question. As if he knew I would require more proof than "yes," he grabbed for his ID and gave it to me. I confess I checked it closely to be sure it was real, and indeed he was nineteen. I was so relieved, because I really did not want anything that might seem awkward or inappropriate. We both relaxed at that point and started making plans of places I wanted to see during my trip.

One of the first things Gez and I did was to visit the Christ Statue that sits atop Rio. Little did I know the spiritual experience that was about to happen. While up on the statue platform, we were walking around looking at the amazing structure. I noticed a door in the back of the statue. The door was open, but nobody was going in or out. Intrigued, I went to peak at what was inside, and I saw a very small chapel. It was very ornate, beautiful, and clean. There were candles burning inside, and it seemed so overwhelmingly holy and amazing that I could not help myself. I walked inside. I looked around waiting to be yelled at, or to see others follow me into the room. Nobody came in. There I was in this holy chapel inside the statue all alone, like in a movie. I just stood there in amazement, taking in the experience. Then all of a sudden, I heard a voice. It was Chaz's voice. It said: "This is for you." I looked all around to see where the voice came from. I knew it was Chaz's voice, so I knew I would not see anybody. I must be crazy, right? I started to tear up a bit. I stood in that chapel, surrounded by lit candles and holiness, and wept. I have no idea how long this all took, but I felt I was in there a long time, and I never felt rushed or that I would be interrupted. Nobody ever came in, including Gez, who should have been right behind me. When I felt I had my time, I calmed and gathered myself, said Thank You to the room (to Chaz), and walked out. I immediately looked for Gez and found him outside looking at the statue. I told him something amazing just happened to me. I recounted to him the details of everything. He just smiled at me in this angelic knowing way and said, "Yes, I am not surprised."

Gez and I did many things and went many places. It was the most fun I had in a very long time. We spent a lot of time at the beach, restaurants, shops, tourist attractions, and many other places. I was beginning to feel very connected to Gez. He had this calming and reassuring effect on me. He was always there for me, always helpful, and always supportive.

We were in a restaurant one day having desserts, and I am not sure if there was something in the desserts, or what came over us, but we started joking around at what other people were doing in the restaurant. We ended up laughing so hard, we were crying and could not even breathe. I nearly pissed myself, I was laughing so hard. I literally needed to calm myself so that I could breathe. We were dying. I totally thought the restaurant was going to throw us out, but thankfully they just watched with amusement. That was the first time I had laughed like that since the "walk-in." In actuality, I have not laughed that hard since, to this moment. Gez gave me a wonderful gift that day I still treasure today, getting me to let loose and laugh like that.

He was able to speak fluent English with me, and then his native

Portuguese back to everyone else. I literally would have died without him there because almost nobody in Brazil speaks English, except in the hotels and car rental places. I had become totally dependent on Gez for my actual survival in that country, just as I had become totally dependent on him for his emotional support all the previous months since the walk-in.

One night, Gez suggested we go to this famous gay nightclub not far from the beach in Copacabana. I had never been to any nightclub at all, and certainly not a gay club. I was a bit hesitant but agreed. This trip was all about letting loose and having new experiences. Plus, I also wanted Gez to get to do some things he wanted also. We walked to the club from the hotel, got to the door, and the doorman needed to see ID's. I showed mine, but then I saw Gez was struggling to find his. I saw the man say something to Gez. Gez would later tell me the man said he was obviously not 18, and there was no way he could go in. I was annoyed Gez forgot his ID and was not surprised the doorman would think he was way too young, since he indeed looked way too young. We had to walk back to the hotel where he got his ID, and then rinse and repeat, tried again, and this time gained entry into the club, even though the doorman was still not convinced Gez could be over eighteen.

I was in awe of the club. All the flashing strobe lights, the music, the people, the vibe. The music was bumping so hard that it was reverberating into, and throughout, my body. It was hard core electronic club music. I loved it! I felt like I was just born into a new world. It was a wonderful world full of lights, music, lots of bass, and so many people having so much fun. It was almost the opposite of the death and silence I had been suffering for months previously. We mostly just stood and watched as I was taking it all in.

The music all of a sudden changed to a slow song. All the people (young guys mostly) started dancing together slow-dance style. They were holding each other, hugging each other, some looking into each other's eyes, and others just resting their heads on each other's shoulders. I admit I was touched by this. I saw the vibrancy of these young guys dancing, and now I was witnessing the genuine love they all had for each other. Gez looked at me and said, "Come let's join them." I did not question it. He took my hand as if dragging me, and I followed. We started dancing like them. I had my arms kind of around his shoulders. I started to lose myself in the music. I was totally present in the moment. Maybe to some, this sounds mundane, but to me being present in the moment was a rare thing. We grew closer as we danced. Then something magical and weird happened. I started to hold him like I meant it. I drew him closer to me, and with more genuine caring. Because I did care. I was holding him, he was holding me, and it felt so good to be held. I had been through so much. Luci being so cold and mean for many months with no affection, having my daughter leave my household, losing Chaz, going through the "walk-in" which shredded my brain for months, and then the whole suicide thing. Maybe what I needed most for months was to be held. Nobody had held me for all those months. Nobody. I started to tear up. I think some would classify it as "crying." I was weeping on his shoulder and he never said anything or did anything. He just let it happen, almost knowing it was going to happen. It was as if all my pain from my losses, suffering, and all my appreciation for what Gez had done for me, all came out of me all at once. Finally. Although it clearly had been sneaking up on and me building, I think I officially fell in love with him at this moment. No words were officially spoken about it, but it was obvious something had changed. From that moment on, we looked at each other differently.

Gez and I continued our adventures, but with the additional element of genuine affection and love. It was nothing I was expecting or looking for. I think it was a natural result of our very intense connection, companionship, and my deep appreciation for him loving and caring about me. I yearned for someone special to care about me after all of Luci's hate, and the losses that followed that.

Eventually, my trip had to end. Gez and I had to say goodbye. Gez was very upset and crying the last day. Although I did not want to leave Gez, I was actually a bit excited to go back home because I was missing my daughter intensely and dying to see her. I promised Gez I would come back soon, and I walked behind the Customs wall, and went back home. But I did not leave without first getting Gez new shoes, new clothes, and left him with all my leftover cash, and then some. He was at least five pounds heavier, and he looked like a prince now.

Gez told me he cried all the way home. But it was not long before I went back to Brazil. In all, I went to Brazil four times. All four times, Gez and I had amazing adventures together, except he was not just my interpreter, he was much more.

During all the trips, I spent time in Rio, Sao Paulo, areas of South Minas, and some beach areas by Angra, Paraty, and Ubatuba. There are way too many adventures with Gez in that beautiful country for me to recount without making this book longer than "*War and Peace*." But it was amazing. We went to places such as Ubatuba, where we had an amazing day on a private tropical beach where we were the only people on the entire beach. I constantly felt like I was in some incredible movie when I was in places like that with Gez. I could open my soul to Gez and we could just talk about anything and everything. My soul was finally healing.

We went to places where the amazing Brazilian hillside looked like it was just under the clouds. We were driving through the beautiful hills headed toward the coastal beach towns, and we reached this area that seemed totally amazing to me. It appeared as if you could touch the clouds from the hills. I immediately pulled over on the side of the road. Gez thought something was wrong and asked why we stopped. I said to him, "I want to touch the sky." I quickly got out of the car and started running up the grassy hillside. Gez totally must have thought I had gone mad. He yelled for me to stop, but then shortly followed me up the hill. I looked up and all I could see were clouds and sky whipping over my head. I reached up. If my arms were only a little longer, I know I could have touched the sky. I felt so free. No other humans in sight. No other cars passed by on the road. It was just me and Gez reaching for the sky. Our moment on that hill was as if we were living scenes from "*Sound Of Music*" meets "*Call Me By Your Name*", all at once. For a short moment on that hill, I truly felt totally alive again.

On another particular adventure, Gez wanted me to see his native home and meet his Grandmother. He lived in South Minas, which was supposedly several hours drive from where we were. Gez loved his Grandmother. She was in very poor health and was pretty much on her death bed. He wanted to see her and wanted me to meet her. I agreed to the journey.

I rented a car. That was the only thing that was easy. From that moment on I was about to embark on one of the scariest journeys I have ever been on to this day.

When we left the car rental agency, I turned the wrong way. I figured it out quickly, but there was no way for me to turn around. All the roads in Rio are one way with NO way to correct for errors. If you end up on the wrong road, you can literally be stuck on it for 10 miles before you can correct your mistake. I had no GPS and no maps. I had no idea where I was. Gez knew the towns but did not know how to fix the one-way road problem. We ended up stuck on this road going all the way across this bridge to nowhere, which must have been the longest bridge in the world. I was in full panic mode having a complete hissy fit mental breakdown. I think I was starting to crawl out of my skin. However, Gez was like a puppy dog going on his first car ride. I think he was laughing actually. I was a little irritated that he did not give a crap, but clearly Gez was just embracing the adventure. I once asked him why he never got scared, and he said to me, "Because when I am with you, I always feel safe."

Well anyway, I finally got turned back around on the island, and took the bridge to nowhere back where we started, and finally an hour and a half later we were just beginning our journey.

I had naturally assumed that Gez knew where he lived and knew how to get there. WRONG. When I started to ask him which roads to take, I started getting answers like, "I don't know." Those are answers I can't handle when driving hours into nowhere land in a foreign country where I don't speak the language and don't have a map. We ended up stopping numerous times at stores and such places so Gez could ask for directions. Gez would come back, and I would say, "Did you get good directions?" He would reply, "Oh yes, I know where to go now." Then I would ask what the directions were, and his "directions" were, "The man said to keep driving this road until we see the mountain in front of us, then take the third road to the right near the old tree." Ummmm okay. Is it because I am American, or because I am too uptight, or is it because those directions are FUCKING USELESS, that I got upset once again? Well, so I drove aimlessly, looking for mountains in front of me, and taking turns "at the large tree," and turning again "at the painted big boulder," and all that sort of thing. We ended up on a dirt road that got worse and worse and worse, the farther into it we got. Finally, the "road" turned into something similar to a horse trail. It would have been two hours to turn back, so I kept going on blind faith. The potholes were so huge and numerous that the drive turned into a crawl. Muddy, wet, dirty, narrow, road to nowhere. There are many roads to nowhere in Brazil by the way. It got so bad that I swear a tribe of natives with spears might jump out of the bushes at any moment and murder us. Seriously. Finally, it opened up and Gez saw what he was looking for and knew exactly where he was. It turned out we ended up in the right place, but we had taken some horse trail instead of the paved highway that everyone else in the world uses.

We finally arrived at his house at some ridiculous hour. The house was actually owned by him. His grandfather had owned several small houses and willed a house to various family members. So Gez technically owned this house, but he was letting his "Aunt" live there. I will explain later why "Aunt" is in quotes.

We knocked on the door, his Aunt answered, and let us in. Of course, like everyone else there, she did not speak English. However, she shined when she looked at me. I could tell she already knew who I was. She could not stop smiling at me, and it made me feel very welcomed. She asked me (thru Gez translating) if I wanted something to drink. I automatically asked for iced tea, if she had any. (Duh, of course she does not have iced tea). But she started making it from scratch. I did not know exactly what she was doing, but by the time I caught on, it was too late for me to insist she not do this, and just give me water. At around 3:00AM in the middle of the night, this little, aging, worn looking woman, who could not stop smiling at me, was "building me" a single glass of iced tea from nothing. About an hour later I got my iced tea and I thanked her profusely. I drank the entire little glass of iced tea in 30 seconds. We then all went to bed.

When I woke up in the morning, I could hear chickens and roosters, and all kinds of animal noises, as the sun was streaming through the window. I told Gez I desperately needed a shower. He showed me where the bathroom was and I went in. It was a very old bathroom in a very old house. I could not figure out how to get the hot water in the shower to work. There was actually a very good explanation why I couldn't figure out the shower. The reason is that there was no hot water for that shower. Ahhh okay. Ugh. So, I took a cold shower. Perhaps I needed a cold shower anyway. But in the middle of my "shower," I heard some commotion, and talking, and Gez knocked on the door and came into the bathroom. He said his horrible brother was there, saw my rental car outside, and wants to use the car. I said, "NO WAY" without hesitation. Then Gez said his brother was trying to get the keys and take it. In a panic I got out of the shower, grabbed the keys to the car, and brought the keys into the shower with me. Apparently, his brother then went away all pissed off thinking I was a jerk. I had known from previous conversations with Gez that his brother was a major asshole of a problem, and he was to be avoided.

After my "shower," we went to visit Gez's grandmother. His grandmother was indeed a very old frail woman lying in her bed. We went in and she gave me the same smiling sunshine look that his Aunt gave me. So, okay, here is another relative who knew all about me and seemed to like me automatically. She insisted on getting out of bed. She was muttering all kinds of things in Portuguese. Gez said she was saying, "Why does God keep me around like this." She got up and hobbled with assistance out to the reception room where I was waiting. Through Gez, she was saying she wanted to pray with us. Gez knew I was not religious, even though I was very spiritual. Thus, I think Gez was afraid I would be uncomfortable with her request, and he asked me what he should say back to her. I told Gez to tell his sweet grandmother that I would love to pray with her, and that I would like to lead us in prayer. Gez looked totally shocked and taken off guard by my response but told his Grandmother what I had said. A moment later, they were both looking at me, as if waiting. I took hold of both their hands, so we were all holding hands in a tiny circle. I said a prayer, in English obviously. I don't remember what I said, but Gez had a tear down his face when I finished. I could tell his grandmother was asking him what I had said. He translated to her. She then took my hand, looked me in the eyes, and said something, I have no idea what. But I could tell we had bonded in that moment. She then said she was tired and would go back into her bed. Gez helped her into bed, and I let them have a moment of privacy. We then left her home, which was pretty much across the road from Gez's house, by the way.

I told Gez I was absolutely starving and wanted to go to a restaurant. He broke the bad news that there were not any restaurants. My heart dropped, and I think a bit of panic jumped into the place where my heart was previously located. Gez said there was a store that prepares food, and then you take it home. I said fine. We went there. The "store" was a hole in the wall storefront with one ancient food case in the back. I looked in the case and determined there was nothing edible inside the case. I looked at Gez with panic and told him this wouldn't work. We went outside and stood next to a miniature horse and carriage parked out front. Really. There was actually a white miniature real live horse hooked up to a carriage "parked" out front in a parking spot. I told him that I will starve to death and die in this place. I told him that between his crazy brother, the shower with no hot water, and the fact there is no edible food for me to consume, I would be dead inside 24 hours if I stayed in this town. So, we literally went back to his house, got our things, and left town. We moved on to another town which was more suitable, and I got a good meal, and all was well. I have to say that to this day I consider myself very lucky and honored to have met his Grandmother and "Aunt" while I had the chance. I never saw them again.

Eventually, after various detours, we were driving back to Rio. We were on the nice correct highway that we missed on the way there and following this other small car on the road. All of a sudden, I saw the car in front of me start spinning around, and then it flipped on its side, and broke through a road sign in the median. I was the only other car on the road at the time. I immediately stopped and was getting out of our car to go and run over to the crashed car. I could see there was a fire starting at the front of the car. All kinds of liquids were leaking from the front of the car, and it was lying in dried grass with fire trying to catch on the grass. There was no sign of the occupants trying to get out. I was able to jump up and look inside the car lying on its side. I saw a man and a woman lying unconscious in the car with a small amount of blood on their faces. I yelled to them (in English ugh) to get out, but no response. I climbed up further to try and open the passenger door that was inaccessible. I heard Gez screaming at me to get away from the car because it will burn. But since I saw no huge fire yet, I kept working the car door to get it open. I got the door open, but I could not reach inside the car, and they both had seat belts on, and I could not grab or pull them out myself. At that moment, some man appeared out of nowhere and was running straight at me with a machete. Now, please recall I am in a foreign country where I do not understand the language. So the thought ran through my mind that I am in some weird twilight zone situation and this guy is coming to butcher me. But no, the "Machete Man" leaped up onto the car like a Jedi, cut the seat belts off, and single-handedly pulled out the occupants. I felt fairly useless in that moment. The occupants came-to when they were out of the car and seemed to not have any major injuries. Seeing that I could not speak the language, and did not have my passport with me in the car, I decided I should depart and leave the occupants in the very capable hands of Mr. Machete Man.

Finally, we made it back to Rio, and arrived back to the car rental place to return the car. I was eager to get rid of the car and get back to my hotel and eat a real meal in the hotel restaurant. When I was returning the car, the man left the counter and went out to do the return inspection. I swear to you before that moment I did not realize what the car looked like. But when the man came back and motioned for us to go outside with him to the car, I then realized the situation. It was then I truly looked at the condition of the car. It was covered in mud from tires to roof, and it was missing ALL of its hubcaps. The man was horrified. He asked what we did. We explained where we had gone, and the man just stared at the car and said he had never seen a car get returned in such poor condition before. I was embarrassed because as a responsible American businessman, I normally would never return a car in that condition. My actual reality came to me quickly in that moment. I agreed to pay for the four missing hubcaps, and that adventure was over.

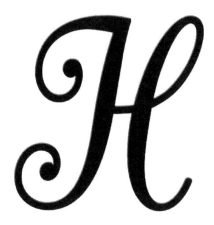

CHAPTER THIRTEEN
Stick A Fork In Me

I returned from my fourth and final trip to Brazil feeling much better within myself. My adventures and time with Gez were amazing and made me realize I was still alive (I think?). Why did I not return to Brazil after this? I wanted to, and I wanted to continue my strong connection with Gez, but when I returned home, I got hit on the side of the face with a board, a shovel, a brick, and worst of all, reality. I got slapped in the face with a horrible new reality. Or maybe it was an old reality, but I was now forced to fully see and accept my business and financial situation in its horrific entirety.

First and foremost, I faced a series of defections from my remaining clients in my business back east. This was followed by a series of defections and even sabotage by my employees, whom I had trusted to run my business.

A person can contemplate and guess as to the various reasons for all this. It could be that I had become too disengaged and detached from my own business. It could be that my employees were not doing their jobs. It could be that there were market forces and economic factors which pushed clients away. I would say it was all three. I take plenty of blame for the downfall of my business. I take all of the blame actually. Even so, it does not absolve my key employees of any guilt from their sabotage and incompetence in doing their jobs they were well trained and experienced to do. But you know the saying, when the cat's away, the mice shall play. So, it's the cat's fault for being away right?

The clients started dropping like flies. Worse yet, I was learning that my various employees were taking these clients for themselves and setting up their own little enterprises. I was being robbed by the people I had trusted for years. But in business, you cannot trust anyone, I know. So again, my fault. I hope I have made it clear by now that I accept full responsibility for the end result. Even so, I still get to call out misdeeds and when people did me dirty.

In no time at all, my key employees had convinced my clients to let them personally service their properties. I suppose they told them my company was crumbling, and they would be resigning, and they should jump ship with them. So that is what happened. Before long, I had no clients left. It was over. Shut the lights off.

There was a part of me that was relieved, because I had been dealing with the declining business, since before I met Chaz and the stress was overwhelming. I was so tired and frazzled from it all. But on the other hand, I now officially had zero income. None. It was the first time since leaving home after high school that I had zero income.

This created a domino effect, and everything started to fall. The first was my large lake house. All mortgage payments stopped. All credit card payments stopped. I fell months behind in most all my bills. It was truly a total collapse.

I more or less just let the business go because I literally had no options. I did my best to get everyone I owed money to paid. There were clients I owed money to, and they were first in line. I diverted money from my own bills and mortgage payments to take care of my clients. Every nickel I had went to clients. I had always operated with the highest integrity and dependability. I think many clients were shocked and confused that I was defaulting and failing. I was the last guy you would expect to default and fail. Yet here we are. Some people I owed money to were very angry, some were hurt, some were just confused. Everyone got hurt.

To this day I live with this guilt. One of those who got damaged by my collapse was Mr. Dawes, who I considered a mentor and father figure. I still literally have dreams (nightmares) about him, and my failing him. For anyone reading this who knows me, I apologize profusely if my business failure caused you any harm or loss. I seriously suffered daily for years over this issue and as I said, I still feel horrible about it today. It is my biggest life failure, and I still live with this failure stamped on my forehead and my psyche. I branded myself a loser from this failure, and it would be years and still on-going before I realized that some things in the past can't be fixed, but we can do positive things in the present and future to make a difference. I could spend the rest of this book listing all my regrets, pains, and apologies regarding my business collapse, but I realize we need to keep moving forward.

It also goes without saying that my credit was totally ruined. That is an understatement. I once had a bank tell me that my credit was worse than someone who had just filed bankruptcy. I did not file bankruptcy because I had no money to file for bankruptcy. Every nickel that came to me went toward food, rent, and debts to clients. There was no money left over to do what I should have done, which was to file for bankruptcy protection. If anyone needed protection, it was me.

But again, I was also depressed. After my return from Brazil with all of this hitting me, I fell back into the deep depression that I was swinging in and out of in different degrees for all these months since the walk-in. Whenever I have fallen into a deep depression, I stop thinking clearly, and I stop making good choices. Most often, I seemed to curl up into a ball and do nothing. That is why living a task-driven lifestyle with task lists you have to complete each day is critical while in depression.

I had Luci hating on me regularly. Luci considered it a sport and hobby to remind me often how much of a loser I was, how I was a horrible father, and how everything in the world was my fault. I knew she was a professional narcissist, and that's what they do, but when you are down, any kind of abuse hurts, even if it's predictable.

I had been beaten on all fronts, but there was one battle I decided to go down fighting on rather than giving up. My dream house, the lake house, was now in foreclosure and I certainly was going to lose it. The irony was not lost upon me that I was losing the house in the exact same manner the previous owner had lost it. Like him, I had a real estate empire that had crumbled, and I was being foreclosed by the bank. Was the house cursed? Who knows? But for one reason or another I decided to take a stand and fight the foreclosure. Why? Did I think I was going to be able to make payments again? No, not really. Did I think I was going to win against a huge national bank that was indeed correct in the fact I had made no payments? No. Did I think I would win a foreclosure fight having no lawyer, while the bank had the best law firms in the state representing it? No. So, what was the point? I have no idea. I really don't. I remember speaking to my mother about this and my mother was confused as to why I was not just letting the house go.

For some reason or another, my psychology would not allow me to give up and let it go. The house represented my life's work. It was a symbol of my success. It was a symbol of my childhood dreams. It was my dream house. I had assumed I would die in that house and would leave it to my daughter as my legacy to her. The house was everything to me. It was my identity. So perhaps I just answered the question of why I felt I could not give up on the house.

But during my depression I pretty much let the foreclosure wheels early on turn against me without doing much about it. But only to a point. Then something weird happened. One morning I woke up with a very strong urge to look at the foreclosure papers. I did. In several days, the deadline for opposing the final foreclosure action would pass. It said I would need to file my opposition by that certain date. So I decided right then, "fuck them." I started that morning doing some research and drawing up my opposition response. I sent off my opposition response to the court. This triggered an endless amount of other motions, hearing notices, and all kinds of things. I had just successfully messed up the bank's open and shut foreclosure action they had against me.

I began to file Motions of Opposition to every single motion the bank would make in the case. It did not matter what it was. If the bank said the sky was blue, I filed a Motion of Opposition. This would trigger delays, hearings, and all kinds of things. Each of these delays would be months. And when I could extend the dates to delay it more, I would file for that as well.

I started seeing chaos on the bank's side. They had very powerful law firms representing them in the foreclosure, but they started firing them one by one. I think the bank went through four major law firms in their fight against me. Mind you, I was doing all of this myself with no help from any attorney. I had no money for an attorney. But I did have lots of real estate law experience, and plenty of veracity.

The foreclosure turned into a part time job. I still had no end game that would result in anything good for me, but honestly it felt good to be fighting and not getting my ass kicked for once. Just the act of not giving up, and fighting, lifted my spirits. I was tired of being a door mat and losing at everything I did. So, this was more of a moral fight for me, even if I would ultimately lose the foreclosure case.

Eventually, all my delays were exhausted, and a judge ruled the bank had won the foreclosure. But I was not done yet. I had one option left that nobody usually exercises. I could write a brief to the State Supreme Court, asking for the Supreme Court to hear the case on appeal. So yes, I had the balls to do this, even though I had lost and made no mortgage payments for a couple years. I followed the instructions carefully and filed a well worded brief, listing some technical errors the bank had made in the foreclosure. Much to my own surprise, the Supreme Court agreed to hear the case. BOOM. So, I had another nine-month's delay in my favor, as this appeal would take that long to be heard. There was a stay on the original foreclosure, so the bank would not be able to take any further action and could not auction the house or take possession from me.

The big problem now is that I needed to prepare a huge written argument to the Supreme Court. I had no lawyer. I had no idea what I was doing. This is when the Universe stepped in. I was randomly contacted by a retired attorney who said he had been following my case in the legal journals. I pictured this attorney having his popcorn out and being amused that someone like me with no lawyer was able to draw this case out so long. The retired attorney said he had been watching and had something he thought I could use. He said he would need to send it anonymously and would not be able to assist me any further. I agreed, yes please, and thank you.

This retired attorney sent me a full case argument he had used in another case similar to mine years ago. It was all there. Endless pages of technical legal paragraphs, legal terms, listed statues, arguments, all the technical parts and pieces of any full court argument and brief, fit for the Supreme Court. Huge breakthrough. So, I used his document as my skeleton, and I just started changing everything to fit my case and argument. It took me many weeks of constant work to prepare this thing. It was like writing a thesis for college graduation. Very intense, very tedious, and difficult. I kept working on it and finally it was as good as I could get it. I had twelve copies printed and bound per the instructions and sent it all off to the Supreme Court before the deadline.

I think the bank figured I would never submit my argument, and was just using this as a delay tactic, and would fold up tent on the actual Supreme Court argument. Wrong. Once the bank saw I had actually filed my argument in compliance with all rules, they filed for an extension on their end. They apparently had not prepared their own argument, because they naturally assumed I would never submit a full brief to the Supreme Court. They counted on winning by default if I did not respond. So now I had an additional free delay because the bank was not prepared to actually argue against my prepared brief I submitted.

Eventually, the Supreme Court ruled. I lost. BUT, in their opinion, I had only lost by a technicality because while my arguments were totally valid, I had not raised one of my arguments in my original opposition years ago, and thus it could not apply to the appeal. If I had been more on it with that original opposition filing a few years back, I would have actually won.

However, not all was lost. After the bank won, they were

obviously looking to move forward and take possession and sell the house at auction. Not so fast. They found a problem in their paperwork. In all the chaos with changing law firms, they forgot to serve me with a certain paper which enforces the original foreclosure ruling. They had a year to serve me with the paper, but they had forgotten to do so because they were distracted by my appeal with the Supreme Court. So, they filed a motion to set aside the missed deadline. I filed a Motion of Opposition. They knew they had been beaten. The attorneys for the bank withdrew their motion, threw their hands up, and got fired by the bank. I had won. Now the bank would have to START ALL OVER AGAIN with the ENTIRE foreclosure process.

Okay great. But let's face it. I had not paid mortgage payments, could not make any payments, and would not be making any payments. Plus, by now the house was starting to deteriorate due to the fact I had no money for maintenance, or to keep it heated all winter. So, the bank made me an offer. They offered me a decent settlement if I would sell the house.

By this time, I was exhausted. Even though I had essentially won, I knew I would not win again, and I knew there was no positive end game. I also wanted to move on with my life at this point. I had proved my point. I had my moral victory I so desperately needed emotionally. Therefore, I decided to let it go. Sometimes you just have to let it go and move on.

I was able to sell the house in short order. The bank agreed to the sales contract, and the house sold and closed. I received my settlement two days before I was about to be evicted for non-payment of my rent. The moment I was informed the house transaction closed, I cried. I cried for two reasons. Firstly, I was so relieved because I so desperately needed that settlement money to prevent eviction, my phone being shut off, and I could list twenty other things and reasons. The second reason I was crying is because I had just lost my dream house. I lost my dreams. My dreams were dead.

I put away everything and anything having to do with the house into a box and shoved the box in my closet. I did not want to look at it or think of it again. It was like someone had died. It was very painful. I mourned it. But it is what it is. Honestly, it still hurts me today.

Right before the house closing, I had a former employee clear out the house and move my things into storage units not far from the house. But my life treasures, I sent to a storage unit out of state, far out of reach of any creditors or people wanting to harm me. My intention was to sell off the things of value in the storage units near the house, so I could get some money. I had the former employee work on selling the things, and I paid him a commission. However, the problem is that when he sold my valuable things, he would just keep the money and never send me any money. Sigh. He was stealing. I could have, or should have, called the police. But I didn't. Just too much work, too much drama, too far away, and I did not want to open myself up to all my own unpaid debts in the area. I had to just give up. I basically let him steal, and the rest of the items were auctioned off by the storage company when I defaulted on storage payments. No point in paying the storage when my stuff is being stolen anyway. Many thousands of dollars in furniture, including my prized desk, huge amounts of tools and equipment from my business, all gone. Lost. To this day, I like to think that my house burned down, and I lost all my stuff in a fire. It just seems easier emotionally. Happens to people all the time and they survive. So, as an inside joke, you will hear me say, "Oh I lost that in the house fire," and everyone knows what I mean by that, except the inside joke is not funny.

As if all that loss and misery was not enough, more disaster was never far away in my life. One Saturday morning while driving on the 60 freeway to pick up my daughter for Disney, my jeep caught on fire. I had an ongoing mechanical problem in the drive train with no money to fix it, and finally time ran out. It was metal on metal while driving freeway speed, and there was smoke, then there was fire, and then I could feel loss of power. There was a ramp off the freeway right when it happened, and I took it. The fire went out on its own, so the entire vehicle did not burn to the ground. But the vehicle was done for. What was my first thought? It was not about my vehicle. My first thought was how in the world am I going to see my daughter and go to Disney today? Remember, my entire weekly existence revolved around doing Disney with my daughter. Without that, life was not worth living.

I called Luci and told her what happened. I was expecting her to say, "Too bad, too sad, guess you won't get Angel then." But instead, Luci offered to come pick me up and let me use their spare vehicle. I was shocked. I am specifically putting this into the book because it was a rare moment when Luci extended any compassion toward me. So that makes it an epic moment. I was very appreciative, as she saved my ass. Without the use of their vehicle for two weeks while I figured out my situation, I would have had an impossible situation to deal with.

My parents ended up stepping up again, since helping me get into the Hollywood apartment, and they came up with the money to have the jeep fixed. Unfortunately, the vehicle started having problems again immediately thereafter. But at least I had a working vehicle for a bit longer, thanks to my parents.

With the house settlement from the bank, I was able to pay off all my late regular bills, my rent, and I decided to replace the jeep and buy a used car in better condition. My jeep had gotten to the point where it was going to die for any variety of reasons, and it was just a matter of time. After the repairs from the fire, it shortly thereafter started making a horrible noise that sounded like the transmission was about to fall on the ground. I shopped online and found a nice BMW that was old but had very low miles. My Jeep barely made it to the dealership. I seriously felt the Jeep would not make it back home, so this car purchase had to work. I agreed to buy the BMW if I could drive away with it today. I had brought cash with me and was ready to go. They checked out my Jeep. Basically, they just started it. My Jeep was clean, it smelled new despite being really old, it started like a Lion, and the engine light was off. That was good enough for them. I drove home with the BMW relieved and grateful. The bad news is after all this, the settlement money was gone.

I came to the conclusion I was going to have to leave my expensive beach apartment. I loved living there. I did not want to leave. But I could clearly see I would not be able to successfully pay my rent there. I decided the logical thing to do would be to move to the center of Hollywood. The center of Hollywood is kind of a shithole, but I would be at the center of the Universe. I would have many options. I could get deep into acting, modeling, or who knows what else. The term "who knows what else" will turn out to be significant further into the story, and not in a good way. But instead of driving over an hour each way for auditions and gigs, I would be within 15 minutes of everything. Plus, because the center of Hollywood is a shithole, the rents were low. I could downgrade from my two-bedroom beach apartment to a one-bedroom shithole and save a fortune and have a fair chance at actually paying the rent. Thus, I found the best least bad option available, and rented it.

However, while I was packing for the move, and before I would make my final move, I would have another heartbreak to endure. My favorite most beloved pet ever, Max, was very ill. He was old. He was 15. I know cats only last so long. But both my cats, Max and Graycee, had been with me for so long, through most of this journey you have been reading. Max especially, was an emotional anchor for me and had been there for all my heartbreaks. Now Max's time was coming to an end. Part of me wondered if maybe he did not want to move and was calling it quits because of that. I had taken Max to the vet and he was diagnosed with end stage renal failure. However, the vet offered me an option that might extend his life for six months. I wanted those six months.

So, I gave the vet my rent money to pay for this. Totally stupid and illogical thing to do, but I could not bear another loss right then. The treatment involved me inserting a needle into Max twice a day, connected to a bag of fluids. I did this without complaint religiously. I had a mishap one day when I somehow stuck the needle into my own finger instead of the cat. I felt a pain so bad that I have not since felt an injury like that. I had hit a nerve in my finger. I was on the floor in agony for fifteen minutes before it subsided enough for me to breathe and get up. To this day, I cannot feel the tip of that finger, and my fingernail of that finger barely grows.

Despite the fluid treatments I had spent my next months' rent on, it was apparent Max was going to die. I felt it was within a day or so, and therefore stopped torturing him with the needles and fluid treatment. Coinciding with this drama was the fact that my birthday was coming up in a couple days.

On the last evening, he laid on my lap all evening. I was petting him, and we spent all evening together. When it was time for bed, I decided to lay a towel on my bed, and then lay him on the towel so he could be in bed with me to sleep. I knew he could not get up to go to the bathroom or anything, but I wanted him on the bed with me where he always slept.

I fell asleep. Sometime during the night into early morning, (and now officially my birthday), let's call it 4AM or so, I was awoken by a horrible noise. I get chills writing this now and I can't adequately describe it, but it was a large loud noise coming from Max. It sounded like a choking type noise, but far more horrible than you can imagine. It sounded like some kind of choking heart attack all at once noise. I knew immediately he was passing. I was immediately traumatized by the noise, but I made myself remain calm, rather than start screaming like I wanted to do. I reached over in the dark and stroked his fur while this was happening. I wanted him to die with me touching him. I finally heard a huge escape of air from him, like all the air in his lungs was going out at once. And that was it. Silence. I kept the light off and kept petting him with tears running down my face. I knew once I turned the light on, it was over, and I would have to face reality. After a few minutes, I turned the light on. I looked at him carefully and could see by his eyes that he was indeed gone. I cried. I mourned. It was not pretty. But then my other cat Graycee came into the room, jumped on the bed, she smelled Max, checking to see if he was gone. Then she came over to me and started rubbing all over me to comfort me. From that moment on, Graycee, which had always been the "second cat," totally stepped into the role of primary cat, and was all over me from then on. Graycee and her comfort is what got me through that experience. Graycee would go on to become just as beloved as Max for as long as she lived.

After Max passed, I wrote this poem:

TIME EXPIRED

Now in the beginning I was presented with a tiny newly born kitten
I was "told" I would have 15 years and then I would lose him
They asked me if I agree to that
I said yes I agree
15 years is a lifetime away, so who cares... I agree
The years went by. 15 years in fact

Then I knew the end was coming, but I still enjoyed him
I asked if I could have another year
They said no
I said, well what if I offer you this money, can you give me 6 more months?
They said, you can do what you want, but you can't buy more time
Then it came that I thought I only had a day or some hours left
I had him on my lap that night the entire time as my remaining time suddenly had become more valuable
I enjoyed him
Then I put him on my bed for us to sleep
I thought I had hours
Then I said, can I have more time please
And they said no
I said...but it was 15 years...what is another day?
Another day is nothing
Why can't I have it?
And the answer was...your time has expired
You used your time
I said, come on...it's been 15 years...can't you give me a few more hours?
No answer
Then I woke in the night with him dying
I said...please...can I have 5 more minutes...please
And they said no
Your time has expired
I said...come on it was 15 years, so what is another 5 minutes....
They said...your time is over
Then I knew he was dying or dead
And I said...
Please...can I have 3 more seconds
Just 3 seconds to feel his fur
I said...it was 15 YEARS
What is only 3 more seconds???
And they said...sorry...your time has expired
And he was dead
I mourned. My time had expired.
Because 15 years turned into only another 3 seconds
Because eventually everything expires

And when it expires it means there is no more
Not even 1 second
No more time at all. None. 0
I used all my time. I used the last second. Then I had none left. And he was gone.

Worst. Birthday. Ever.

With one less cat, I moved a week later. My parents were good enough to cover my rent which I had spent on trying to save Max. I said goodbye to the apartment and beach town I loved and moved to a new city and apartment I did not want. Hollywood here we come.

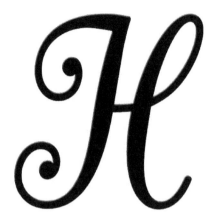

CHAPTER FOURTEEN
The Hustler

I was about to enter the darkest times of struggle. You would think the previously mentioned events would have been the darkest of times, wouldn't you? Well, the next few years of survival would prove to challenge that notion.

There I was standing in my new home in Hollywood. What a tiny dark dump, UGH. Sigh. It was a small one-bedroom apartment consisting of two rooms, because the "kitchen" area was included in the living room area, as was the "dining" area. What I mean to say is that there was a bedroom yes. There was a bathroom, yes (with an old rusting tub/shower). Then the main room had space for my desk on one end, and a kitchen sink with a couple cabinets on the other side of the room. Between the desk and kitchen area, I crammed a couch and a small dining table. There was very little space to even walk from one area to another after that. I even managed to carve out a couple square feet for my daughter's toys. It was tight to say the least. I had windows on one side of the apartment, but they looked out onto a brick wall, along with windows, belonging to the adjacent building, which was about twenty feet away. Thus, no natural light got into my apartment. It was always dark in there, and I always had to have the light on. Even with the light on, it still felt dark. Quite depressing really.

My first night there, I enjoyed my new neighbors. Some poor soul in the building next door was coughing and hacking all night and sounding like they were actually dying. This went on every night for months. Several months later, there was a blissful silence coming from their window for several nights, followed by an ambulance, which arrived to remove a body.

The other neighbors from the building next door liked to stay up all night and talk excessively loud until 4AM. Then there were the pot smokers who should have just come up into my apartment if they wanted to get stoned, because that is where most of their smoke ended up. Very unpleasant for a non-smoker like me with asthma.

Another bonus was that if you looked out my window on a Saturday night, you could watch one of the Walk of Fame street performers, who lived next door, screwing his girlfriend. After the first time, I didn't want to watch anymore though. It was not that inspiring really. My game plan for when my daughter stayed over was to close all the blinds and leave the TV on all the time, so she could not see anything or hear anything. That plan worked out okay.

There was some good news. My building was located at the center of the universe. I was a stone's throw from the Chinese Theater off the Hollywood Walk of Fame. The Oscars was held a few buildings down from me, and the police would literally stage themselves on my street during the Oscars. I had to show my residence papers to get in and out of my building during Oscars lockdown time. There were also conveniences, as I could walk down the street for groceries and the ATM machine. For the most part, I did not have to drive my car at all unless I had to go to a specific appointment.

The whole purpose and silver lining of this move out of my beloved home at the beach, to this dump in Hollywood, was to make it possible to get by financially. My rent at this Hollywood place was a lot cheaper, and perhaps I could more easily find work, gigs, and opportunities, being right in the center of the universe. My parents had been nice enough to pay my first month's rent and deposit, but I felt I could not get any additional help from them. In case I might forget this fact, they reminded me of this as well. The assumption is that I was in a cheaper, more convenient place where I could survive on my own, right?

One problem. My business was now totally gone, and thus so was my income. I had NO income. None. Zero. For the first time in my life, I was just sitting there, all alone, with no resources, no business, no opportunities, and no further help available. It finally hit me that I should be terrified about all this. How was I going to eat? What about the next month's rent? Gas? Cell phone? You name it.

My parents had jabbed me many times about getting a job doing anything. McDonalds, sweeping floors, anything. Yeah, just go ahead and work minimum wage full time, and see if you get by in Hollywood on your own. Impossible, as the cost of living is too high. A traditional minimum wage job was never going to cut it.

Thus, the Hustler was born. Craigslist was my friend. Best friend. I looked for gigs in acting and modeling. I was in Hollywood after all, right? I had my acting training and the beginnings of a resume under my belt. Perhaps it was time for me to pursue acting with more vigor. I started auditioning more heavily. I was successful at getting plenty of non-paying or low paying roles in tiny no-name films, shows, and student films. I signed up with an "extras" casting service to do "extras work." However, to get paid any decent money doing that kind of work, you needed to have your SAG (Screen Actors Guild) card. To get your SAG card, you had to do three solid days on a SAG set with SAG paperwork. To get onto a SAG set with SAG paperwork, you had to have a SAG card. Does anyone else see the problem here?

So back to Craigslist. I picked up some low paying non-SAG extras work off Craigslist to pay for food and stuff. I also started doing small modeling jobs. The problem with being a young male in Hollywood is that almost all "modeling work" means you have to take off your clothes. I am not necessarily talking about porn either. It is more about underwear and fetish stuff, and shoots for boy magazines, gay magazines. If you were lucky, you could do shoots that were purely for "art," but the "art" also was meant for people who wanted to see naked young men, so it was all the same.

I remember my first nude modeling shoot. I was offered $300 for an art shoot. Black and whites. There were no other models, nobody touching me, and nothing sexual. But I was terrified. I was comfortable with my body because I was in great shape and had gotten enough positive validation that I was attractive, or at least not ugly. However, I was still shy to be naked, and all the complications that go with young guys being naked for too long before something odd or embarrassing might happen.

I arrived at the studio, and the male photographer was super nice and professional. He never tried to do anything inappropriate. I took my clothes off and we started shooting. It turned out to be lots of fun and I became very relaxed. After a couple hours it was over, and I grabbed my $300 and left. Wow, that was not that bad. So, I started going after those jobs in earnest. However, the "good paying?" gigs like that were not super common.

Thus, back to the acting extras work. How could I make this work out better for me financially? I HAD to get my SAG card. But how? Well, I finally saw a potential opportunity. I randomly made contact with a guy who had seen other people successfully get their SAG card. He told me what I needed to do, and said he had a contact that could help me. He knew a low-level producer who was working on the big TV show at the time, *Entourage*, staring Jeremy Piven and Adrian Grenier. To make a long story short, I was advised to "sneak onto the set," and his contact would be willing to sign a SAG voucher for me after I put in the day's work as an extra on the set. So that is what I did. I was given the location of a shoot *Entourage* would be filming at for several days straight.

I showed up early morning at the *Entourage* set and simply acted as if I belonged there. I had to stand in line to "check in." I was nervous because obviously I would not be on the casting list. I got to the front, and the guy asked my name, and I told him. He looked up and down the list and could not find my name, obviously. He looked at me and said, "You are not on the list." I replied, "(my contacts name) told me I would be on the list." The guy looked at me for a couple seconds as if processing what I had just said. Then he said, "Oh yes, okay," and in I was. He gave me a SAG voucher, and I put in my full day's work. He signed the voucher at the end of the day. Success! Since I needed three vouchers to get my SAG card, I was one down and two to go. I was able to rinse and repeat this whole process all three times over three consecutive days. It was also a lot of fun. I was chosen to do a scene where Jeremy Piven enters a club, and it was my job to give him a hard shove. I was nervous at first because I did not know how hard to push him. So, on the first take, he walked by me and I gave him a light push. After the director yelled, "Cut," Jeremy Piven came over to me and said, "Hey it's okay to really push me; push me hard, like for real, you won't hurt me." So, on the next take, I pushed him like I meant it. The scene was great, and the director liked it. We did many more just like that, and all was good.

Having my three SAG vouchers in hand, there was only one problem. I had to pay around $2,000 in initiation dues. I did not have that kind of money. So now what?

As always, I would pour over the Craigslist ads for a couple hours every day, applying for anything and everything that was acting or modeling related. I would pick up small jobs regularly. However, I was barely making enough for rent and food, and there was never enough left over for the SAG card initiation dues.

Eventually, I was faced with a bad month. I was not even going to make my rent, let alone pay for the SAG card. Without the SAG card, I would not make the money I needed to pay rent and bills. I knew if I could just get past the SAG dues thing, I would make more money, and could pay rent and bills easier.

It soon got to the point where I was going to be facing eviction. To me, eviction was not just about having no place to live. Worse than that, it meant no way to have visitations with my daughter. As I have previously mentioned, I was taking my daughter to Disneyland every weekend, and having her spend the night. She was the only reason I kept living. Without her and the visitations, there would be no reason to keep fighting. So, I HAD to make more money, or no place to live, no daughter, no life. Death. It was a very simple equation.

I could act, I could model, and I could take my clothes off for the modeling. So hmmm. Let's think. Well, so I saw this vague post about some guy who wanted a male model to put on a "private show." I was not stupid, and I knew what this meant. I remember thinking, and thinking, and thinking. Am I really in this much of a desperate situation? Has my life really come down to this? Is this my new life now? Am I really going to go down this rabbit hole?

Could I actually perform the required duties for this? There was only one way to find out. Try it.

I nervously went to the location of this "gig." It was the guy's house. I walked into his home wearing my tight jeans and tank top, the official uniform for such an activity. He saw me and looked like a pit bull staring down at a steak. I was wondering how, where, when, what way was I supposed to act and do this "private show." I had never done anything like this before, was not made for this, and should not be doing this. I had no clue what to do. I did not have to wonder long. He just simply dropped to his knees in front of me. He unzipped me, and he got to work. I was a bit surprised and terrified, and my legs actually started shaking. I think he thought I was just getting over excited, when in fact I thought I was about to faint. I was thinking in my head, "Really? This is what the private show is? I just stand here and let *whatever* happen?" I was kind of expecting to perform a private show by my own hands, I think. I closed my eyes. The guy was gross. He was nice and seemed clean, but ugh, he was old and had baldish bad hair and a moustache, and oh my, maybe I will puke. He started to yell at me to "*Bleep* his face." (See, I cannot even say it.) Not caring about his request, but wanting to get it over with, I complied. I kept my eyes closed and thought my own thoughts. I thought about how I had entered the gates of Hell. I thought about how my quality of life was no longer worth having a life. But I also thought about the money I needed to survive for "A." Sorry, I can't say her name in the same paragraph with all this shit. Anyway, thank goodness through some miracle I was able to "finish" with a bang, and he seemed extremely satisfied with it. I was thinking I might puke, cry, or run, or something. But I just awkwardly put everything back where it belonged, put myself somewhat back together. He had my "reward" ready, and he said, "Wow I would love to do this again sometime." I just nodded, took my reward, and walked out of his house. Walking back to my car I felt dirty and horrified. I got into my vehicle, and for a moment thought I needed to puke. I started to drive home. Then I had this moment. I calmed. I looked down at the passenger seat where I threw the "reward," and thought, "Wow, look at what I got, and it only took 15 minutes, and now I can eat and live." By the time I got home I was feeling better, and I was thinking this was a totally viable enterprise. I immediately took a shower and felt almost back to normal after my shower, and I kind of just pretended nothing ever happened. The difference is that now I had much needed funds sitting on my desk that I did not have before. And so there you go. The Hustler just added another tool to his toolbox. We will call this my "other job."

I quickly figured out how to most efficiently "book" such gigs for this "other job." My daily routine was to look for acting jobs, extras jobs, modeling jobs, and then pick up a late-night gig for my "other job." My hope was that one or more of those would work out each day. For the most part they did. Before too long I had enough money to pay for my SAG card. I was a proud and happy member of the Screen Actors Guild. Sadly, I doubt I am the only person who had to pay for his or her SAG card this way. This kind of fuckery is the way of Hollywood. But having the SAG card meant I now had all kinds of doors open to me. I could be considered for legitimate paying acting jobs, and for extras work that would pay much higher union wages.

I was building a fairly nice acting resume for pathetic standards. I was also becoming somewhat known locally within the underground community of modeling in Hollywood. Additionally, I was gaining more confidence and coping skills in dealing with the "other job." So, things were looking up. "Looking up?" Did I really just say that?

With the "other job," I developed all kinds of rules and

procedures. I would only go to certain parts of town. I would never go into bad areas. I would never agree to be in a situation where there was more than one person involved. I would only allow one certain act to be performed. I would not perform any acts on another, and the person was not allowed to touch me with their, umm, "thing". So, I was strict. I was not sure why anyone would even be interested, because I made it pretty obvious by my rules that I was totally not into doing this. Despite this, older men did not seem to care about my lack of enthusiasm, and were crazy for it, and me, at the time. I knew what to wear, how to act, and I even had a routine for where I would put my keys and phone in case I had to leave quickly, and so I would never forget them. I usually kept my eyes closed, and under no circumstances would I ever make direct eye contact with them. I had it down to a science. Like everything in my life up to this point, I became good at it. As long as I could get home quickly and take a shower, I was good. After my shower, it was as if it never happened.

The downside of course, apart from the obvious fact that I had to do it in the first place, was that I had to always "save myself" in case I needed to "perform" each night. So, there was no way I could date, and I was not master of my own domain. Who would want to date someone like this (me) anyway? Nobody. I had no control over my own sexuality. I basically sold my sexuality to the devil in order to make ends meet.

Additionally, I felt dirty, ashamed, and now I was now part of the underbelly of society. I felt I was garbage. I had no dignity left. I was just an object, rather than a full person. I had given up part of my soul. In a way, I had sort of "given up," period. When you give up, things get easier in a way. You forfeit your joy of life, but you gain in return a certain numbness that helps you cope with each day. Part of you dies inside, but at the same time, it does not hurt as much anymore. You just let it go. It's both sad and necessary.

I told Gez everything that was going on. Gez and I were still talking daily, and I would tell him about all my adventures. We got to the point where we would laugh about it, discussing each "client," how it went, and so on. He knew I hated doing it, but he also knew I had no choice. I think he was always kind of sad for me, but he also encouraged me to not let it bother me.

I met all kinds of people. There were crazy people, gross people, rich people, famous people, weird people, pathetic people, and super nice people. I actually liked the super nice people. I will confess straight up there was a small handful I looked forward to seeing. Not because I enjoyed the physical aspect, but because with the nice ones, we would chat for several minutes first, and get caught up with each other as if we were friends. I had several people like this that were very nice, and it was quite a painless experience.

I also noticed after time, that the Universe or God seemed to be using this situation as a vessel to reach out to others in need. There were plenty of "clients" who were sad and lonely. Visiting with me for a short time really seemed to give light to their lives. There were even a couple who seemed to have terminal cancer, and my time with them was the only and last bit of joy they would have. I would meet others at critical moments in their lives, where they needed someone to talk them out of harming themselves or making bad choices. Plenty of times, I would actually counsel them and provide comfort during our initial verbal exchanges. So, before you judge me harshly as I am sure you will, consider that even in the worst circumstances, a person can be a true light to others who need light in that moment. God and the Universe was both torturing me and teaching me simultaneously. I learned to shine light in the very darkest places.

So yeah, there was a huge variety of people and experiences that came out of this. Okay, twist my arm. Go ahead. Ask me to recite some of the various experiences. Ahhh okay, sure, since you are twisting my arm, I will confess and share at the risk of horrifying us both with such memories.

Let us start with "Leather Man." Leather man would come to the door wearing nothing but leather straps, with tiny parts hanging out. Dude, if you are going to have parts hanging out, make sure they are not tiny okay? It was like some 70's gay Village People leather nightmare every time.

One of my favorites was "Two-minute man." He was a successful business owner from Canada who would come down for business purposes, and he liked to see me when he did. His whole game was that he wanted me to walk into his hotel room and see how fast I could "perform." He would be totally ready when I walked in, and the faster I could finish the better. My record was two minutes, or 110 seconds to be precise, thus "Two Minute Man." I would literally show up, perform, and be back inside my vehicle before the song on the radio had changed.

There was "Dog Man," who had this wonderful little dog that LOVED me. I would arrive and the dog would remember me and go absolutely crazy for ten minutes. It got to the point that I think sometimes the man had me over just so his dog could see me again. He was a very sweet man and would always have some gift for me, such as some clothing or something, because he worked in a department store and always got freebies. Long after I had retired from my "other job" and had not seen the man in a long time, I received a note from him where he wanted to tell me that his beloved dog had passed away; and he just wanted me to know since the dog loved me so much. I wrote him back with my sympathies, along with some nice thoughts I came up with for comfort. The man wrote back expressing how truly touched he was by my words and what a great person he thought I was. He was one of several people who were truly very nice good people, and it was actually nice to have met him.

I had several celebrities also. You already know from reading previous chapters that this is not a kiss and tell book where I expose others. So, I am sorry, no names. My story is not about causing problems for other people or cashing in at the expense of others. This book is about telling my story so that others might benefit from my experiences. But yes, I had some very interesting famous people.

One celebrity is a very well known "B list" actor known to be a train wreck. I had no idea who he was when I was going there. I ended up in an old Hollywood "C list" neighborhood. As soon as he answered the door, I knew exactly who he was, but I pretended to be clueless. He had me sit on his couch for like 45 minutes and just chatted with me about meaningless random bullshit. I was beginning to wonder what he wanted, and how long I had to stay, and if I should say something. He eventually asked me to take off my jeans. I did. He looked at me and said my legs were not doing it for him, but not to worry as he would still cover me for my time. What a flake. In person, he is even more messed up than his public reputation, and that's saying a lot.

Another celebrity who I saw many times was a professional in the music industry. He lived in the Hollywood Hills, and I was up there often to see him. I actually enjoyed going up to see him because he was very interesting, and he hung out with interesting people. He had done projects with Michael Jackson, Prince, and Whitney Houston. It is not lost upon me what these three have in common, as his client list seemed to pass away one after the other. This man had pictures of himself with these performers, and many others. His house was also full of signed memorabilia. I was fascinated just to look at the pictures and all his keepsakes. His house was literally a museum, and I was star struck.

He was very easy to be with, and I felt more at ease and relaxed than usual on these "gigs." Very often I would just hang out there after business was done, and we would make fun of his fans that were fighting on his Facebook page. He would also talk to me about certain projects he was working on and ask my opinion on things. It was very surreal at the time. Eventually though, the man made things complicated by wanting to change our "relationship" from "contractual" to "genuine." He suggested dinner dates and that I go to public events with him. He was on the red carpet often and wanted a companion to go with him. This idea was simply out of my realm, and not something I could be comfortable with, for many reasons. My resistance resulted in him not seeing me again.

A dubious celebrity meet-up occurred in a different area of the Hollywood Hills. The man instructed me to enter through the garage and to be very quiet. I was accustomed to weird instructions, so it did not faze me. I arrived and entered the garage as instructed. Inside the garage with me, were two of the most beautiful Ferrari's I had ever seen. The man greeted me there and motioned for me to not speak. Once I saw him, I was fairly sure who he was, however I still can't say for certain. He led me upstairs into the house, where all the lights were off. He whispered to me in his thick accent that his wife was sleeping in the other room, so we had to be quiet. I was horrified. But I think because of the man's celebrity status, I just went along with it in a daze. I sat on the couch in his living room in the pitch darkness. Afterward, he led me back down into the garage and sent me on my way. I still wonder what would have happened if his wife had walked out into the living room and turned the lights on while I was there.

I had other celebrities that I was not sure exactly who they were until I got home and did some Google research. Sometimes I had a rough idea of who they might be but needed more pictures to confirm. There were plenty of actors, directors, producers, executives, musicians, and others of various types. Two of these were musicians. One was on tour and had me meet him at his hotel. When I found out what band he was in, I was totally star struck, as it was a huge band from my childhood. Another one was a retired musician who had a "one hit wonder" many years ago, and I was equally amazed to be in his presence.

The absolute standout was when a man gave me his address that led me into a weird neighborhood that has a mix of regular nice houses, and a few mansions. It was at night and I could not see the numbers on the houses well. I had it pretty well narrowed down to which house it should be. But it did not seem right because there were about four nice houses, and one gigantic fancy mansion that stood out like a sore thumb. I checked my notes twice, three times, and indeed the correct house was the massive fancy mansion. I got nervous and was afraid maybe it was a fake setup. I parked and sheepishly went to the gate. He opened the gate for me automatically, so I knew he was expecting me and it was the right house. I walked into the house, and it was a very normal looking, nice man, all alone in this gorgeous mansion. There was a very fancy antique dining table with red velvet chairs adorned with gold trim. There were statues, and many ornate decorations. He guided me to his study, and we sat and talked. He seemed to be kind and have empathy for me. He smiled at me and said, "What you do is pretty rough." I said, "Yeah, but it's okay." He said that things used to be rough for him also. He told me what he used to do. I will not say because it's too identifying, but it was a very simple low level, low pay existence, what he used to do. I then asked him, "How did things change for you?" He looked at me, as if fully realizing that I actually had no idea who he was. He seemed amused by this. He said, "I got lucky; I got very, very lucky." He made it as simple as that. My mind wondered of course. Did he win the lottery? Or did he sell a screenplay? Or what? Well anyway, we completed our business there. He then said he liked me and that I seemed different. He said I did not seem like someone who would do this kind of stuff. I replied to him that I was not a person who would do this stuff, but yet here I am (honest answer). I could tell he was intrigued and felt bad for me at the same time. He asked me if I was comfortable "doing more." I said, "No, not really." He said, "Ahhh okay, too bad." Then I left and rushed back home, took my shower, and started Googling furiously. I did not figure it out that night. But about three weeks later, I was watching something on TV, and THERE HE WAS. I was like: AHHHHH MY GOD, YES! I knew who he was finally. He was an A list producer/director/writer who was involved in some of the biggest movies of all time. Very famous. I just did not recognize him because I live under a rock, and people look different in person much of the time. His astronomical net worth between $500 Million and $1 Billion Dollars did not result in any extra for me though. Nice man. Cheap bastard. He could have shown compassion and changed my life. He chose not to.

If you ask me the most difficult traumatizing one, I would have to say there were two; but by far the most entertaining of the two would be, spoiler alert, "Cadaver Man." One afternoon (yes, during the day. Odd.) I had an address for the Hollywood Hills. I went up there. I found myself at a large beautiful home at the very top of the hill with one of the most amazing views in all of Hollywood. I was actually kind of excited at that point, because I was going to get to go inside this house, and I was willing to pay the price for admission on this one so that I would see inside it, and plus see who lived there. HA! Careful what you wish for! I knocked on the door, and who opens the door? A living cadaver. Now, please forgive me, no disrespect intended, okay? But seriously. It was a cadaver. He did not just look old. He did not just look like he was 98 or in his 100s. He looked dead. He literally looked like someone you would expect to see in a coffin at a funeral. I don't even know how he was able to get to the door. I was shocked when I saw him. I initially assumed it was just an awkward situation of him perhaps being the father of the man I was supposed to see. But no. That was the actual man who invited me over. How did I know? Well, he said nothing. It was as if he did not have the ability to speak. I am not sure how he still had the ability to breathe actually. However, taking my eyes off of him for a moment, revealed an amazing home interior. The house was made of crystal and glass inside. Everything was crystal and glass; the walls, the stairs, some of the furniture, everything. It was stunning and amazing. I had never seen anything like it. He had the highest house on the hill, and the best view in that area of Hollywood. Stunning, just stunning. But then my eyes went back to the man. He had somehow made his way over to some stairs, where he sat. So again, how did I know *this* was the man I was supposed to meet? Well he was sitting on the stairs with his eyes fixed on my crotch while he had a very long string of drool dripping from his mouth. In fact, there were a couple strings of drool dripping from his mouth. I was kind of frozen and shaken. I had gotten used to my "other job," and I had seen almost everything. But this, I had never seen. I was appalled, revolted, and freaked out. I was actually afraid he might die if he tried to do something. I was afraid if I moved slightly, and it pushed him over, and maybe would kill him or something. I moved slowly over to him where he just stared at my crotch and drooled. I was in NO mood to do this, and so far, it was not happening "downstairs," if you know what I mean. It is difficult to perform when you are that horrified and revolted. I felt kind of embarrassed actually. But I unzipped because he was clearly waiting for this, and he was unable to move his own arms to unzip me himself. He tried to touch, and I tried to get going with it, and he was trying, and I was trying, and oh my gosh, there was no way this was going to happen. Zero chance. I was getting agitated knowing that I was going to fail on this one gig. Just impossible. No thought in my mind could possibly be enough to conjure myself up for this task. I was getting sweaty and upset and I said to him, "I am so sorry I just can't do this." He kind of just nodded as if he was not surprised, and he walked me to the door. I went to my vehicle, started to drive away, and started to cry. I am not sure what was so upsetting. Was it because I had just failed? Was it because there was no reward, which I always needed? Or was it because I just tried to engage with a cadaver? Horrifying. I took a shower, which usually made things better, but the thoughts of this interaction haunted me for weeks.

But the absolute worst experience that scarred me, was a man I met in Santa Monica. It seemed normal at first. He seemed like a middle-aged gruff angry man who just wanted what he wanted. Seemed routine. But during the process, he started to grab my head and force me to do something to him. I resisted. I told him I don't do that. He started to really grab me and force me more fiercely. It turned into a full struggle. I was officially being attacked. I pushed him away from me and jumped like a jackrabbit to the door. He saw I was free of him and getting away, so he gave up. He said I was a piece of garbage and belonged in the trash. I left with a ripped shirt and a scratch on my face. But worse than that, I left feeling like a piece of garbage that belonged in the trash. When I got into my vehicle, I just let loose and cried. I was more upset than I had been in quite a while. I felt so horrible about every part of this encounter. I ended up crying out to myself, "You are a piece of garbage." In that moment, I was indeed a useless piece of garbage that belonged in the trash. That was the moment I felt the worst about what I was doing. It traumatized me. I had to take a break from my "other job" for a week. I think the man was the first person to fully verbalize what I was suppressing in my own subconscious of how I felt about myself regarding what I was having do.

I saved that one for last because even though my stories are funny and amusing, it is important to remember that I was living in my own personal hell much of the time doing this. I did not choose this lifestyle. I did not like doing this. I would not choose to do this if there had been another feasible way. I was as low as low could get doing things that the underbelly of society does when there is no hope and no way out. And that is how I felt. I felt like there was no hope and no way out.

However, it would also be one-sided and unfair if I did not mention the many wonderful people I met. Yes, that's right. Some of these people were truly nice people I enjoyed meeting. In addition to others I already spoke of, one man in particular, would sit with me for a good fifteen minutes first, and ask me how I was doing. He would listen intently with true caring. I recall once he said, "I feel dirty doing this to you; do you think I am a horrible person for doing this?" I of course told him he was not horrible, and by doing this, he was helping me eat and live. The truth is that the very fact this man was thinking this, and asking me this, proves he was indeed a nice good man.

He was not the only one. I had another man who would be very kind and give me designer clothing that no longer fit him. I had others who ended up being more interested in my intellect and gift for interesting conversation; and would reward me just for talking with them, without anything else being required. It's proof that even within the underbelly, there are many very good people. I am grateful for any kindness I received. The bottom line is that any contributions made to me, went toward food, rent, and going to Disney with my daughter.

As previously alluded to, I also met some very good people who seemed to need me on a spiritual level during the moments I met them. On many occasions, I would show up at someone's door when they needed counsel or guidance on a human spiritual level. I was always more than happy to provide this, as I always viewed it as God sending me to these people when they needed. In fact, on many occasions I would end up at the door of some very sad or distressed people, who really just needed to talk to someone.

After talking with them a while, they would say, "God brought you to me at just the right time." I heard this many times, from enough people to wonder what the hell was going on with this, and why would God send me to people in such a weird manner. Sometimes we just don't know all the answers. But most certainly, my visits were not always as they seemed, or for nefarious purposes, and often they were more meaningful and spiritual in nature.

The other silver lining to all this is that I somehow managed to survive all this without ever catching any disease. Perhaps it was simply because of my rules limiting the contact and extent of things I would allow. But I still want to give thanks for this and my good health and safety during this time.

I am obviously embarrassed about all this. But it is part of my journey. Even in all the darkness, I tried to shine as much light as possible. Additionally, I am very grateful for some of those I met through these experiences, a few of which who became genuine friends. I was trying to survive, and I was trying to show kindness to others at the same time. There will be people who judge me for all this, but those people are not stuck in my journey and have never walked in my shoes. Part of the lesson in this, is to learn not to judge others for what they do, without first understanding why they do it, and the circumstances surrounding them.

CHAPTER FIFTEEN
Star Trek Alien

Despite the supposed moments of adventure and amusement, I remained in a very dark depression every day. My weeks consisted of the heaven of being with my daughter on the weekends, the pain of dropping her off on Sunday nights, and then the horrible reality and daily grind of my various gigs and "other jobs" during the weekdays. What a nightmare. The adjustment between heaven with my daughter at Disney, to the despair and horror of what I had to do during the week, was so stark it was hard to comprehend. But that was my life, and this existence went on for several years.

At one point, my own struggle would become more complicated by problems Gez was having. It was all I could do to keep up with my own daily nightmare of trying to endure and survive each day so that I could buy food, pay bills, and pay my rent. I was always running behind on everything. I was a rat on a wheel, not keeping up.

But I was still close with Gez, talking every day, and I depended on him for moral support, and he depended on me for advice and guidance. Gez had a complicated family situation. His "mother" was a crazy evil psychotic woman. She was abusive to Gez when he was younger, and was still abusive with him as an adult, but was getting even worse. She was getting more psychotic and dangerous. Some months earlier, I had sent Gez some money so he could travel to an old unoccupied family home in a different area of Brazil. The plan was to shelter him there so he would be safe from his mother and brother. Gez was young and had no way to support himself. I had to send him money for food during this time. Eventually he ended up back at his house, and his mother persisted with her abuse. I am not sure what was wrong with that woman, but she was really declining mentally, and increasing in her psychotic behavior. She had been making threats to burn Gez's house down with him inside it.

I constantly had to send him money despite the fact that I was starving myself. For some reason I felt responsible for him. I ended up having to move him around to different locations and houses, and make sure he had the basics to stay alive, such as food and electricity.

One night he sent me a message saying his mother was screaming outside his house. I told him to immediately lock all doors and windows, and do not let her inside under any circumstances. He messaged back five minutes later and said he did everything I told him to do. But ten minutes later, he messaged me again and said his mother was banging on the door and she had a gun in her hand. I totally freaked out. But what can I do? I am sitting in Hollywood. I told him to call the police and stay away from the door. He said he already called the police. I heard nothing from him for a long time. I was in agony wondering what was going on. Finally, 45 minutes later, he messaged me and said I will never believe what just happened, and that he could barely breathe. I was wondering if he could not breathe because he was shot? What was going on? He finally spit it out and gave me some clear messages. He said his mother was unable to get into his house and went out into the street in front of his house and shot herself in the head. The police arrived shortly after that, Gez went out to meet them, and they ended up putting Gez into a police car while they tried to figure out what happened while a river of blood was running down the street in the rain. I, myself wondered what happened. Gez told me what happened, but part of me wondered if maybe he couldn't take it anymore, and snapped and shot her? It's a horrible thing for me to say, but the whole thing was just so insane I did not know what to think. I specifically did NOT ask him that because I did not want him admitting anything to anybody, including me. Nor did I want to know. However, it turned out that a neighbor had witnessed his "mother" shoot herself, and the police released Gez.

I personally was relieved that woman was dead. Again, sorry if this sounds bad or insensitive, but that woman had caused my life to be a hell because I had to spend my time and money helping Gez dodge her for years. For me it was a "the witch is dead, the witch is dead, Wizard of Oz" moment, and I was relieved.

After the burial, which Gez did not attend, Gez was summoned to his Grandmother. Through some miracle, his Grandmother was still alive, although not well at all. His grandmother had some major earthshaking news for Gez. His grandmother told Gez that his mother was not dead. Gez was obviously confused, as anyone would be. His grandmother then confessed and explained that the woman who had been his "mother" all his life, was not his mother. His real mother was his "Aunt." Ahhhhhh. Ah ha moment. What had happened is the aunt and the mother were sisters. Well, Gez's real mother got pregnant with Gez, but was not in a position to take care of him. On the other hand, his aunt was in a marriage with money, and wanted to take Gez. So, they decided the aunt would raise Gez as her own, and they would just switch places, saying the aunt was the mother, and the mother was the aunt. Hope you caught all that.

So, the "aunt" who had always been so kind and loving to Gez was actually Gez's real mother. So, when I met the "aunt" at Gez's house, I had actually met Gez's real mother and did not realize it. So, it was Gez's real mother who made the iced tea for me and would not stop smiling at me, not his aunt.

This raised other questions though. Who was Gez's father? Gez had always thought the man married to his "mother" (really his aunt) was his father. But obviously not. So, it turned out Gez's real father was a man who had stepped out of Gez's life when he was born, but this man still lived in the area.

Being the mature adult pragmatic American in the room, I asked Gez where his birth certificate was. Gez said he never had a birth certificate.

I was really beginning to go back to my original theories when I met Gez, that maybe he was an angel and not a real live person at all. This guy does not know for sure who his parents are and has no birth certificate. Is he really alive? Is he a person? Can he prove it?

So, I did some research and told Gez to go to the government office in a certain town and request his birth certificate. I sent him some money so he could do this. He did as I instructed and obtained his birth certificate. It indeed listed the correct parents as his grandmother had indicated.

Shortly after all this drama, his beloved Grandmother passed away. Gez was very sad but took it in stride. I know to this day that he misses her because he still mentions her sometimes. I am very grateful Gez figured out his parental situation before she passed.

Incidentally, Gez's father would shortly pass away from cancer. Gez did have a chance to meet the man, but there was no chemistry between them, and no relationship formed before he passed.

Gez's real mother continues to live in Gez's house to this day as I am writing this.

Meanwhile, back at the ranch in Hollywood-land, I was really struggling. To make matters even more depressing, my remaining cat, Graycee, finally passed away after a long decline. It was really rough, but I was expecting it. I had decided I would take a break from having a pet for a while. But right when I decided that, I had an immediate image pop into my head of a large fluffy white/beige cat. I assume this was my way of envisioning my next cat, but I brushed that thought aside, and went catless for several months, and solely focused on my financial and rent problems.

My various gigs and jobs and such, usually barely got me by, but if I had a slow month, I would not make ends meet. I had several instances where I ran behind and could not pay my rent. I received eviction notices routinely. I would usually be able to pay it before the trigger was pulled on me though. The landlord was growing impatient with me. I was warned they needed me to pay on time every month or I would be out. I knew it was impossible for me to pay on time. I knew I was screwed.

I started to develop this mentality that I was going to be on the street eventually. I started to spend time planning a life on the streets. I had plans laid out of living in my car, getting memberships at gyms so I could shower, and figuring out where I could park and sleep every night. I seriously made a file folder on this and did research. I still have the file folder full of information.

One night I wondered what it would be like for me if I had to sit on the street and ask for help. I took a short walk down to Hollywood Blvd on the Walk of Fame and found a clean spot, sort of out of the way, and sat there as if I was resting. In my mind I pretended I was really homeless. I just sat there watching people walk by me. 95% of everyone would not even look at me. So, in that sense it was not even awkward. The other 5% were men who would look at me and give me that look that I get in my "other job," so I knew they probably would help a homeless guy if the homeless guy was attractive and "willing." Ugh. I was already in that position anyway, I guess. It was getting cold, I was uncomfortable, and I did not want to deal with any man coming up to me, so I decided I had enough of this experiment, and I walked back home. I decided being homeless on Hollywood Blvd was not going to work for me.

Ever since that "experiment," whenever I saw a homeless person sitting in that same spot on Hollywood Blvd, I always gave them something, whether it be $20 or $5.

In fact, I started to develop a passion and hobby for handing out money to homeless people. Even if I had very little money for myself, I would go out for short walks and choose a homeless person and give them money. It was therapeutic for me. I lived in a cruel world. I felt forsaken by God myself. I knew nothing but struggle and pain. In giving money to random homeless people, it was my way of keeping faith in humanity alive. If I was THAT person who helped others, then that meant humanity still had people who helped. Be the person you wish you had in your life. Be the change.

It turned out the landlord would indeed try to evict me when I only paid partial rent. After being served the notice, I refused to move. I told them we could go the distance in the legal process if they wanted. I put on my old real estate legal hat, looked over my lease carefully, and I found a provision the landlord was violating.

California state law indicated I was entitled to peaceful enjoyment of my dwelling. The circumstances of my building were that they were renovating every single apartment. Just my luck (and annoyance) that they had renovated every apartment adjacent to me, and I actually in all honestly never had a moment's peace for two years. I wrote my landlord and told them if they proceeded with the eviction, I was going to counter sue and demand two years of rent refunded back to me. The landlord backed down. I eventually paid and caught up with my rent. Life went on, and they never tried to evict me again.

Eventually, I finally had a major positive breakthrough. I had seen a casting call for guys my age, size, and appearance, who were in great physical condition, to audition for a "special project." I applied and was invited to attend the audition. I went to the audition not knowing what this project even was about. At the audition were a bunch of others who looked similar to me, with exact same appearance and build as me. They asked us to line up and take our shirts off. They asked us questions about our physical condition, and our willingness to wear masks and prosthetics. I knew I fit all the requirements. Just by luck, I was in the best shape of my life and looked great. It was a case of being in the right place at right time and being the right type of person ready to do the right thing.

I was informed I got the job. I was told to come back on a certain date and time. I showed up, and there were about fifteen others present, who had also gotten the job. They had us sign all kinds of non-disclosure agreements first. Afterwards, they told us why we were there. We had all been chosen to work on the new Star Trek film, *Into Darkness*.

When they said those words, there were audible gasps. Personally, I could not believe my ears. I had always been a huge Star Trek fan, and to think I would now become part of that franchise was a dream come true. I was beyond stoked. I felt I had hit the lottery.

The Executive Producer came down and showed us the outdoor set (initial scene running through the red forest), and said it would be difficult and long, and if anyone could not do it, drop out now. Everyone stayed. We ended up having a week of choreography training for movement, as we were the aliens chasing Kirk and Bones thru the forest and needed to move like aliens. We had fittings at Sony studios for our costumes and makeup work.

Filming was intense. I had about six hours of makeup prep work in the morning, then shooting all day. After that, a couple hours of cleanup at night. It was a very long couple weeks with lots of running. Most everyone was injured at some point. Personally, I was impaled into a tree. I was knocked out for a few seconds and had some scrapes but was fine after a five-minute break. I loved every minute of this project.

I had a couple of fun scenes. In one scene, I had the camera sliding down on a wire right at me, and I had to jump out of the way just before it hit me. The other one that I will treasure forever is that I was chosen for a scene with just three of us. JJ Abrams personally directed us in the scene, so I got to work with him directly on that one scene. He was a very nice regular guy, and very respectful. How can life get better than that?

I never wanted it to end. If only that could be my only full-time job, I would be in heaven. But eventually filming ended for us. Our three weeks of work amounted to a few minutes in the movie, and me appearing for only several seconds on screen. Because of this, I did not get any screen credit or anything. Does not matter to me though. It was all about the experience. Epic. The best acting experience I ever had, as of this moment. Not only that, but I walked away with a nice sum of money. Life was a bit better. Finally.

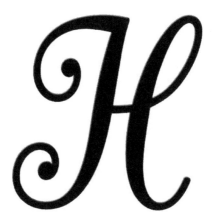

CHAPTER SIXTEEN
Professional Psychic

After Star Trek, I was feeling much better. It had been a few years since the walk-in, and my mind and body had made substantial progress healing. I was in the best physical shape of my life, and although my depression was coming and going, it was no longer constant. Plus, Star Trek put some money in my bank account and allowed me to catch up on everything.

Not only that, but after a few years of conversing with Gez daily, his English had become excellent and totally fluent. I coached Gez into finding a job teaching English. Gez was successful and managed to find a solid job teaching English at a school near his home in Brazil. He would go on to teach at a few different schools and developed a solid resume as a professional English teacher. He was finally able to take care of himself financially, and the moments of me needing to rescue him became infrequent.

While maintaining my connection with Gez, I was also still making new friends on social media as a means of human socialization. Most were younger than me, because that felt more like my tribe. Chaz, Gez, Jackson, and others I had lasting conversations with, had all been five to ten years younger than me. I also had started posting my modeling photos and such, and this attracted many young people, many of them gay, bringing with that many more family and social issues. But I have never been hung up on sexual preference, especially after the walk-in, since Chaz was gay, and I have had amazing friends of all sexual preferences. I relate to them all equally well. I was married to Luci by a lesbian for goodness sake. But one thing I did discriminate about during this time was age.

In my prior business years, I had always been the youngest person in rooms, full of middle aged and older businesspeople. I always related well to older people because I was very mature for my age and had an old soul. But since the walk-in, I for some reason preferred people much younger, more similar to the age of people Chaz used to hang out with. I assume all this was another symptom and result of the walk-in, whereas if you had not noticed by now, I had become more and more like Chaz.

Swimming in these younger circles exposed me to younger people (guys and girls) who had all the normal classic problems of youth found at that college age. Many were depressed, lost, had issues with parents, had issues with boyfriends and girlfriends, and had issues finding themselves.

I felt compelled and empowered to reach out to them and give advice and comfort. I had suffered so much in my life, experienced many things, and even though I was unable to help myself, I found I was very good at helping others. I slid into a big brother, or mentor role, for many of my social media friends.

Suicide was an issue that would come up often. I was shocked at how many young people were suicidal to some extent. I took it as my mission and personal hobby to reach out and help anyone who had suicidal issues. There started to be instances that people would tell me they were thinking of ending their lives, and I would have to talk them down from it. I felt a huge amount of satisfaction from this. It made me feel worthwhile. I really took it seriously and spent lots of time chatting and helping. I was not being paid for any of this obviously, so it was just a hobby, and I still had to keep up all my other gigs. But for sure what I enjoyed most, and wanted to do most, was help others. I wanted to make a difference. I wanted to take away people's suffering. I wanted to do for others what was never done for me. I wanted to be the person who reached out and made things okay.

It feels a bit self-righteous of myself to list or get into too much personal detail of how I intervened into some of these young people's lives to save them. But for the purpose of this story I have to confess with humility and gratitude, that I feel I prevented many suicide attempts, and saved many lives. This alone, gave me much needed validation for my own pathetic existence.

Not all stories ended happily. There had been one young man who I had been chatting with maybe weekly. He was clearly very depressed with many issues. I talked him down from suicide attempts maybe three times. I did the best I could. But after some break in communication, I received an email from a friend of his I had never spoken with. The friend told me that unfortunately the young guy in question had committed suicide. He said he was writing me because his friend had left a suicide note. In the note, the young man named me specifically as the only person who truly reached out consistently to help him, and that he truly appreciated me for that, and he was sorry.

Although I was obviously sad that I lost one and was not successful in his case, I found it very fulfilling and validating that he actually validated that my efforts were not worthless. My efforts were appreciated. That taught me a lesson. I realized that even if you lose the war, it still matters how you treat other people. This strengthened my perspective that taking people's suffering away was valued even if it did not solve their problem. Of course, it's always nice to accomplish both, but sometimes it is not possible.

I have always tried to apply this concept in all my work since. For example, many in society don't give money to homeless people, thinking "they will just buy alcohol or drugs with it so I won't give." But my thinking is, "If I can give money that will relieve suffering for even a day, it's worthwhile." The truth is that homeless people use money for a variety of things. Sometimes it's alcohol or drugs, but sometimes it is food, socks, or something they need. Who are we to withhold compassion just because we judge what they use it for? Compassion must be given unconditionally. Compassion is love for humanity. Compassion is love for what is right. Compassion is never to be judged. Making excuses to withhold compassion is wrong. The more pain you have suffered in your life, the more you would understand everything I just said above.

So along with all my various gigs and "jobs," I also had this nearly full-time passion of counseling and helping young people, people I would never meet in person. While my depression was trying to wane ever slightly, my psychic abilities were strengthening over time. I started to feel pretty Jedi-like, but still needing to do pathetic things to live, and was still living a pathetic life.

I have not wanted to brag about much in this book. Instead, I have been exposing every embarrassing or shameful thing I have ever done in my life. With that said, the truth is that my mental and psychic "abilities" had only become more and more powerful since the walk-in. All the things Chaz used to say to me that made no sense back then, all began to make sense over time since the walk-in. I also learned to control my empathic abilities forward and backwards. Frankly, I can see and sense things that others cannot understand. I look at the Universe, world, and people, differently than the normal person. I consider the human psyche a puzzle to put together, even if pieces are missing. What I am trying to say, is that I was ready for "prime time" as a professional helping people. All I needed was to figure out how to get started.

One day I had a breakthrough. Larry, an older man I had met in the psychic circles, contacted me and told me about a project he was working on. He had been cast in a pilot for a new TV series that had psychics and detectives working together to solve cold cases. Larry asked me if I wanted to go to the first shoot with him and just watch. I was lucky enough to not have any obligations that day, and I enthusiastically accepted his invitation.

I arrived on set to watch the filming. I can recall the producer/director asking people who I was, and why I was there. Larry told him I was a psychic and that he invited me to watch. Not sure Stefan, the producer/director, was too happy about this. But there I was.

The case they were filming involved a married couple who had been kidnapped, taken to a remote area, killed, and buried. Stefan knew all the details of the case but did not share them with the cast of psychics and detectives. He wanted to test and see what the psychics could come up with, and how close it was to the facts he already knew from the case. So, the location we were at was in fact the location where the police had eventually found the bodies.

Each psychic cast for the project was filmed going out into the desert scrub brush area and giving their impressions of where the bodies might be buried, and what exactly they thought happened. I watched.

After everyone was done, one of the psychic cast members, Christine, suggested to Stefan that they let me give it a shot. Stefan had this look on his face like, why waste his time filming someone who was not even on the show and he did not even know. But he reluctantly agreed anyway. So, they put a mic on me, and out I went. I was surprised at how easily information was coming to me. I actually FELT the horror, dread, and fear of the victims. I felt the energy. I scanned around like a metal detector until I found where I thought the bodies would have been buried. I could feel a distinct difference between the energy of that exact spot vs. the rest of the area.

It turned out that I had nailed the correct spot of where one of the bodies had been found.

I was immediately hired onto the TV series pilot.

We ended up filming four different episodes, meaning four different cases. The dynamics of the cast fell into place. I ended up working closely with Christine out in the field, as well as doing the "counseling bits" of the episodes on my own. I ended up being a prominent part of the show, and I think Larry resented it a bit, as Larry was supposed to be the star of the show but was not. Christine and Bobby Brown (from Dog The Bounty Hunter) would end up being the stars of the show, but I worked closely with Christine on film, and had many scenes I did on my own. I am certain Larry regretted inviting me to the set that day.

I recall another instance where we were at a cemetery filming a scene, and we were tuning into two graves. It was husband/wife dual graves right next to each other. We, the psychics, were trying to tune into the spirits of the husband/wife. I was able to tune into the husband fine, and I relayed the impressions I was getting from him. But when I tried to tune into the wife, I got nothing. In fact, it felt so empty to me that I felt the grave was totally empty. There was literally no energy there, as if the grave was empty. Larry took Stefan aside and was telling him that he thought I was crazy and did not know what I was doing. Okay fine. But days later, one of the other producers had done some research, and it turned out that the wife's grave was actually empty, because one of the relatives had decided to keep the wife's ashes instead of having them buried in the grave. BOOM. Sorry Larry. So, there was only the memorial stone for the wife next to the husband, but no remains.

The show was great and we did amazing work, including helping police solve a major case outside Los Angeles. However, for one reason or another, the show was never picked up by a network. Both Discovery and OWN came very close, but no cigar. Even so, my experience working on this TV series was amazing and solidified me as a legitimate professional psychic.

As a professional psychic getting increasing attention, I made the decision early on to keep my daughter a part of my private life, and not include her in my public life. She was still kind of young and I wanted to protect her from any intrusions. Thus, nobody would ever know that I even had a daughter. My policy in general was to never talk about my personal life at all. My professional life was about helping other people. When a client pays for my help, it's all about them. It is not about me. It was best for me to leave my entire personal life out of the equation. That included Angel. This book is the first time I am revealing my personal life to the world.

Additionally, Angel had started showing some psychic ability. Angel has abilities similar to mine, except more energy sensitivity in nature, whereas mine are more empathic in nature. I wanted to give Angel the time and privacy to develop in her own way and time, without public expectations or interference.

I put out my shingle using my professional psychic name and started offering sessions and readings. I had an instant positive response. I was able to officially retire from my "other job," and I officially had a new job as a Psychic Counselor and Life

Coach. The acting and modeling took a back seat as well, and pretty much faded away as I was getting too old for that stuff anyway. There comes a point when you hit a certain age and nobody wants to look at pictures of you in your underwear anymore, you know?

Word got around within the psychic circles regarding the work I had done on the TV series pilot. People were intrigued and I was invited to various internet radio interviews where people got to know me better. I always presented myself as a psychic counselor because I never had any interest or talent for "fortune telling" or "reading palms," or any of that. My talent was for using all my God given, walk-in given talents, and use them to help solve problems for people, take away suffering, and improve lives. Over time, I would actually become more of a Life Coach.

I did countless traditional psychic readings which included predictions and things involving relationships, and all the normal stuff you expect from psychics. But my best work was always involving people who were broken and needed to be fixed. I used my abilities to do this. I also excelled at mediumship readings where I communicate with people's deceased loved ones. For some reason I was able to look at a picture, look into their eyes, and they start talking to me.

Over the years, I have been able to rope in all my mental resources to maximize my abilities. I use my own personal abilities I was born with, all my personal experiences in life, all the knowledge from my walk-in, all the information offered to me from my Spirit Guides, and my entire practical medical, psychology training, and general knowledge of many subjects. I have tried to create a perfect storm of light, power, and knowledge, to give the client what they need, customizing a special approach for each individual client.

I don't talk about my clients, but I ended up with clients ranging from kids, to housewives, to businessmen, to Hollywood celebrities. I became known as the "psychic's psychic," because many other psychics would commonly ask me for a consult or advice on their own lives or professional cases. I ended up working with clients from all over the world. In one publication I was listed as one of the top 50 psychics in the world.

I ended up being invited to be one of the original members of a prestigious psychic network. Incidentally, I would end up meeting a person in that group that would change my life forever.

However, before that were to happen, I had a debt to pay. I had fallen out of touch with my TV series cast since the series was never picked up, but one day I received a message from one of them. She informed me that Larry had been diagnosed with terminal cancer, and she thought I should know. I tried to call Larry, but there was never an answer or reply to my voice mails. I got back in touch with the person who told me about him, and I asked where he was. She told me he was presently in hospice, and where. The next day I made a trip up to the other side of town to see Larry. It was indeed a hospice facility. The front desk told me which room Larry was in. I found the room and walked in. Larry was lying in bed, half-unconscious, with oxygen and tubes coming out of him. I was horrified and shocked. I was obviously way too late for a proper visit.

But when I walked closer to him, he woke and saw it was me. He seemed really surprised and I said, "Hey Larry." He responded, "Hey Brian, how are you doing?" There was something funny about it because he was acting like everything was normal and totally fine, as if we were meeting on the street or something.

I told him I had only heard about his situation recently and that I was sorry. I knew he had bone cancer and clearly, he was very end-stage. Then Larry said something from under his mask. He said, "Heal me. Try." I gulped because, ummm, it looked a bit late for that. But I took his hand and focused. What I "saw" in my mind was a body completely littered and covered with tumors and cancer cells. There was seriously no way. But I acted as if I was giving it a good college try as a way of showing Larry I cared enough to try. I knew he was dying. So, I thought to myself that if I can't save him, maybe I can help him pass. So, I got all determined, looked at Larry, and said, "You won't have to do this alone." "I will come back." "I will come back in a few days." "You need to hang on until then." Larry nodded and motioned to me goodbye and I left.

In my car on the way home I contemplated when I should return. The message from the voices in my head came in very clear. "Thanksgiving Day." Thanksgiving was about a week away and I actually had no plans for Thanksgiving that year. So, I waited until then.

The morning of Thanksgiving, I drove up to Larry. I was hoping he would still be there, if you know what I mean. Sure enough, he was. I walked in, and he seemed both surprised and relieved I was there. By this time, he could no longer speak. I could tell he knew it was me though, and he could understand when I spoke to him.

I told him it was good to see him and that I was honored to spend my Thanksgiving with him. I am not a touchy-feely guy, but I took Larry's hand and just held it, as if praying with him. I was trying to tune into him and determine where he was at with his process. I could tell he was very close to the end. So, I started talking to him. I told him it was going to be okay. Then I just started launching into my "instructions" on how to "do this." I told him to relax. I told him that if at some point he felt an urge to just "push off," he should gently "push off." I told him I would be with him and guide him to the light. He seemed to truly focus on what I was saying and be determined to follow my instructions. That day Larry fell in and out of consciousness. I could tell when he was in pain, and I would get the nurse to give him more morphine. I also had to have his oxygen turned up regularly all day until it was on full blast. He had two visitors that day besides me. His best friend, a woman, who I had never met, came by. I got to meet her, and we visited and bonded. She left.

Then Larry's daughter showed up, whom I had also never met. I introduced myself to her and explained what I was doing. I told her that if she preferred privacy and wanted me to leave, that I would do so with no hard feelings. She enthusiastically asked me to stay. We visited and got to know each other, and we bonded as well.

I monitored Larry all day and into the evening, making sure he got his morphine shots. I observed him closely and stayed tuned into him empathically. He woke up momentarily when his daughter was there and they had a moment together, but then Larry was out again.

Eventually I could tell Larry was fading. I could sense he was seeing things and interacting with someone, or some presence. I could sense he was very close to death, and he was "talking" to whoever was perhaps meeting him in heaven/spirit world. My senses were very heightened, and I even told his daughter that I thought it was close.

Larry got "quiet" psychically, and I watched him. I am pretty sure I sensed the "push," or he was trying to push up. For some reason, I felt like I was intruding, and I looked the other way almost as a way of giving Larry some privacy. A minute or seconds later, I turned my head to glance over at him, and I saw this huge flash of light. I was a bit startled by it. I immediately asked his daughter, who had been watching TV in the room, if she had just seen that flash of light. She indicated she had not. But I was sure of what I saw. I got closer to Larry and looked at him. I tried to sense him. Nothing. He was still breathing slowly, but I could not sense any brain activity. He was gone to me.

I explained to the daughter what I felt had just happened, and I told her I felt he was gone. We kind of had a moment and I just stared at him. We had a nurse come in and check on him, and he was still breathing, but he was totally cold and barely had a pulse. I stayed another hour, and then I really felt I should leave. I really felt Larry was gone. I felt Larry no longer needed me because he was actually gone. I felt him push off, I saw his soul leave his body, and I sensed his soul meet the light in spirit world. It felt complete to me.

So, I asked Larry's daughter if she needed me to stay. She indicated it was okay if I left. I said my goodbyes to her and left. Shortly after I returned home, his daughter texted me saying, "He stopped breathing and it's over. Thank you, Brian."

I have often contemplated that entire event. Helping Larry was a way for me to repay him for helping launch my psychic career. But Larry allowing me to witness every inch and aspect of his passing was an amazing gift. I learned so much from going through all that. It helped me further understand death, from decline to reaching spirit world. Amazing. Simply amazing.

Larry's best friend, who had been taking care of his cats, offered me Larry's prize companion cat, a huge fluffy white/beige rag doll cat. Since this was the exact cat I had seen in my vision when my cat Graycee died, I accepted. Larry's cat is still with me today as I write this. I am his third owner, and all of his owners have been psychics.

My psychic abilities continued to grow and expand since Larry's death. In addition to everything already mentioned, I also developed an ability to do some healing for people. I started focusing more on energy work, and found I could also "influence," or even "manifest" certain outcomes for people. None of these skills are effective on myself, or those too close to me, but I can be quite effective for strangers. It seems I am only limited by willingness to truly connect with the Universe, and my own personal and physical energy available. All of this work is extremely draining for me and I can only do so much. This story is certainly not over when it comes to my abilities, as they continue to grow, develop, and shift.

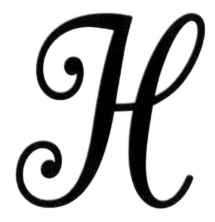

CHAPTER SEVENTEEN

European Adventures

Through the psychic organization I had joined, I was able to network and socialize with other professional psychics. It was a great platform to pick up business from the public, but its greatest value was the interactions with other psychics.

One day I received a message from one of the other member psychics that she was interested in getting a reading from me. This in itself was not unusual because I had developed a reputation as someone that many other psychics would get readings or consults from. But this one was a little unusual because the woman wanting the reading was a major powerhouse in the industry. She was quite famous in Europe and tended to operate very independently. But okay, I'm game. I'm here to help.

At first she just wanted an email reading. She asked me her questions, which mostly centered around where she should, or would, be living. She gave me some choices, and I gave her my thoughts on what she should do, and where.

After the ice had been broken with this email reading, she started chatting me up informally, and I took the bait because she was always easy to banter with. It was not long before she started asking me if I had ever been to Europe, specifically England or Ireland. I said I had never been to Europe and did not think I would ever go to Europe. She told me she had plans to come to the USA for a visit, and maybe even move to the USA. She told me she had "some dogs," and that started what would become our big inside joke in the future.

She suggested that maybe I could come to Europe and watch her dogs while she came to the USA. But the truth is, she was looking to personally meet up with me, whether in Europe or USA. So the conversation somehow twisted around to hinting at me coming to Europe for a visit.

I never thought she was serious. I was also thinking that I really did not want to get involved in anything at this time, such as a relationship, or whatever this thing was, or trying to be, or whatever her intentions were. The facts of my life were that I was still stinging from the poison of divorce from Luci, the heartbreak of Chaz's death, and I was still chatting with Gez, and had a strong connection with him. But most of all, I was 100% focused on my daughter. I just wanted to spend time with my daughter really. That's it. So, I really felt "done" with any kind of drama or relationship adventure. Stick a fork in me, remember?

But Serena persisted. Oh, excuse me, how rude, I forgot to introduce her to you. Her name was Serena. As I said, she was a very prominent psychic with her own huge reputation, and from her pictures you could see she was an absolutely stunning blond woman with large cleavage, and even larger confidence.

It did not take long before Serena boldly offered to fly me to Europe for a visit. She offered to pay for everything. Plane ticket, car to her house, food, hospitality at her home, and some interesting sightseeing. She laid her winning hand on the table and called me on it.

I was only left to stutter and stammer and look for ways to squirm out of it, but she had sealed off all the escape routes. I was trapped. There was nothing I could do but throw my hands up, yell "uncle," and say, "Okay fine."

When I agreed, I think she was almost amused that I had actually agreed, as if she was expecting me to just run away. But I don't run away. If given no other options I will jump. So, I jumped. I agreed to fly to the other side of the planet to a place I had never been, to meet a person I had never met before.

Oh wait. I've done that before, haven't I? Well here we go again.

The day came to set off on my twelve-day trip to Europe. I refused to go for longer because I did not want to miss much time with my daughter. Serena had booked the tickets for me and everything. I just needed to show up at the airport. I boarded and found my cramped coach seat on the impossibly long flight and settled in.

The next day I landed in London. There was a driver at baggage claim holding a sign with my name on it. Wow, this Serena woman was solid, reliable, and on her game. I was super tired and not feeling well from my flight, but glad to be off the plane. I started on my car journey with the driver. I seriously did not even know where I was going. I neglected to even ask Serena what city she lived in. Notice I used the word "city." You will see how funny that is in a moment.

After it felt like we had been driving way too long, I asked the driver how much longer we had to go. The driver replied that we were probably halfway there. OH MY GOD, UGH. Really? Are you kidding? So just like on the plane, I wanted to shoot myself to get rid of the pain of travel. I'm not a good traveler. I get cramped quickly, as well as travel sickness.

We had long cleared out of London and surrounding cities. We were now driving by sheep pastures. Then it turned into a skinny winding road where we had to follow farm equipment crawling up to their next field. Then it turned into a one-way tiny road in a small town that consisted of stone homes with grass roofs. This is the point where I actually started to become afraid. I was wondering what I had done and gotten myself into. Was I headed into a trap and my certain death? Flashback images of when I got lost in Brazil finding Gez's house popped into my head. Would I never be seen or heard from again? I was not in Kansas anymore Toto. This town was out of some fantasy novel. It looked like maybe Snow White and Shrek lived there. I once again asked the driver if we were almost there, because I was wondering if I should just ask him to take me back to the airport. However, a couple minutes later, the driver pulled up to an old stone farmhouse with an old stone barn to the left of it. The farmhouse looked like it would be lucky if it had heating and plumbing. "Here you go," he said. I looked at him, and honestly there was a moment where I froze time to contemplate if I should get out of the car or just tell him to take me back. But before I could finish that thought, Serena came out to the car to meet me. Yep, it's Serena. She seemed normal enough, and acted normal, and I felt more comfortable right away. So, I got out and retrieved my gigantic roller suitcase from the trunk of the car.

I looked at Serena, waiting for her to guide me into the house. Umm not quite. Serena said, "Oh no, I am over here in the barn." I looked at her confused and wondering if she was messing with me or not. She wasn't. She was headed right for the barn. One problem. It had been raining that day as it does almost every day there, and it was very muddy. Complete mud from where I was standing at the car, all the way to the door of the barn. I was wearing my regular LA sneakers, leather jacket, and was pretty much dressed as if I was going to check into the Marriott. But that was not the only obstacle. Anyway, I walked through the mud knowing my shoes were fucked, and my suitcase as well. Then I got to the second obstacle. Standing between me and the door into the barn was a horse blocking almost the entire narrow passageway. I looked at Serena like WTF. Serena never missed a beat and said to just gently walk behind him. So, I very carefully and gingerly tried to go behind the horse. It was a tight area to pass through, and the horse's ass was inches from my face, and I was terrified it might kick me or do something even worse. I somehow made it past the horse's ass and to the door of the barn.

I entered the barn and what I found was a place that looked like a barn (because it was a barn), which had been turned into a huge studio "apartment." It had a bed at one end, a sitting area in the middle, one little wood stove as its only heat source, and then a table at the other end. But it was missing something. A couple things actually. It was missing a kitchen. And most horridly, it was missing a bathroom. The kitchen thing I let go by. But I immediately asked where the bathroom was. Serena motioned to the back door going outside. I had horrible visions at that moment of the bathroom being an outhouse, or even just a tree. But fortunately, there was a small separate building that had a full bathroom in it. Well sort of. It had a real sink with real water, a real shower with real hot water, and then a pretend toilet which was a chemical toilet (not good). But okay, it checked off a few of the boxes anyway.

The barn came complete with something else. The barn had animals. Dogs. Lots and lots of dogs. You will eventually pick up on the inside joke, but I will start by saying that Serena claims there were only five dogs. We will take her word for it, okay? But to me, there were at least fifty dogs. Little sausage dogs. Barking. Lots of barking. Lots of dogs everywhere. Barking. They would move around constantly, and if I tried to count them, I would end up counting the same dog more than once, and thus I could count up to fifty dogs. It seemed like fifty dogs anyway. I don't mind dogs I guess, but I am not a dog person. Well, I had a dog as a child that got run over by a car, but that's a different story. I am actually a cat person. And if the dog is barking or shitting, I am even less of a dog person. Serena's dogs specialized in barking and shitting and deserved an Oscar for their talented performances at both.

In the USA, I am pretty sure this situation would be classified as "being homeless," "camping," or "living in a dog kennel." But for the local standards in that area, it was apparently quite reasonable accommodations. More interestingly is that Serena seemed totally comfortable, as if she chose this, and loved living there. In fact, she did love living there. But I digress.

I was starving. Serena knew this. She's psychic, remember? So, Serena asked if I wanted to eat. I said yes please. But I glanced at the lack of a kitchen and wondered what would happen next. Well, Serena snapped into action. She took a camper stove, some old pans, along with some bread, eggs, bacon, and went outside near the bathroom. She set up near the bathroom door and started cooking a full course breakfast meal out in the elements. By this time, I was just exhausted and over it, so I just rolled with it. I took a shower while she cooked, and thankfully it was a fully satisfying hot shower. Breakfast was ready.

Serena had a full breakfast spread laid out on the table inside. It was one of the best breakfasts I ever had. She somehow had managed to whip up an amazing high-quality breakfast by slinging some ingredients out on a camping cook stove in the light drizzle outside. Serena would prove over and over that she was a master chef and could cook under any circumstances. It could be dark out, raining with gale force winds, and her meals would all be first class without her even breaking a sweat. It turned out that Serena was indeed a chef. She had done this during her early days before she started doing psychic work.

Serena and I consummated our new "friendship? slash relationship?" that very first night. I am not sure if it was the fact I had just had a long trip and needed to blow off some steam, or if it was that it was cold as fuck in that barn and the bed was so cozy, or was it because I was in bed with a beautiful kind woman? I could have been a gentleman and slept on the hard, cold leather couch, but that never happened.

I woke up the next morning to find a huge sheep staring at me through the window. Serena told me that was Rodney. Rodney the sheep would spend the rest of my time there staring at me through the window. Yeah, I don't know. But setting aside my debilitating jet lag, shock, and discomfort of where I ended up, we settled into a very nice routine. Serena always made sure there were endless amounts of Earl Grey tea, snacks, and amazing meals she would prepare on cue without ever complaining once. That's another thing about Serena. You will never hear her complain. She will debate you on any topic until you are beaten into the ground, but she will never complain about anything. She would go out and drag wood inside for the fire, cook endless meals outside under impossible conditions, and she would walk her dogs twice a day, regardless of the weather. Never a complaint. I believe I had pretty much found the opposite of Luci.

Serena showed me around the little town, and I found the entire place very odd. It had stores and restaurants, but there were never any customers inside. It had its own elementary school, but I never saw any kids. I had come to the conclusion that the town was some vortex where vampires lived. The man who owned the property where she was living, would have little white birds hanging in his shed one day, and gone the next, as if they were his vampire snacks. He was also always burying something in his backyard. While at the one restaurant we actually ate it, I saw an old photograph from the 1800s, and there was a man in it that looked EXACTLY like Serena's landlord. To sum up, it was a very creepy place. The entire town. Creepy, creepy, creepy. But it was also beautiful. Rolling hills, sheep, and a pretty view of the ocean. In some ways, I found myself reconnecting with my childhood home in New England, because the topography and environment was so similar.

Eventually, my twelve days were up, and I returned back home to LA. However, I would return back to "the barn" and Serena for several visits at close intervals. On one of those visits, we had a paranormal event happen at the town church. This church was named after a specific Saint, and I was wanting to exercise my psychic skills, and was frequently trying to connect with various spiritual entities. We went to this church, and conveniently it was empty, and we had it to ourselves. I felt very comfortable in there and started to feel a presence. I got into my sort of high intense focused meditation mode and tried to pick up what I was sensing.

I ended up having a psychic interaction with some entity that I felt could have been the Saint. He was talking about twisting and turning energy for power and heeling. I automatically spoke out loud what I was being told so Serena could listen to my words and maybe capture them. Serena did indeed take notes. So, I had this interaction, and then there seemed to be some intense swirling light that appeared up on the second floor where the church bell was located. I focused on that light to continue my connection with the entity. It became too exhausting and I finally broke connection. We went back to the barn and contemplated Serena's notes and what it all meant. We would learn a few days later, that for the first time in two-hundred years, the church bells at the church had broken for some reason. Some mechanical part mysteriously gave way and broke, after no problems for a couple centuries. We smartly kept our mouths shut.

Eventually, Serena realized that I was tiring of the barn. Although I loved visiting Serena, the barn was really below my standards of comfort, and it was wearing on me. I was also having huge problems sleeping in that one bed with all her millions of dogs piled around me and on me all night. Plus, since the walk-in, I was more comfortable sleeping alone in total silence without being around anyone else's energy. I know it's weird and unromantic, but it is one of the side effects of the walk-in. I remember Chaz also saying he preferred to sleep alone, far from others. So anyway, I just couldn't deal with it anymore. The needle that broke the camel's back was when the chemical toilet started malfunctioning and I think it was about to explode. I had reached my limit with the barn, and Serena sensed this.

So, one day, Serena surprised me and said she was moving. I asked where, and she said back to Ireland where she had lived for a long time previously. I was skeptical, but excited. Would we end up in another barn in Ireland?? It did not matter because staying in that barn we were in was no longer an option. We packed up her little car, stuffed all her numerous dogs inside, and off to Ireland we went.

After much driving and a ferry ride, we arrived in Ireland that night, and Serena just had to pick up the key to the house she had rented. I was still skeptical and nervous of where we would end up. She retrieved the key, and we found the house. We walked into the little house and what did I find? I found a fully renovated, completely clean modern house. It had two bedrooms, living room, dining room, full huge kitchen, dishwasher (which Serena refused to use), clothes washer, clothes dryer (which Serena refused to use), full bathroom INSIDE, and everything you would expect from a house. It was fully furnished, and it was a real home done to American standards. I really thought the doors to heaven had just opened up. Then I did something really rude. I found the guest bedroom, I went in, and I shut the door behind me. I never slept so well in my life. I woke up feeling like a normal person, same as back home in LA. I apologized to Serena, but explained I just needed to be alone and sleep for once. She actually thought it was funny and totally understood. She has a full understanding of all my oddities and habits resulting from the walk-in, and me just being weird, picky, and annoying in general.

I loved that house. I loved Ireland. What a wonderful beautiful place. Granted, we were living in the "Beverly Hills of Ireland," so it was a really nice, safe, high class town right on the bay in the Dublin area. This was a place I could live. I had many visits there. I had fallen in love with the area and developed a real comfort level with the house and town. So, because of all this, of course something had to ruin it.

It turned out that Serena never got approval from the owners to have all her dogs there. The owners ended up finding out two years after she moved in about the dogs. Please understand that however annoying I found her dogs, the dogs did no damage to the house at all. There really was no reason for a landlord to have an issue with these dogs. But they did. So, the owners started action to try and get Serena evicted from this home I loved so much.

That was not the only drama that was ongoing. As you may or may not have thought of in the back of your mind, what about the whole Gez vs. Serena situation? Even though I had not seen, or been with Gez in person for years, I cared for him a great deal and we conversed daily. Serena had known about this and never liked it, but it started to bother her more and more. On the other side,

Gez had caught on to the fact I was making way too many trips to see "the witch," as he called her, and he was getting intensely jealous.

I am great at helping other people. I could possibly negotiate world peace if given a chance. But when it comes to my own life and situations, I am a total and complete idiot. So, I lay myself down at the mercy of the court right now and am subject to your judgment. But I cannot help my feelings, I do not control my circumstances, and it is what it is.

So, I was in a situation where Gez hated Serena, and Serena hated Gez. I loved both of them and wanted both in my life. Gez was in my soul and there was no way I would walk away from him, but Serena was my everyday life partner who I also would not part with. Giving up one or the other was not an option. This drama between the two of them, and me getting squeezed in the middle, would go on for years. It resulted in Gez and I becoming a bit more distant, and Serena always being suspicious and sensitive about the issue. I have no solution, and I am just telling my story here, okay? Yes, Serena should have just left me; and Gez should have just written me off. It is one reason I have always felt I would end up alone. I just cannot cope with other people, and I am impossible to cope with as well. I accept all this.

But other than that, things were pretty good. All of these trips Serena was funding were paid back in the form of me working on most of her client cases. She had a huge book of business providing various psychic and energy work to many various clients all over the world. She put me to work giving consults on all her cases and doing much of the energy work for her clients. We ended up working together on many things. We did not necessarily advertise ourselves as a team, but most people ended up finding out and fully accepted and embraced us as a team.

One of the talents I developed while in Ireland was the ability to choose lottery numbers. Ireland has a wonderful and fun way of hitting on the lottery numbers. Through a local betting house (bookie), you can place bets on partial lottery numbers. For example, let's say one of the Irish lotteries draws 6 numbers. Through the bookie, you can place a bet on choosing 3, 4, or 5 of the 6 numbers. So, you can still pick up a huge win of many thousands, by betting on 4 numbers, instead of the impossible 6 numbers.

Well, I seemed to be pretty good at picking 3 or 4 of the numbers each draw. Serena had clients that wanted me to choose numbers for them. I chose each client's numbers based on their individual energy, along with the numbers I felt might come up.

I hit success several times for her clients. One particular client received a large lottery win with the numbers I had given him. I was very grateful to have helped him. Too bad my talent seemed to work for others better than they worked for myself.

Eventually, we lost our battle to stay in the Ireland house. Despite my endless begging and pleading, Serena decided to move back to England to be close to her parents. I was not only disappointed, but you could say I was actually irritated and angry about it. I had loved Ireland (and that house) and wanted her to stay. But she is stubborn, and nobody will ever tell her anything. She ended up renting a house back in England close to her parents.

This move had some silver linings though. Firstly, I got to finally meet her parents. I was nervous like most guys in my situation would be, but my worries were not warranted. After entering her parent's beautiful marina flat, Apt 345, her parents turned out to be the kindest people ever, and immediately accepted me into their family without hesitation. Serena's dad was a retired medical doctor, and her mom a retired nurse. Her mom and dad met one day in a courtyard while her mom was carrying a bottle of urine. It was love at first sight. It was not long before I had met her entire family. All such nice people.

Serena's new home was actually much bigger than the Ireland house. Her new place had three levels, a quiet, dog-free third floor just for me, and plenty of room for her kennel of dogs on the levels below. I admit in fairness it was a nice house, but I will always be grumpy about her move away from that house in Ireland.

The other silver lining is that in England there was so much to see, and we had many adventures. We focused all our adventures on visiting significant spiritual, holy, or paranormal sites.

We went to countless churches, chapels, cemeteries, and you name it. We visited Roslyn Chapel where the Holy Grail is purported to have been stored for a time. We toured the Knights Templar church in London. We went to Stonehenge where I got to see a pile of rocks set out in the middle of nowhere, which to me appear to be a sundial built in someone's honor. But of course, we do not know for sure what and why Stonehenge is there. At least I can say I was there and touched it. We went to Westminster Abbey where all the crypts, coffins, and remains containing many of England's kings and queens are interned. I had many spiritual connections in there. We also went to Windsor Castle where the current Queen Elizabeth actually lives. She was in residence when we were there, but we would not see her until we traveled to Scotland, and I was only a few feet from her as she went by in her car for an event there. I waved at her, and she waved back. I'm sure it's only a matter of time before I receive my Knighthood, but I digress. I loved all my visitations, and our adventures were many and broad in scope. I truly got to see and experience all of England. Our favorite place to stay was in a nice hotel next to Big Ben, and Serena always made sure we got the same room with the most amazing view, room 345.

My favorite of all the adventures were our couple of trips up to Scotland. Scotland has such a wonderful dark mysterious old-world energy that really suits me. But the best part was Serena's choice of where to stay. She booked us into an exclusive place called "The Witchery." It is not for everybody though. It has a small select amount of rooms located in two different buildings which are clearly very old and very haunted. We have since stayed in most all of the rooms. The rooms are all decorated in very old dark mysterious decor. Even if the place was not haunted, you would still get creeped out due to the decor.

By far the most interesting of all our stays was in a suite called "The Inner Sanctum." The suite has a very ancient four-poster bed, an elevated dining area with a view out onto the street, a sitting area, and a bathroom with a huge claw tub, and a full-scale portrait of a creepy gentleman who stares at you from any location within the bathroom. The suite is decorated with antique furniture, lamps, and books. The centerpiece of the entire suite is a bust statue of Queen Victoria, which sits on an antique table in the center of the suite.

Upon checking in and entering the suite, Serena was immediately drawn to the Queen Victoria statue. I was very amused by the statue. I love creepy things. Creepier the better. But Serena does not like creepy things as much, and she found this statue very creepy. She responded by taking out some kind of holy water from her purse and splashing a tiny amount of the water on the statue. My reflex action was to yell at her for doing this. I told her, "How would you like it if someone threw water at you in your home?" She of course responded that she needed to deal with that creepy thing in her own way. I responded by saying she better hope she did not piss off that statue, because she probably made the situation worse, and she should have left it alone. We commonly get into these ridiculous banters about ridiculous things. So, it was not a fight, rather it was us just having our normal dialogue.

We enjoyed our day there and turned in for the night. Sometime during the night, we both woke up. The moon was strong and streaming moonlight into our room. The moonlight was hitting the Queen Victoria statue in a perfect creepy way. I started to notice some strange things on the statue. It appeared to me that Queen Victoria now had little stubs of horns coming out of her head, and now had grown hair on her chest. I thought this was kind of funny. I told Serena to look at the statue and tell me if she could see what I see. Her reaction was, "Oh my God, there is hair growing out of her chest." And I said, "Yeah but look at her head." And Serena said, "Oh My God, are those horns?" I said, "Yep." Serena got really freaked out and grabbed me. I just watched the statue with amusement. Again, everyone reading this is entitled to come up with their own opinions and theories. But there was indeed hair coming out of the statue's chest, and what appeared to be horns on her head, even if they were shadows or whatever. Somehow, we drifted back to sleep because we were tired from the journey to Scotland.

When we woke up, I noticed the statue had moved. Queen Victoria was still on the antique table, but it had swiveled around to the left, such that it was staring directly at Serena with a very disapproving look. I was a bit shocked and confused at this. I told Serena to look at the statue, and she immediately lurched and almost jumped out of her skin. The statue was staring right at her looking very disapproving.

Thinking there must be an explanation, I thought it was funny and laughed at Serena. I told her, "See, you should not have thrown the water on her and pissed her off." Serena did not take that well and started to get angry at me. Sorry, I still think this is totally funny and did not care how scared or annoyed she got at me. I kept rubbing it in. However, my own curiosity had to be satisfied, so I did get up and check out the statue and check out the table. I tried to swivel the statue back around, and I was able to do it, but it took a huge amount of effort. That thing weighed a ton. I don't think Serena could have moved that statue herself. I also looked underneath the table to see if there was some kind of mechanism. There was no mechanism. I was also certain nobody had entered our room in the middle of the night, and nobody would not do that anyway since it would be inappropriate.

I have no explanation. And that is what makes it so awesome. To this day, I desperately want to stay in that room again, and Serena desperately wants to never stay in that room again. Serena is also still afraid of Queen Victoria. I sometimes joke to her that Queen Victoria is still pissed and is coming for her. Yeah, I'm an asshole, I know.

My adventures with Serena continue. She is the kindest most generous person I have ever met. Her patience for all my problems, complications, and bullshit, qualifies her for Sainthood; and she has been a treasured companion and source of support for which I am very grateful.

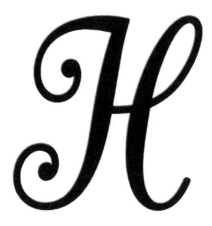

CHAPTER EIGHTEEN
Forsaken

Things had been going pretty well. With my retirement from the "other job," the start of my psychic/counseling work, my adventures with Serena, and so forth; I was in a much better place in my life and feeling somewhat stable. The centerpiece of all this was still my weekly Disney visits with my daughter. She was always my anchor and ultimate reason for living.

She was getting older now and turning twelve. She was starting to have all kinds of social drama, school responsibilities, and more adult issues, as girls transitioning into womanhood have. Angel always had constant problems with her mother, and they were not close as a result. Despite Angel's many efforts, she was never able to build a good trusting bond with her mother. Therefore, I was the one she relied upon for her emotional needs. Angel and I had a tradition of sitting down in a quiet place at Disney for our official snack time, where she would bring up all her weekly issues and problems. We would go down through her list of topics and discuss each one. It was her chance to get what was bothering her off her chest, and for me to give all the advice I had to offer in order to help her navigate her personal life on a weekly basis.

As some fathers will tell you, there comes a moment when your little girl transitions to your best friend. This was happening. We would have many open free exchanges of discussions. It was my way of connecting with her, the center of my universe, and keeping me grounded and grateful for life. It was her chance to be with someone who truly cared about her daily problems and life. I was always willing to discuss any topic with her and give her all the advice, love, and support I could humanly offer. This weekly connection was critical for both of us.

As long as all the glue that kept my life together remained, I felt I was making great progress and was going to be okay. But that was not to be.

One day, Luci called me and said she needed to talk to me. I called her back and asked her what was on her mind. She diplomatically and pragmatically informed me that she and her husband had decided to move. Up to this point, they lived inland from me an hour away. I was in Hollywood, and they were in a wealthy suburb of Anaheim near Disney. So, while they were not next door, I was easily able to do the weekly visitations with Angel. Luci informed me they were moving up to Montana near the Canadian border, where Luci's husband had lived with his first wife some years ago.

I was shocked. Luci knew to pause and let it sink in. There was a total silence on the phone while my mind seized up and grinded to a halt. When Luci tried to break the long awkward silence, I immediately said, "Oh I see." "Well then I guess Angel will be moving in with me then." Luci immediately turned on her bitch switch and said Angel was part of HER FAMILY and would be moving with them. I reminded Luci that our divorce agreement had a clause that stated Angel was not to be moved out of southern California. I then also asked Luci what Angel had to say about all this. Luci paused and told me that they had not told the kids yet. I was like, "WHAT???" I asked Luci when she was planning on telling Angel and her husband's kids. Luci said they were going to wait until they were just about to move before telling the kids (this is an example how evil she can be). I told Luci she must tell Angel, or I would. I gave her until my weekend visitation to tell Angel herself, or I was going to tell Angel. Luci put the bitch switch in overdrive and started her usual ranting, swearing, and insults. As with most our calls, it ended with Luci screaming and hanging up on me. After the call I was visibly shaking. My world as I knew it had just ended.

After I gathered myself together and calmed down, I realized that I would simply hold her to the divorce agreement and not allow Angel to be moved. I had the idea to call my parents and see if I could confirm their support in helping me, in case I needed to get a lawyer or something.

So, I called my mom and I did my best to remain pleasant and calm, but my heart was beating through my chest. I was sweating and totally worked up over the situation. Oddly, my mom seemed super calm as if she was expecting my upset phone call. I explained to my mom what had just happened regarding Luci's announcement. I was expecting my mother would get equally upset and pledge their total support to me in keeping my daughter near me. Nope. And it's even worse than that. My mom calmly informed me that Luci had already talked to her, told her about the move, and that she (my mom), and Dave, were fully supportive of the move.

I again paused due to my mind seizing up. I took a breath and calmly reminded, explained, to my mom how my entire life and existence depended on Angel remaining close to me. I also reminded my mom how much Angel needed me also, since she had a horrible relationship with her mother. My mother was unmoved and explained that she and Dave always felt a more rural upbringing would be better for Angel, and they thought the move would be great for their entire family. My mom wanted Angel to have a more traditional rural upbringing, far from the horrible things a big city can offer. My mom thought Angel would be safer, healthier, and simply better off up north in the middle of nowhere.

I then pulled out all the stops and told my mom that if Angel moved away, it would be the end of me. I would have no further reason to live and would not want to live. In not so many words, I told my mom that if I lose Angel I would die (one way or another). My mom was unmoved.

I then realized I had been set up and betrayed by all of them. In my mind at that moment I was DONE with my parents. DONE. But I never said anything of the sort and remained calm so that I could ask my mom one last question. I asked my mom how long she had known about this and why she said nothing to me. My mom had an uncomfortable pause that she gets when she can't say something, but she also does not want to lie (because my mom doesn't lie). She simply said Luci had discussed this with her a while back, but she did not know how serious it was at the time. There was nothing left to say, and I was done with the conversation.

A few days later I received a frantic hysterical call from Angel. Angel had obviously just received the news. I called Angel back and she was crying. At first, she was angry at me because I had known about the news a few days before and had not called her. I told her all the circumstances and that I agreed to let her mother tell her. Since Angel's mother had a habit of lying about certain things, Angel and I always had a routine of telling both our sides of a story so that we could compare notes and figure out what Luci was really up to. Thus, we did it in this case as well. Angel calmed down and I asked her how she felt about the news. Angel said she absolutely did not want to move, and she wanted to stay near me.

I told Angel I would fight for her to stay if that is what she wanted. Angel asked what that would mean. I explained to Angel we might have to go to court to enforce the divorce agreement. Incidentally, I had previously let Angel read the divorce agreement because her mother was lying about some other things, and I wanted Angel to see for herself what the divorce entailed. Luci had previously told everyone I had not paid her credit cards that I was obligated to pay. In actuality, the divorce agreement clearly said that Luci was responsible for all her credit cards. We both had debt coming out of the divorce, partly due to Luci actively trying to destroy my company and me during the breakup. So, Angel had read the divorce agreement for herself, and knew the divorce agreement said that she would always stay in southern California. I explained we might need to go to court to enforce it. Angel asked if she would have to do anything, and I replied she might have to give her wishes to the court, or talk to the judge, as well as answer questions about parental issues on both sides. I explained to Angel that she would have to tell the truth about all parental issues. She could tell the judge anything she wanted about me, and I was okay with that, but she would also have to tell the judge about how her mother treats her. I told Angel to think about what she wanted, and we would talk about it at our next Disney visit.

I lived on pins and needles the next few days while I waited for our Disney visit. While Angel was just my twelve-year-old little girl, it all of a sudden felt like she was a forty-year-old Judge about to render her decision upon my life that would impact my actual existence.

Saturday morning came and I picked up Angel for Disney. I could tell she was really nervous. I was even more nervous. I was almost too sick to eat my usual frosted cinnamon roll I always got. The initial part of our day was very tense, quiet, and awkward. It was killing both of us, I think. So finally, snack time came, and I dropped the hammer, and asked her what she was thinking about the move.

My sweet beautiful daughter, who I knew loved me very deeply, made every effort to be very gentle with me. It was not long before I felt her decision rip through my heart.

Angel was scared of her mother, as was I, and had conflicting feelings. Angel was used to living in a nice house with her mom and her stepsister and stepbrother. I think she was a bit scared of my unstable financial situation, and the fact I would have to move to a new satisfactory school district, which was uncertain. But most of all, she was afraid what would happen if she said something bad about her mom in court. So, Angel quickly determined that she absolutely did not want a court battle. She obviously wanted to stay in LA, and stay near me, but not at the expense of a scary court battle.

For a twelve-year-old girl, Angel did a great job of dropping the news on me. It was like a beloved girlfriend breaking up with her fragile boyfriend. I felt pretty pathetic, and the only thing that kept it from reaching all-time lows, is that I somehow managed to remain calm and not break down sobbing in front of her. Believe me, I wanted to break down sobbing. But I hugged Angel and told her I loved her very much and that I would always support what she wanted. I told her it was okay and that I understood her entire argument for her decision, and that I was very proud of her for being so adult and making a difficult decision like that.

We continued with our Disney day, and I was able to remain

normal for the day even though I was on the verge of tears the entire day. I kept my sunglasses on the whole time just in case. I dropped Angel off at her mom's, hugged her, told her I loved her as usual, and then walked back to my car. I drove a half mile down the road, pulled over, and cried and sobbed uncontrollably for many minutes, after holding it in for so long. My little girl, my best little buddy, my anchor, my everything; she had rendered her decision. And it was not in my favor. I was destroyed. That was it.

At this point, my situation was that Luci had dropped a house on my head, my own parents had completely betrayed me and turned their back on me, and my daughter had asked me not to fight to keep her in LA because she was terrified of a court battle. I was beaten. I was done.

I died inside, and I was back into a very dark depression. I was back to contemplating suicide. I thought maybe what I would do is wait until my daughter had moved, and then I would just end it. Why live? I lost my daughter, my own parents had betrayed me, and thus I was done with them as well.

There is this dark time and place I think most people find themselves in at least once in their life. It's a moment when they feel totally worthless and of no value. Not loved by anyone and having no purpose. It is a dark lonely place which I believe is actually hell. It's that place which causes suicides. I had been there before, but here I was again. Except this time, it seemed darker because it involved my daughter who truly was the center of my being. The pain that entered my soul from this event still remains today.

My depression was so deep, I was once again unable to do anything. All work ceased. I was unable to do any of my psychic/counseling sessions, and was unable to work at all, period. I had completely crashed once again, and all I wanted to do was sleep and mope around the apartment in hopelessness, waiting to die.

With all that said above, I was not about to make things too easy on Luci. Thus, even though I had already made a deal with my daughter not to fight, and the war was over, Luci did not know this since Angel and Luci did not talk much. So, when Luci called to ask if I had talked to Angel about the move, I told Luci I was still considering my options. I told Luci that if she took Angel across state lines without my permission, I would call the police and have her arrested. This hit Luci hard, and the ranting swearing psychotic bitch switch came on again. Except this time, I was enjoying it. I wanted to see her squirm. She told me I was a horrible human, horrible father, a loser, garbage, and blah blah, and she told me to go fuck myself, and hung up. All the usual stuff. That is all normal talk for Luci.

But shortly thereafter I got an email from Luci. She wanted to talk again, and she felt bad for me and knew I was a good father to Angel and so forth. Luci ended up offering to fly me up to their new home once each month to see Angel. She would let me stay in their guest cottage and would provide me with a vehicle to use. So basically, she offered to pay for monthly visits to get me up there to see Angel for visitations. Furthermore, she sweetened the pot by agreeing to pay for Angel's college education.

For me, this was a pretty good deal considering I had already lost the war. I accepted. I agreed to let Angel move with her, and I would not take any legal or criminal action against Luci.

Despite my seeming acceptance of my fate, I secretly kept hoping and praying things would somehow change, or there would be some divine intervention to stop the move. I had agreed to go along with my daughter's wishes, and I had received a visitation arrangement from Luci. But still, I had full intentions of my life being over without seeing my little Angel every week at Disney as we had been doing since she was five.

On one of our last Disney visits, I decided to do a special prayer. Okay, so back-story. Through-out the years, my daughter and I had a tradition, where in this particular special place to us in Disney (California Adventure in this specific case), I would have my daughter pick a tiny pine twig from a tree. I would have her make a wish upon it, and then I would place the pine twig up in a secret place where it would not be touched by anyone, or cleaners, or anything. Over the seven years (almost every weekend) we had been going up to that point in time, I had placed many twigs in this spot. We only did this on special occasions, several times a year by the way, so don't start thinking that Disney has no trees because of me. So, it had got to the point that the oldest twigs at the bottom of the little pile had actually turned to dust, but the dust was still there. Lots of silly sentimental history there. So, for this visit, I decided to pick my own twig and make my own wish.

I chose my twig carefully and with love. I made my wish. I asked, I wished, I prayed, that my daughter would not move. I gave this prayer with every meaning in my body and soul. If a person only has a few wishes or requests from God in their lifetime, I was using one of my requests in this moment. So, I meditated over this twig while Angel watched. I suppose she knew what I was doing, although we never talked about it. I did my thing and placed the twig in our special place. I went home praying and asking the Universe/God to grant my wish. I had faith that it might even work.

It didn't. The date certain of Angel's departure was set and upon us. The plan was that I would take Angel to Disney for one last day together, then I would drop her off at her mom's, and they would then drive off into the sunset, driving north to catch up with their movers who had come to empty out their house that day.

I had a couple surprises in store for Angel. First, I had a special

Disney day planned where we would do all our favorite things, eat at our special places, do one last special pine twig wish, and basically do everything and anything we considered traditional and special. Our seven consecutive years of Disney, almost every weekend from ages five to twelve, was ending. Up to this point, we had probably gone to Disney nearly 350 times over the years. Quite possibly, that is some sort of a record for a twelve-year-old.

I had one other surprise for Angel. I had been working on a picture book for her. I gathered together pictures of her and I together, starting at her birth, and running to the present. I had organized all these pictures and had them published into a hardcover book. I would present this book to her as I was dropping her off. It would be my way of saying goodbye without making a long speech and causing me to sob uncontrollably.

We had our Disney day, and even though I had a lump in my throat all day, it was a nice, fun, beautiful day together. There were even a few moments when I think I forgot what was happening. So at least we had a nice day. As I was driving her home, I feared that I was going to cry, as it was all hitting me now. I know she was also very nervous. I think she was afraid I was going to cry or something.

As a quick aside, Angel once remarked to me that she was surprised she had never seen me cry. I remember it was one of the funniest things I had ever heard her say, because while it's true Angel never saw me cry before, the fact is that I spent almost her entire childhood crying and sobbing about one thing or another. But she just never saw it, so she thought her daddy never cried about anything.

Anyway, we arrived at her house. I parked on the road so I would have a quick easy exit. We got out of the car. I grabbed the picture book. She just stood there very uncomfortable in this very horrible sad awkward moment. I calmly gave her the book and told her it was her going away present from me. I told her that I had an exact copy for myself also. I told her to look at it whenever she felt sad, and to know I am always with her, and will be with her forever in her heart. I told her I loved her more than life itself, that she was in my soul forever, and that I was in her soul. I told her she could call me anytime she needed me. I hugged her. I let her go. I turned away from her and started walking back to my car. I was starting to cry. I think she knew this. I got into my car and drove away. I stopped down the road and cried and sobbed like I never had before. It's so personal to me, and the pain was so deep, that I really can't express it fully in this story. I guess I will just leave that with myself. Another piece of me died that evening. Angel would tell me at a later date, that she ran to her empty bedroom with her book and cried. She was inconsolable for hours, while her mother ignored her, and was busy getting everyone out of the house that night for the long drive away from her daddy.

I had lost my business, my house, my money, my dignity, had my brains scrambled by some paranormal event, was forced to live like an animal doing unspeakable things to survive, had been betrayed by my family, and now I had lost the one thing that mattered most to me. I had lost my daughter. Why did God hate me so much? Why did I have to suffer so much? Why did I have to live in such intense eternal pain? Why was I forsaken?

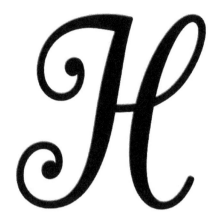

CHAPTER NINETEEN
Is Murder Illegal?

After Angel's move, my latest deep depression reached an even deeper low. I was dead inside. I had come so far after Chaz's death and the walk-in, and now here I was back to zero again.

Although my connection with Gez had faded significantly because of my relationship with Serena, Gez was still very heartfelt in his support, as he knew what my daughter moving would mean to my soul and my life. I think he feared for what I might do.

Serena, for her part, was truly amazing. Serena totally stepped up. Not only did Serena offer herself as my total support on an hourly/daily basis, but Serena stepped up financially. Since I could no longer function and do my work due to depression, I was in danger of once again having eviction issues, not to mention starving to death. Serena was able to help me financially to stay afloat. This also served as a way of keeping my mind engaged, as she used it as a fully justified excuse to ask my help on her various client cases. Without Serena at this point, I would not have made it.

So, while Serena helped keep me afloat, and helped/forced me to stay engaged with client matters, I also made sure I got outside often, and I started doing three hour runs/workouts in the area mountains. While others would have said I should have been working to pay my bills, I feel this daily reconnection with nature, self, and fitness, is what kept me from slipping off into the abyss forever. After a while I started feeling a bit better and was able to function and work.

That's all the "good news." Now here is the bad news. Shortly after Angel's move, I contacted Luci to set up my first visitation. I suggested I come up for a week, and I gave her my suggested dates. Luci responded by informing me that she would not be able to pay for any of my visitations, and the guest house promised to me was no longer available because her husband's mother was now living there, full-time.

I can't say I was that surprised really. Luci had long ago proved she was a liar and really had no honor, conscience, or anything else that decent people have. But still the same, I fought back and called her out on her promises and lies. It was a pointless waste of time. The bottom line is that all the promises Luci made to get me to allow the move, were rescinded. I guess they were all just lies from the beginning. I had a couple of choices. I could either go to court and enforce the divorce agreement, or I could just stay in my hole and die. Since I promised Angel I would not force a court battle, and I would receive no support from my parents in such a battle, and because I was already snugly dying in my hole anyway, I decided to just stay in my hole dying. I had to let it go and hope that the Universe had some mechanism to deal justice to people like Luci. In case you were wondering, yes, I informed my mother of the promises Luci made, and how she was went back on those promises, and my mom just shrugged it off. No big deal, I guess. Nobody cared except me.

However, that eventually changed. It did not take long for Angel to start having emotional problems. Like me, Angel had grown dependent on our weekly snack-time sessions at Disney, where she could talk about anything, and I would listen, discuss, and give my advice. Her weekly visits with me were her chance to be the 100% focus of attention, receive infinite hugs and love, and to actually have the full engagement and support of a parent. I feel the sudden lack of this created a gaping hole in her life and her emotional well-being.

While I was always accessible by phone, and we spoke somewhat often, Angel has never been a phone person. She prefers to be engaged in some activity and talk in person in real time. I think she felt distanced from me, and even if I had called her every other hour every day, it was not going to fit the bill for her.

Angel started having depression issues and behavioral problems. None of these issues were her fault. Her mother would instigate and exacerbate every issue that arose. It was not long before Angel became impossible for her mother and stepfather to deal with. Frankly, I agreed with everything Angel was doing. I know I am supposed to be supporting the other parent and co-parenting with Luci, but from what I was hearing, Luci could often act like a psychotic bitch, and her husband in some instances was apparently cold and rude to Angel, even if non-deliberate. It was understandable that all of Angel's behaviors and actions were totally in line and acceptable under the circumstances. I had raised Angel to not accept shit from anyone, and to not accept being a victim. She was raised to listen and respect her elders, but to also question authority if conscience dictated. Angel was doing everything I taught her. With me, Angel was a perfect Angel. She was very respectful, well behaved, and I was very proud of the person I had raised. So, I knew Angel was only misbehaving with her other parents because the conditions dictated it.

Eventually, Angel found her first major boyfriend and that immediately calmed her down and smoothed her out. Angel had seemingly found a replacement for me, in the sense that she had someone she could confide in and receive love and affection from. Angel was still confrontational with her mom and stepfather, and had a weak and poor relationship with them, but within herself she was no longer as depressed, and she felt good about life. She was doing well in school and had settled into her new home. Things were pretty stable for over a year. I was able to go up and visit her a couple times on my own steam, even though it was a month's rent out the door every time I went up there. It was hard enough to come up with one month's rent, but during months I went up to visit Angel, it was like paying rent twice, and it wreaked havoc with my finances each time. This severely limited my contact with Angel.

However, two boyfriends and a couple years later, I noticed some problems within Angel. She had become more distant and withdrawn. During our regular phone conversations, I noticed she seemed very depressed, as if she no longer cared about life. She also told me many disturbing stories about what was going on in her house, and what she was doing outside the house. My shy perfect Angel had become a bit out of control.

Within the house, I heard stories of increased drinking and pot smoking by her mom and stepfather. The other kids in the house were also doing things that were out of control. Angel was sneaking out of the house, going to parties, and nobody seemed to be monitoring anything. Yes, Angel was now a teenager, but I know my daughter, and this behavior was not expected or normal for her, even given the fact she was a teenager. Mostly, it was the depression and total "I don't care anymore" attitude that bothered me most.

This behavior continued for months, and then I was informed that Angel had been taken to a doctor and psychologist; and it was suggested she be put on antidepressants. I am totally fine with antidepressants for people who need them. I most definitely needed them for myself, even though I never took them, because I never had any medical attention when I needed it. So, I could understand the need. But when it comes to antidepressants for children, I am not in favor of this, and have always felt the root cause must be identified and fixed, rather than covering it with medication. Covering with medication is for adults who need to work every day, take care of kids, and run a household. Kids do not need to do any of those things, so their emotional problems should not be superficially covered. They should be cured with counseling or environmental changes.

I had a call with Luci and specifically informed her that she did not have my consent to put Angel on medication. I suggested that if her household was so awful and fucked up that a kid needed medication just to live there, that maybe it was time to discuss Angel moving back to LA. That call ended with the same screaming, ranting, swearing, insults, and hang up, as they always did.

Not long after that, I was on another call with Angel and she sounded really bad. I was very concerned. I told her she either needed to talk to me about things, or I was going to take action to move her to LA. She paused many times. She then offered me a deal. She made me promise that if she told everything that was going on, I would promise to keep it a secret between me and her, and that I would not take any actions against anyone. I agreed to her deal. Then she dropped a bomb on me that would shatter me and send shards of my soul flying in every direction.

Angel confessed to me that many months ago she had been raped. When she said that. That sentence. That word. My stomach went up into my mouth, and I had to swallow sharply to get my stomach to descend back down where it belonged. This is something you can never understand unless you are a parent who has heard the same words from your child. It took all my strength to remain calm and not explode with every emotion imaginable. Such rage, anger, sadness, desperation, and every emotion, came to the surface all at once. But as I have done throughout Angel's entire life, I was going to keep my promises to her and not lose my shit, not tell anyone, and not take any action against anyone. I very calmly asked Angel to tell me what happened.

Angel told me who it was. Again, I was shocked. It was a previous boyfriend who I thought was a good kid. She told me the story. They had gone over to the boy's house to watch some TV. You have to first understand she had been with this boy for months, and it was common for them to cuddle together and watch TV. But this time something was different. Apparently, days previously, the boy's big brother had been abusing him by whipping him with a belt and bullying the boy by telling him he was a pussy and would never get laid, and that he couldn't even get laid despite having a girlfriend. You get the picture. So, the boy, being a young stupid idiot teenager who clearly had major emotional and mental problems I was not aware of, had decided he was going to show his brother he was a man.

So, I believe the boy planned this from the beginning, but that's just me speculating. So, Angel was with the boy at his house, and the boy rolled on top of Angel in a playful way. No problem so far. But then he started getting aggressive. My daughter is a small girl. The boy was not huge, but he was on the high school wrestling team. The boy managed to hold her down while he got her pants down, and he started to force himself on her. She told me she yelled for him to stop. She begged him to stop. She said she would have cried, but it was so shocking and scary, that she actually didn't cry, and instead she became silent. There was nobody else home at the time, and nobody could hear her pleas anyway. She said she struggled against him at first, but she started to feel some pain in her privates like something had torn or something. She totally gave up, died inside, and just laid there totally lifeless and let the boy do it.

When he finished, he started talking to her as if nothing had ever happened, and nothing was wrong. She was bloody and dirty, so he dragged her into the shower and told her to take a shower. She sat in the shower feeling dead and lifeless for almost an hour, crying single tears of trauma. The boy eventually came back and took her out of the shower. He got her dressed because she was too weak and traumatized to do so herself. He then walked her outside, still as if nothing bad had happened; and she went back home. She was scared, traumatized, confused, and afraid to tell anyone. However, thank goodness she told her stepsister. The stepsister took her to a health clinic, and they examined Angel. Angel said the doctor said she had some minor damage and trauma to her vagina, but they would need a parent's consent to do any further treatment. Angel did not want anyone to know, so she went home with no further treatment, and refused to answer any questions the doctor asked her, about what happened.

After Angel finished telling me her story, I had two thoughts in my mind. Firstly, I was going to kill the boy. My life sucked anyway, and I was simply going to go up there and kill the boy. Very simple. Slit his throat, watch him bleed out, and be done with it. Drop dead serious. I was shaking with the thought of it. Not out of fear, but out of THIRST for wanting to do it so badly. My second thought was that I needed to be absolutely supportive in the most epic way for Angel. I engaged in the second thought first. I told her how sorry I was, and that it was not her fault. Angel then said to me, "Yeah but now you think of me differently, don't you?" I immediately replied by saying, "YES, I am even more proud of you now, and love you more now, than I ever have in my life." I told her how brave she was to live through this, and to finally tell me the truth. I told her she had my full support, and we would do anything she wanted that would make her feel better and heal her from this. I told her she was no longer alone in this and that we would work as a team to make things okay again.

That is when she gave me the bad news that what she wanted and needed most, was to put it all behind her without protracted drama and problems. She was telling me that my first thought of killing the boy was not what she wanted, nor was calling the police, which was my next suggestion to her. It was a bitter pill for me to swallow. How could I let this boy still exist and breathe? How could I not call the police and make him pay? But I chose to focus on my daughter. Thus, I had to repress those feelings of rage and violence.

After I hung up with Angel, I started crying. I felt like I had failed my daughter. I failed to protect her from harm. I immediately had a flashback of when she was very young and I would hold my innocent little baby on my lap, and always promise to protect her. I am guessing this is common with most parents in this situation. You remember them as innocent little kids before anything bad happened. Then you are hit with the present reality that a horrible thing just happened, and you did not prevent it, and it's too late and done. I was devastated for days. Also, due to my promise of secrecy to Angel, I was not able to tell Serena, which I really needed to do in order to access my own support system.

The incident changed me forever. I became even more cynical than I already was. I had trusted this boy. I was fooled. I also realized there were some things I could not protect my daughter from in life. I felt stupid, naive, and powerless. What I valued most in life had been violated. I was deeply damaged and traumatized by this event. However, I knew it was not about me. I had to put aside my own traumas and focus wholly on my daughter who needed me.

I started talking to my daughter daily, and I could tell her mood lightened. She was coming out of the darkness since confiding in me, and it bonded us together closer than ever. But then she made a mistake. One day during her frequent almost everyday fights with her mother, she blurted it out. I am not certain the exact words or how it happened. But Angel ended up blurting out to her mother that she had been raped. Angel told her mom the story and told her that I knew already. I then received a frantic angry bitter call from Luci. Luci started yelling at me that I never told her what happened, and that it was a violation of our co-parenting trust, and so on and so forth. I explained I HAD to promise Angel to keep it a secret or NONE of us were going to ever find out what happened, and we would still not know what happened. Luci didn't care. Luci has always only seen things from her point of view, so she was offended that she was the last to know.

At this point, Angel made her mother promise she would also not take any action. Luci promised she would not take any action, and that she would only arrange for counseling up there, which I wholly supported and backed Luci in doing.

Luci lies. Always.

Luci called the police. At this point, the incident had taken place many months ago, things had smoothed out for Angel, and in fact she and the boy were co-existing at the school with no incident or problems. Obviously, the boy realized what he had done was horribly wrong, and he was terrified of getting into trouble. Thus, the boy always made sure there was a mile distance between him and Angel at all times. So really, the time for rage, police, and drama, had long since passed. Angel was healing emotionally and just needed to focus on school and move forward in her life, instead of being stuck in that most horrible moment.

Angel found out that her mom told the police when she went to school the next day and people were talking. The school had assigned a bodyguard to follow her around school since the boy was still at the same school. Angel was also informed the police would be coming to take her statement. The boy's friends started bullying Angel and threatening her. She was embarrassed and humiliated in front of the entire school. She was completely derailed from the healing and stability she had managed to achieve.

Angel was so upset at her mother for betraying her trust on this issue, that it permanently damaged any shred of trust she had in her mother. Angel became very despondent, depressed, and I believed she might become suicidal. I would learn later I was correct, but fortunately the stepsister once again intervened to prevent tragedy.

I decided enough was enough. I wrote Luci. I told Luci she had broken our daughter. I told Luci it was time for Angel to move down to LA with me, and there would be no judge in the world that would disagree with me. For the first time ever, Luci conceded. Luci replied, "Fine, she hates me anyway, you can have her." "But I'm not paying to move her shit down there, so that's your problem."

The understanding was that I would move out of Hollywood and into her old school district in the expensive Anaheim suburb. Then Angel would move down after I was all set up and ready for her. I started laying down my plans to do just that.

This is when my parents re-entered my life after their betrayal a couple years earlier. Apparently, Luci had called my mother and told her what happened to Angel regarding the rape. I have no idea why she did this, but she did. My parents were horrified and mortified. My parents approached me and told me they found out what happened to Angel. They asked what they could do to help. I informed them of my plans to move Angel back down to LA, that Luci had already agreed, but that I had to move to the expensive neighborhood she lived in before to be in the correct school district. Not only that, but I had to upgrade to a nice acceptable two-bedroomed home. Without hesitation, my parents offered to fund the operation. I had not even asked them for anything. They volunteered. They also did not flinch when they saw how much the whole move would take. They gave, and they gave freely. Once again, my parents would step up very unexpectedly when I needed it most.

So, I moved out of Hollywood and into a beautiful home in the expensive suburb near Anaheim. I set up the master bedroom suite for Angel. I took the guest bedroom for myself. I was ready to take Angel now.

Not so fast though. During the process of my move, several things had happened. Firstly, Luci had shriveled up in a corner and was no longer harassing or attacking Angel on a daily basis. Also, Angel had been inspired and empowered by me taking such major steps to give her the option of moving into a nice home in her previous great school district. I think it touched her, and proved I was indeed willing to do anything for her, because yes, she is that important, and has always been my number one priority. But sometimes we need to see proof of this, right? Also, things at school had calmed down. The boy ended up moving away to live with his uncle in a different state. But finally, the biggest factor of all was that my daughter met a new boyfriend. This new boyfriend was a seemingly nice, young man who treated Angel in the way she was seeking and seemed to love her very much. He was that typical young man that you hope for in a boyfriend for your daughter. He was well-mannered, polite, good grades, brought flowers, chocolates, ice cream, and most importantly follows my three rules.

What rules, you say? Well, since Angel started spending time with boys, I had laid out three rules that she should watch for in determining if a boy was a good boyfriend or not. I recall making Angel recite these rules to me often so that I was satisfied she knew them by heart. My three rules for a good boyfriend are as follows: 1. The boy must treat you as well as your daddy does. 2. The boy does not make you cry. 3. The boy is loyal to you. By the way, I also make sure the boys know my three rules as well.

Well this particular boy re-opened her heart and soul and let the sunshine back in again. My daughter started to get straight A's in school and was very happy again. This of course, made me happy and caused me to give full approval of this boy.

So here I was sitting in this nice, large, high rent district home in a neighborhood I did not even want to live in, sleeping in the guest bedroom with the master suite empty; and all of a sudden my daughter was doing amazingly well, and did not want to move anymore. Sigh.

So, what to do? Am I going to make her move against her will, leave her boyfriend, and interrupt her schooling in which she was getting straight A's? Well if you know me by now, you realize the answer is no. I would once again accept the short straw and lump it. For me, the whole point of my existence has been to do what is best for my daughter. If my daughter is happy and doing well, then I am winning. So as long as that remains, I'm happy, I guess? Well, not really, but you know what I mean.

So, I remained in this home that is too big and too expensive for me. I continued to live in the guest bedroom while the master suite was empty. It was since pointed out to me, that me being here ready to take her at a moment's notice was also a major factor in keeping Luci in check, because she knew if she misbehaved, Angel could leave her and be down here in an instant. Therefore, if I had to stay here to keep things stable and good for my daughter then so be it. The things daddies will do for their daughters.

CHAPTER TWENTY

The Devil's Den

Now that things had smoothed out for Angel, and I was feeling much better within myself, I had to refocus back on my own challenges and problems. For better or worse, I was in this nice home, and it was expensive. My parents had been good enough to help me get into the place, but they left me to cover everything on my own from here on out.

My psychic, counseling, and life coaching work had slowed due to all the drama, depression, and time taken off due to Angel's issues. Serena was experiencing a slowdown in her income as well, and therefore she would be unable to help me or bail me out if I got into trouble. So while I worked to increase my counseling and life coaching work, I needed something else to supplement my income. What could I do? Get a job? WHAT??? Doing what exactly? At this point I would not even know how to get a job, nor would I be qualified to do anything. My resume of running a failed company, modeling, acting, being out on the streets, and being a psychic, was not a glowing resume for a traditional job, except for maybe something in the circus or a patient in an insane asylum. So, I came up with an idea. Let's go to the casino!!! Yeah, okay, I know you are laughing; and if you are not laughing, you should be laughing. This is the dumbest possible idea anyone could come up with. But one thing is for sure, it could either totally work, or it could totally ruin my life. Thus, it was a perfect option for me!

Now let me first preface something. Well actually, I may end up prefacing a few things, so bear with me. I had gone to casino a few years ago with a client and had dabbled in it on and off, over the last several years. So, I did have some experience and knowledge of what I was dealing with.

I was raised to believe gambling was stupid and wrong. Gambling was something adults did as a sin, like drinking, or smoking pot, or having meaningless wild sex. I carried this thinking through my business years. As a businessperson, I never considered going to a casino or engaging in gambling of any kind. I naturally assumed it was stupid and would result in definite losses at the least, and an addiction at most.

With all that said above, I ended up with a client in my counseling work who had several addictions. In fact, he was a master of addictions. I had never seen one person with so many addictions. I can't even list them all, but a few of them were drinking, coke, pills, pot, porn, sex, and gambling. Considering how many addictions he was managing at once, he was doing quite well. I was impressed. So, this client asked me to accompany him to a casino to see if I could implement some coping mechanisms to help him tone it down, because he would easily get out of control, which would result in heavy losses.

So, with him, I entered a casino for the very first time. I was immediately overwhelmed by all the lights and noises. Holy crap!

Let me also say that considering nobody will admit they go to casino, casinos sure are packed with thousands of people at all times. I was intrigued to see what it was all about. I had not brought any money to play with, nor did I want to. I was there to watch him and get paid for doing so.

However, I got carried away with the excitement, and was looking at the machines to figure out which one might be a winner. My client sat down at a machine, and I immediately told him to play this other one instead. He looked at me funny because I was playing the weird mystic who thought he could pick winning machines, but he humored me. He tried the one I suggested, and in five spins won $500. So maybe I was not a stupid useless mystic after all. I watched him throughout the day and will admit it was kind of fun. I never played, but it was fun watching him. He played until late night, and then said he was going up to his room to bed. He paid my fee for the day and went up to his room.

I was not ready to go up to my room yet. I had been shadowing him all day and trying to help him. I just needed to unwind with some "me time" before bed. I decided to take a $20 bill from my pay and slide it into a machine, and just see what would happen. I chose a machine I liked that my client had played earlier. It was $1.25/spin, which was an entire dollar down the shithole every time I pushed the button, but nothing too outrageous. The machine was "friendly" and it went up and down for a good ten minutes without taking all my money, until it shocked me and gave me a $500 win. I couldn't believe it. I was used to working really hard for my money, so getting $500 with a single push of a button was mind-bending to me. I tried my luck at a few other machines and kept winning. $100 here, $50 there, and so on. I got my winnings up to $1,000 and was so delighted with that nice beautiful round number, that I stopped and went up to my room for bed. I had officially caught the bug. A casino monster was born.

After some weeks went by, I got the itch to maybe go to the casino on my own and see if I could win more money. I was having a good month and felt I could spare a nice bankroll to try. I took $500 and decided to go to a casino in southern California, which for this story we will call Pennacook Casino. I booked a room for one night and went. I played most of the day and into the evening, and was able to stay mostly even, plus I had fun. I went to bed. When I woke up, I decided to crawl down there and try a machine I had a feeling about that I had tried to play the previous night, but it was always occupied. So, I went down half asleep early morning and took a few spins. I got lucky and hit a bonus round. During the bonus round, I saw lots of lights. Lots and lots of lights. It went by fast onto the next free spin though, so I did not really see what had happened. When the bonus round finished, the machine locked up. It froze and had a message on it saying, "Jackpot call attendant $6,000." WHAT? I had not even realized I had hit something nice in that bonus round. I think I nearly had a heart attack when I saw the jackpot message. I stood in shock. The slot technician came and paid me my money. I had not even fully woken up yet, and my pocket was bulging with hundred-dollar bills to the tune of $6k. Holy shit! Now a MASSIVE casino monster had been born.

Okay. So that is how I caught the bug and got started. Now let's do some more prefacing, as now we are ready to jump ahead in time to where we are now in my story. Firstly, that $6k win all went to bills, rent, and car repairs. There was nothing left. But good thing I won it. Secondly, let's talk about the casino.

Pennacook, my casino of choice, is huge. Once you enter through the doors, you are in an alternate universe. The color scheme is mostly reds and very dark wood. The lighting has a low dim quality to it. There are statues, bars, and endless machines. It has a rich dark feeling to it. It's the devil's den. If the devil had a man cave, it would look like this. The reds, the rich dark wood trims, dim lighting, and all with dubious intentions. Casinos are designed to take your money and ruin lives. If they did not take your money, they would not be in business. And they ruin lives because too many people get sucked in, addicted, and never leave until they are an empty ruined shell of nothingness. I would not want my own daughter going to a casino, nor would I suggest it or wish it upon any of you. Stay away. Almost everyone loses.

I said, "almost everyone." I did not say everyone. There are a few who win. This is my story. Don't assume my story will be your story. My prefacing, and "soapboxing" is over.

So, needing to supplement my income after the Angel episodes and depression, I decided to enter the devil's den. I had become familiar with slot play and had learned how to play video poker. I had actually become a great poker player. I was super-fast and super accurate. Mostly in the beginning I played slots. I figured out some good machines to play and I started winning $1,000 regularly. Then I started winning more. I also would lose sometimes. Sometimes I left with a thousand. Or more. Sometimes I left with nothing and suffered losses. But mostly, I was able to win something when I had the discipline to leave after a win. It was not long before the casino monster within me got fully cranked up.

But first, I was to meet someone at casino who should serve as a cautionary tale. One day, I was walking by a machine that a middle-aged woman was playing, and as soon as I walked up to her machine, she hit a nice win. She yelled at me, "Don't move." "Stay there." "You are good luck." I laughed and stood there. She kept winning. She then gave me a hug and thanked me, saying she had been losing until I walked next to her machine. We introduced ourselves, but I missed her real name. But let me introduce you to "Hug Lady." This is actually what I really call her. She got her name from that first hug, and all the hugs to come. Nothing romantic, just casino friends.

I would end up seeing Hug Lady all the time in that place. She pretty much lived in there. Oddly, every time I would see her and stand next to her, she would hit a win, and then hug me. This happened several times. We became casino buddies and would sit and talk and catch up on which machines were "hot" that day, and how we both had been doing.

Hug Lady's husband had passed away and left her a retirement fund and a house. Hug Lady was drowning her sorrows by spending all her days in the devil's den. She started out small, but gradually built up her level of play. It was not long before I would only find her in "High Limit." One day she asked me for some tips on which machines to try. I had become very familiar with the casino, so I actually knew some good machines I felt were going to hit wins, but they were above my pay grade. One was $27/spin, and the other was $5/spin, but would require hours and hours of playing and sustaining losses before it hit in my opinion. She agreed to look at the machines with me. I showed her the $27 machine and told her the $3,000 progressive jackpot was going to hit, and I explained why. I then showed her the other machine and showed her the $16,000 progressive was going to hit soon.

Later that night I received a text from her that she won the $3,000 jackpot on the exact machine I said she would hit it on. One week later, I got another text saying she had won the $16,000 I said she would win. She thought I was magic.

Her winning was actually the magic. She would not stop winning. She won $37,000 one day, and she won $3,000 - $5,000, routinely, almost daily. She became one of the top players at Pennacook. She was invited on a cruise with the owners and other top players. She was a top VIP player who could ask for, and get, any perk she wanted.

There was one problem. Hug Lady never left the casino. She would spend a few days there without even going home. She would often go without sleep for two nights, and just play constantly. Her famous story is when she passed out on a machine one night with her elbow on the spin button. The machine kept spinning for who knows how long while she was passed out sleeping. She was later woken up by a slot attendant who informed her she had won a $4,000 jackpot!!

But the constant playing with no stopping, the chasing of more and more wins without stopping, her increasing the bets after a win, her not leaving a machine after a win, all contributed to her starting to sustain regular losses. All of these things are also classic symptoms of a gambling addiction. She couldn't stop. She just kept playing. For days, weeks, months. Recklessly. She started losing more than winning and started running through her retirement fund. Eventually it was gone. Then after that, she ended up losing her home. She crashed. She ended up with nothing. I ended up seeing her looking homeless and playing with $5 bills to amuse herself, while she slept in her car in the parking garage. She still goes there, and she pretty much lives there on premises in her car. It's the saddest story I ever saw there. Whenever I see her, I always give her money out of respect and compassion, but it's very sad. She serves as a constant reminder of what going to a casino can do to a person who can't control their compulsions.

I would meet and see many other interesting characters in that casino. There was a man I called "Lemming." I named him Lemming after those little rodents that purposely march toward a cliff and simply plunge to their deaths. This Lemming man at casino would sit at a losing machine and incessantly push the spin button very quickly. The more he was losing, the faster he would push the button. Faster, faster, faster, as his money went down and down and down. And then he would look at the machine as if he was surprised and confused that he ran out of money. It's like he literally was in a race to march to the edge of the cliff as fast as possible and plunge to his financial death.

There was another man I called "IV Man." I called him this because he would sit at the same poker machine for hours, or maybe even days. I would never see him eat, drink, or take any break at all. There were times he looked like he was going to die and needed to be hooked up to an IV bag for his survival, thus the name.

Then there was "Cheshire Cat Man." He was this very old man in his 80s or 90s, who would sit at these progressive "Quick Hit" machines, which could give wins ranging from $1,000 to $50,000. I very often would see him sitting at one particular machine, and he would very often win $2,000 most nights. But one night he was sitting at a machine waiting to collect a $50,000 jackpot he had just hit. That old man had a grin on his face just like a Cheshire cat that night.

Of course, there were also the many dubious looking characters who would constantly come up to me asking for a spare dollar, or five, saying they missed their bus, or had no food, or had been stuck at the casino for days and wanted to leave. Clearly, if these people can't afford a french fry or bus fare, they don't belong coming to a casino in the first place. But that is the kind of thing, and kind of people, you get in a casino.

There was one time I was actually attacked inside the casino. I was playing this particular machine and had stopped pushing the spin button in order to check my phone. I was still standing at the machine completely in front of it, touching it, with my money in the machine. This crazy woman on some kind of pills most likely, barged up to me, pushed me aside, and started to shove her money into my machine. I yelled for her to stop and she didn't. I yelled again, saying I had money in the machine already. She ignored me. I then grabbed her arm and pushed it away from the machine. She then started screaming for security, claiming that I had attacked her. I suppose this was some kind of scam or something? Security came and the woman was ranting about how I completely and violently attacked her. Obviously, I was the one who was attacked. But when casino security gets involved in a "brawl situation," they have to investigate.

They told me to cash out of the machine and come with them. Yep, I had casino police escorting me to a "holding area," where I felt like I was in a police station after arrest. The woman was demanding I be thrown out of the casino, and she was ranting on and on. The casino detectives explained to the woman that they would need to review the tapes from the internal security cameras. The woman did not like this answer and started being aggressive and rude to the casino detectives. The woman ended up making some excuse that she could not wait around and had to leave and dropped the accusations against me. The woman left, but I stayed until the casino could review the tape. They clearly saw the woman had attacked ME. The detectives came out and apologized profusely for holding me so long. The Head Detective said he would have done exactly what I did, had he been in my situation. They could not apologize enough, were very kind, and offered me beverages.

I marched out of the holding pen and went right back to the same machine where it all happened. I slid a $20 bill in, and after 5 spins, hit a $1,000 win. I looked up at the security camera and said, "I accept your apology." While I was waiting to get paid on that win, I played the machine next to it, and hit another $1,000 win. I thanked the security camera again. Call it a coincidence or whatever you want, but that's what happened.

Regarding my regular routines and strategy, I usually played $3

- $12 per spin, so it was a substantial investment. But the wins could be substantial also. I would hit massive bonus rounds and end up with $2,000 - $5,000 jackpots.

There were times I was hot, times I was cold, and times I pulled off miracles. There was one trip I was not doing well and almost out of money. I had $19 left and had resigned to the reality I was leaving with nothing. But I didn't. With only $19 left, I hit a $2,500 jackpot. I immediately left with the money and paid my rent. Another time I was having a good visit and playing three huge machines at once that were all side-by-side. Each machine was $10/spin. They were huge machines with blazing sevens, and if you played the max bet of $10/spin, the machine would have flames and fire on video shooting out if you hit wins. I had all three machines firing off flames. I had a little bit of a crowd watching me as I was spinning $10/spin on three different machines at once, as fast as I could spin them. Fire and flames everywhere. $700 win here, $900 win over there, $300, $900 again, and so on, until I hit $3,000 on one of them and it froze for the jackpot, and I stopped all of them at that point. Sorry folks, the show was over. I am sure all the folks watching were shaking their heads at how crazy it was to play three machines at once at that much per spin. But it worked.

There was another time I hit $5,000 on a machine, and then each machine I played after that hit around $1,000. It's like I couldn't lose. The slot technician actually followed me around and paid my jackpots as we went, and I randomly played the machines I felt were "ready."

It was not long before I developed a reputation and was recognized by the staff and some other players. I had earned VIP status, and that came with perks. I had reserved parking, unlimited access to free hotel suites, unlimited access to free meals at any casino restaurant, and a casino host which would accommodate my requests. I would typically arrive and sometimes walk into High Limit, play poker at the bar, and the bartender would automatically give me an iced tea because he knew that was my only drink. He also knew if I won, he would get a nice tip. I tipped everyone. If I won, the slot technician got a tip, and the bartender would get a tip. Also, if another player was standing next to me watching and cheering me on at the time, I would often tip them as well. I believe showing respect, humility, and gratitude, is essential in gambling. It's a good karma thing. There were a few random players who were familiar with me, who would follow me around in hopes I would hit a win while they were there, and I would tip them.

But I would also lose. Let's keep it real. I would sometimes lose a few times in a row. There was one particular time I was on a losing streak, and I also really needed money for rent and bills. So the pressure was really on. I was tired of losing, and rent was going to "go critical" soon. I was growing very frustrated, and anyone near me could tell.

I went on a certain holiday weekend hoping the heavy money going into the machines would play to my advantage. I arrived and started playing. And started losing. Another losing trip, really?? But I kept at it. Even though it was very crowded, I noticed a bank of machines I loved were totally empty. I love playing empty banks of machines in a crowded casino. So, I ran over there. There were four machines each row, back to back, so there was a total of eight machines. They are all $5/spin. I started on the back side, giving each machine a few spins. $0 every spin. I tried the machines on the front side. $0 every spin, except for the last machine. The eighth machine was keeping me even, so I kept playing it.

I played it for a good fifteen minutes maybe. It was late in the evening and I was frustrated, getting angry, and my attention span was wandering. I spun and heard the noise it makes when a

"Triple" symbol drops down. The first one dropped. This caused me to turn my head back around to look at the machine to see what was happening. The second "Triple" dropped, which made a higher pitched noise than the first. Then I heard a noise that very few people ever hear. I heard a very loud intense high-pitched noise, indicating the third "Triple" had landed. I heard all the triples drop but I think I was not sure or was in denial or something. The machine screamed. I knew I hit something decent. I knew it was a jackpot. But what? It tallied. And tallied. And tallied.

I saw the jackpot notice and I saw the amount. $20,000. I think I lost air in my lungs. My eyes came out of my head. I looked again to be sure it was not $2,000. I stared. Looked again. Stared. It was indeed $20,000. I just stood there in shock. I think I could have cried, but I was too cool in that place to cry. A crowd started to gather as it often does when somebody hits something big. Finally, a cool looking young slot technician pushed through all the onlookers, and said, "Holy shit dude, you just won $20,000." He said he would be right back. A few minutes later he came back with an entourage. It was him, his floor manager, and a very distinguished man with two security guards flanking him.

Serena and I had always joked whether or not there was a "Mr. Pennacook" hiding behind the walls, and if he was the devil in the devil's den, or whoever he was.

All I can do is call this distinguished man flanked by his own security, "Mr. Pennacook." This man was tall, big in stature, wearing a perfect grey suit with a black shirt underneath. It was as if he was dressed all in black and put a grey suit over it. He had perfect slicked hair that looked more like a helmet. He was tan in complexion and looked like he got regular facials. He had finely french manicured nails that appeared to come to a point on their ends. He was clearly "someone." I say he was Mr. Pennacook, and that's what I'm sticking with. He extended his hand and said, "Congratulations, I hope you are happy now." I thought this was an odd thing to say since it would indicate he knew I was previously unhappy. He was right, but how would he know that?

He then said, "Follow us please," and the entourage led me to a counting room in a hidden side area like you would see with safe deposit boxes at a bank. They had stacks of $100 bills waiting for me. $20,000 worth. I thanked them profusely. Yes, I had won it on my own steam, but I felt I needed to thank them personally for some reason. I gave the slot technician his $100 tip, Mr. Pennacook winked in approval, and then he disappeared behind the wall. I had trouble picking up the stacks of money and was trying to stuff it all in my pants. My pants were too tight, so I had trouble fitting all the money in my pockets. I stuffed money in all four pockets, front and back. I then waddled out of the counting room, hoping my pants were not going to rip open. It was so ridiculous, I had to leave because I could not walk with all the money in my pants.

I know to some that might not seem like much money. But to me, that money was a game changer. I was about to default on rent and many bills. I paid everything off. I paid ahead. I sent Serena some money. I paid some old debts and fixed my credit. I now had good credit again for the first time in ten years. It fixed me up. I am still beyond grateful for that win. It was a true blessing that came at just the right time.

After the $20,000 win, I decided I did not want to start losing it, and slots had proven to be a very scary prospect. Therefore, I decided to mostly switch to poker (video poker), which was more stable, more of a difficult grind, but less risky.

The poker turned out to be even better. It became very common for me to win $2,000 and $4,000; sometimes multiple times in the same trip. On one trip, Hug Lady would repay some of the good karma I had always given her. I was losing so far that night, and Hug Lady of course was slumming around there as usual passing the time, even though she had no money to play. She sat down next to me and we started to talk. She then said, "Brian, you are going to win a jackpot, I can feel it." About two minutes after she said that, I hit $4,000. It was my turn to hug her, and I did. I also gave her a crisp $100 dollar bill, and she hugged me back. Casino is full of stories like this. It's a place where anything can happen at any moment.

There were also times Serena came in handy. Serena, being a very powerful psychic, would often get ideas of where the wins would be. She nailed it on several occasions. On one trip, she told me to go to this specific bank of machines and play a specific machine on the end. She said I would win a Royal Flush. I did exactly as she said. I won a Royal Flush. The win was only $1,000 because I was playing a low denomination, but still, $1,000 is $1,000, and she was totally correct. How did she do that?

Another time, she told me to go to a different part of the building to a specific bar, and to a specific machine at that bar. I informed her the bar would be totally crowded at that early hour on arrival, and no machines would be open to play. But I followed her instructions anyway. Upon arriving at the bar, I saw it was totally crowded, EXCEPT for the one machine Serena told me to play. Okay.

Well I played that machine, and ten minutes later hit a $4,000 jackpot. Anyone who does not think Serena is highly psychic and magical is crazy and has not seen what I have seen. She really is magic.

Sometimes casino and poker is magical and easy, but usually it is really difficult, and can make you sweat blood. The downside to poker is that it's almost always a very long grind. What I mean by this is that you have to be prepared to play for many hours before anything good happens. I would typically show up late evening and play all night long, and not hit anything until early morning. Once I start, I don't stop. No eating, little drinking, maybe two bathroom breaks. Your mind starts to bend and do weird things playing for endless hours. I get to the point where I don't even see the cards anymore. My mind and fingers just react and make the correct moves based on shapes and what my subconscious sees. Eventually, sweat starts getting into your eyes and burning them. Your fingers get bruises on them, and your hands get painful with cramping. Your feet hurt, and your back hurts even more. This can go on for 14 hours straight. Also keep in mind, it can often cost you $3,000 before you win $4,000. It's not easy. But I found if you stick with it, and then leave right after the win, you can come out ahead. But it's work. It is not leisure.

    My general win ratio with all this, was something like three steps forward and two steps back. So, I would tend to win, but then I would lose also. So, believe me, there is plenty of losing that goes on. Lots of wins and lots of losing. But three steps forward and two steps back still leaves you one step ahead.

    I enjoyed this winning ratio for quite a long time. There were bad dry spells where I got into trouble for a bit, but then I would more than make up for it during the hot spells. There came a point when I was winning almost every visit. I would go once or twice a week and rotate between three different casinos. I did not want to wear out my welcome, go to the well too often, or test my luck by being greedy. I really was not being greedy after all. I was just trying to make enough money to pay my rent and bills. It worked amazingly well. Until it didn't.

    One day, I didn't win. Then the next time I tried I also lost. Then I lost again. Then I lost again. Two of the casinos in particular, seemed to have shut me off cold. This obviously is not, should not, be possible. I am not a conspiracy person, and I realize casinos follow very strict rules. But somehow, I went from winning every single time for many months, to losing every single time.

It was very frustrating and confusing. I became very rattled and unnerved. Had I lost my touch? How did I lose my touch? What was different? I was playing exactly the same as always, at the same places, at the same times, in the same ways. But now I was losing every time. There were even times when almost every hand on the machine resulted in a loss, which is statistically impossible.

I can only speculate that the casinos had realized what I was doing. I was going in during the middle of the night, playing mostly alone, and winning. Maybe they saw that as a hole in their operation? They could have then changed the programming, server settings, or chips in the machines. Perhaps they changed the pay-out settings for the particular type of poker I was playing. Or perhaps they made changes that would make the machines more dormant during the night when I was usually playing. Or perhaps it was just impossibly bad luck. I don't know. But I was losing. And I was not there to have fun or feed a gambling addiction. I was only there to win money. It was my income. So, I had to stop.

I decided, while I still was ahead and had plenty of money in the bank, that I would stop before I lost it all. It just seemed to me that I was losing every visit, and I was unable to change or correct this. I was not about to keep trying and lose my last penny. So, I made the very sad, depressing, and frustrating decision to give it up. And just like that, my career as a casino poker player was over.

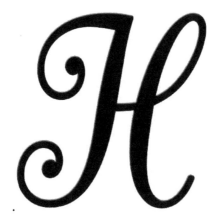

CHAPTER TWENTY-ONE

The Books

I was left deflated by the apparent fact that my career as a professional casino poker player was over. Although it was stressful, part of me enjoyed the thrill of the chase, and the satisfaction of frequent victory. However, the reality was that I seemingly could not win anymore, and thus I would be an idiot to continue. Fortunately, I still had a decent sum of money remaining from my good months at the casinos.

Not only that, but with my casino winnings I was able to put down a nice down payment on a new jeep. The BMW was old, breaking every three weeks, and had an eternal engine light on. I was grateful my poker winnings were able to get me into a beautiful, brand new white jeep SUV like I had before.

So, I was left in an okay position financially, but no longer had a future on-going income, and no longer had an outside focus other than my regular client work. A vacuum had been created, and I was about to transition into a new world.

And so it happened. One morning I woke up quite depressed and bored. I randomly for no reason whatsoever decided it might be time to tell my story. It was as if I felt my life was over, and I was like a salmon swimming back upstream to die. I felt a natural compulsion to put my story down in writing before I left the Earth.

I cannot stress enough how totally random and unexpected this was. I went to bed the night before expecting a totally normal boring day to come. I remember waking up sad, depressed, and bored. But then I remember having this definite moment in time, an epiphany kind of, where I just decided I was "done," and that I needed to document my story.

And so it began. I threw all other peripheral thoughts aside. I turned on some music really loud. Then I sat at my computer and stared at the keyboard. I scratched out the entire outline of my life story in about ten minutes. It was as if I had already done it in my head long ago, or that it was channeled from some outside source. It took zero effort. I just jotted down notes as fast as I could in the form of chapter titles, which seemed to be in the correct order. I then wrote notes under each chapter in the form of highlights I wanted to cover in each chapter. Again, it was effortless, as if someone else was writing it, and it was only my hand needing to move to do the work.

Then I started from the beginning at chapter one. That began one of the most amazing experiences of my life. It was a great adventure of emotion and memories. I listened to music, and I typed endlessly without much pause. There were moments I would cry. I learned to keep a tissue nearby. There were moments I would laugh out loud. Then there were moments I would cry and laugh all at the same time while wiping the mess of tears off my face. It was like a huge celebration of life. It was cathartic. It was the biggest release of emotion I had in perhaps my entire life that did not only include misery and pain from loss.

In fact, I felt no misery or pain at all. I felt nothing but celebration for an amazing adventure lived. However horrible, hideous, embarrassing, awful, painful, shameful, disappointing, and deplorable my life had been, I was amazed and celebratory over what an incredible adventure it had been. It made me eager to want to share all I had lived and learned, in the hope that some people might understand what I had been through, and that I was trying to be a good person, despite everything. I just wanted people to learn from my life so that maybe they could have a better life for themselves. If nothing else, perhaps my daughter could read it someday and fully realize my soul, and what I had been through, allowing her to connect more deeply with her own soul, and better understand whatever it was she was going through.

So, I wrote my story. Day after day. Same routine, every early evening until late into the night. It was like a nightly party that never ended day after day. This went on for about three and a half months. I obviously had to take some days off due to client sessions and other activities and obligations that would come up. That three plus months included me going through the finished draft for the first round of editing. After the three and a half months, I was satisfied that it was done. I had the entire manuscript printed, including table of contents, and all pages numbered.

I brought the printed manuscript home from the printer and set it down on my desk. I stared at it and thought, "What now?" I decided to send it off to a large and prestigious literary agent in Beverly Hills. I waited, expecting an immediate response of interest.

Those of you in the publishing business are likely laughing at me right now because you know what would happen next. For the rest of you, let me tell you. Nothing. Nothing happened next.

Why? Because nobody cares. I was a first-time author with no reputation or fame. No literary agent would have any interest in representing me or my book. I did not know that then, but I know that now. So, nothing happened. I'm guessing it is either sitting in some storage room unopened, or it was just thrown in the garbage without even being opened. Or perhaps it was opened so that the staff could get a good laugh before they threw it in the garbage. The end result is the same.

The next option I considered was self-publishing the book on Amazon. I started to seriously consider that and get my head around making it happen. Then I had another epiphany. I thought about everything I had written about. I thought about my family, friends, associates, and clients reading everything I had just written. This made me realize that there was no way I could publish the book. I had written too many personal and embarrassing things in the book. All my personal secrets were there. I have always been a very private person, and even my own family knew little about me. So there is no way I could drop this story out there for all to see. I started to actually have panic attacks at night before falling asleep. I would imagine those close to me reading certain things that I had written. I thought about my mother and daughter specifically quite often. I obviously became concerned I would bring embarrassment and shame to those closest to me, and I did not want to do that. I had written many truthful but hurtful things about many people. I had written many embarrassing and shameful things about myself. I would be insane to let those skeletons fall out of those huge walk-in closets.

I just couldn't let this book get out. Not in this lifetime anyway. So, I decided to take the story and literary work that had meant so much to me, and given me so much joy to write, and permanently shelve it. Perhaps I would leave instructions for it to be released after my death.

Therefore, there I sat. With nothing to publish. Nothing to show for all my work and effort. Nothing but nothingness.

A day or two after shelving the book, Serena had a thought for me. Serena suggested I write another book that I COULD actually release to the world. My immediate response was to moan and complain about how tired I was from writing *The Walk-In*, and how that was the only book I wanted to write and would ever write. I dismissed her idea and went to bed, sad and depressed with no purpose.

Then as before, with the epiphany to write my life story, I woke up the next day remembering how much fun I had writing *The Walk-In*. I realized how much I actually loved the adventure of writing. I was starting to miss the process already. Maybe I could have more nightly parties after all. Maybe I had another book in me somewhere. After considering ideas, I quickly realized that I should write a book that detailed all my spiritual thoughts, ideas, and theories, especially those I had gained from my walk-in experience. I had all this information in my head from the Universe, and maybe it was time to document those thoughts so there would be a reference book documenting my thoughts, messages, and theories. And so, *The Hunter Equation* was born.

For those of you familiar, the phrase "The Hunter Equation," applies to a universal equation given to me by the universe, but it also refers to the title of my book by the same name. So, the writing process began every evening or so, in the same routine and fashion as I wrote *The Walk-In*.

The one major difference was that *The Hunter Equation* was much more difficult to write. The words did not come automatically like before. I had to carefully think and work for every paragraph and chapter. Thus, I painstakingly designed and planned out the entire book thoroughly before starting. It was a much more detailed outline involved and took much more effort.

It was exhausting and sometimes not as fun. But I knew I was writing something meaningful that I would be proud of.

It took me another good three months to write and edit *The Hunter Equation*. When it was done, I was very happy with the finished product, and this time was entirely eager and excited to publish it and release it to the public. So, without any agent, publisher, or fanfare, I released it on Amazon. It was my first book. At least that is how everyone looked at it. In my heart, I considered it my second book. It was like having two children, but the world only knowing about the second child. I still considered *The Walk-In* to be my first book, but I quickly had to change my thinking so that I would refer to *The Hunter Equation* as my first book.

It was exciting to have it out there. It sold a few copies the first couple of weeks, and I quickly grew disappointed with those results. I am not sure what I was expecting. Again, anyone in the publishing business would be laughing at me. The reality is that over 95% of all books published, only sell a few copies here and there. It is only the few books at the very top of the pyramid that sell a decent number of copies. I learned this soon enough as I saw not much happen with my book.

I decided to put some money into marketing with Facebook ads and such. I started working that type of marketing, and immediately saw results. I then put even more money into marketing and started marketing the book all over the world. I very quickly saw my sales rankings on Amazon skyrocket. It was not long before *The Hunter Equation* was the #1 Best Seller in many of its categories. For example, in The United Kingdom, it was the #1 Best Seller in Philosophy and Metaphysics. Serena suggested that since it was now the top selling philosophy book in the UK, that it should be required reading for all Philosophy majors at Oxford. I am not sure who started laughing first, me or her, but we were both rolling around on the floor for about five minutes. While I did not take the rankings or myself too seriously, it was indeed true that the rankings were fantastic, and something I was very pleased and encouraged by.

The book ended up being one of the top 100 of all books in Australia. It briefly got as high as #36 or so I believe. The book also was ranked very high in Canada among all books. It routinely sat in the #1 Best Seller position in Canada for the Reincarnation category. The rankings were not as spectacular in the USA with all the intense competition, but it did manage to be among the top selling books within its categories off and on.

I believed my ship had finally come in. I was seeing all kinds of activity all over Facebook about the book in the countries I was advertising in. I was seeing some amazing sales rankings from Amazon. I was excited. But one thing I did not see was any money. I was to learn that there was a two, or more, month lag-time before an author got paid. I was also to learn that for books sold outside Amazon's network, that lag-time could be four months. I guess I had to patiently wait before my payday would come. While I waited to be paid, I threw money at marketing like confetti at a parade. I was spending all my cash on hand from the casino days, and I was going deeply into debt piling marketing expenses onto credit cards. I did not worry much, as the excellent sales rankings seemed to indicate the money train was on its way to my station.

Not all the feedback about the book was good though. Many Evangelicals hated the book. Call me naive, but I was actually surprised by this. I did not think I was that disparaging toward Christianity or religion. In fact, I made it clear I actually believed in God, and believed in Jesus. I even wrote a chapter on why and how I believed the power of prayer was real, and that I believed it worked. But oh my goodness, did the haters come out against me. Many of them called me the Devil and said my book was the Devil's work. There was one post in The Philippines that seemed to indicate someone was organizing a protest specifically against my book. I was very disappointed to realize that many extreme religious folks were hating the book before they even read it. They hated the title, hated the front cover, and hated the entire idea of the book. I had never come across so many loving Christians who hated so much, before in my life. I was also discouraged by how many people judged a book by its cover without even reading a single word inside.

Honestly, I was dumbfounded over the whole thing. I had written the book with love, and with love toward all humans. I was trying to respect all beliefs and all religions. But yes, the point of the book was trying to get people to think independently for themselves. THIS is what many folks found so offensive. In most religions, it is heresy to think for yourself. The whole point of religion is to give total faith in a religious structure that tells how you should think and act regarding issues of morality and beliefs. I really did not think people would be so offended by my sincere and genuine thoughts and theories. I was wrong. And this folks is why we don't discuss religion or politics at the dinner table in mixed company. Lesson learned.

But I still stand behind everything I wrote in that book. I remain very proud of what I produced, and the reality is that many more people love the book than hate it. So, I watched the sales rankings fly high, and I watched the haters hate. But what next?

After the release of *The Hunter Equation*, I was actually really tired. I had written two books, one after the other, within a six-month time period. I was tired from all the writing, but also exhausted from the editing phase, in addition to the actual publishing and marketing process and tasks, which could be daily. I was really needing a rest and long vacation on a very comfortable island somewhere.

But I had no money. In fact, I had less than no money. I had no money and I had lots of debt. I was just waiting and hoping for my royalty payments to start coming in. This was when Serena made another suggestion. She suggested that while I was waiting for my payments to come in on the first book, I write another book. This time, I may have responded with some expletives. I was seriously very exhausted and seriously not wanting to write any more. Yeah, *The Walk-In* was fun, but *The Hunter Equation* was not as fun. It was exhausting work. Two books in six months was a lot, and I just needed to be done for a while.

However, as Serena often is, she was very convincing as to why I should put out another book. I had grown concerned over the royalty situation with *The Hunter Equation*, and perhaps I better put out a second book for insurance. Plus, *The Hunter Equation* had lots of haters due to the spiritual nature of the content. So why not put out a book that is a pure self-help book, without any reference to religion or anything that anyone could find offensive. It made sense, and I had an idea for a book that I wanted to do in order to help people who were down-and-out, or needed help rebuilding and re-booting their lives. Thus, *Rising To Greatness* was born.

For one reason or another, the thinking on my part and Serena's, was that I should hammer out this second book (which was actually my third book) very quickly. The book was very clear in my mind, and I felt I could write it quickly. So, I did. But I would regret doing it that way.

If *The Hunter Equation* felt like a difficult book to write, I would soon realize that *Rising To Greatness* would be even more difficult. I had to totally focus, concentrate, and engross myself into each chapter in order to get it done clearly and effectively. This meant no music, no party, no fun. Just work. It was grueling. I was hammering out one or two chapters every night without any breaks. There were moments when I felt like crying because it was just too much. I had to force myself to do it. I found myself actually using many of the skills and coping mechanisms inside the book, in order to survive the process of writing it. *Rising To Greatness* was a book that I wrote while living out its concepts in real time. While I was writing the chapters on Motivation and Discipline, I was clinging onto strategies and coping methods of those principles while I was writing them, so that I would endure the process of writing about them.

I wrote that entire book in only 30 days. I do not recommend doing that, nor would I want to ever do it again. But I did it, and I was very delighted with the end result. I really felt I had put together something that everyone could love, appreciate, and benefit from. No haters, no trolls. Just a solid self-help book that was good for anyone of any age and any religion or background. YAY! So, after a very quick and intense editing by Serena and myself, *Rising To Greatness* was released on Amazon.

The book had good solid immediate sales, mostly based upon the coat tails of *The Hunter Equation,* that had blazed a strong trail for a follow-up book. The book did really well in the USA with solid sales every day, without as much marketing required. I had pretty much run out of money from *The Hunter Equation* marketing, so I had to release *Rising To Greatness* with very little marketing, and keep the release focused only on the USA and UK. The book quickly went to the #1 Best Seller slot in the UK for Women's Spirituality, despite the fact that it seemed just as many men were buying the book and loving it too.

I was very pleased with both books, and proud of what I had accomplished. I had written three books in a period of nine months. Two of those were published and released. I was done writing. I told Serena to not even suggest anything to me about writing for a long time. I was really tired. At this point, what I needed, and all I needed, was my money. Where were the royalties?

I was broke. I had blown through all my casino poker winnings, all my credit cards, and I had not been working on building my client business, because I had been a full-time author for almost a year at this point. So now I had concerns about paying rent and basic bills. If I did not have those royalties coming, I was totally screwed for sure.

Therefore, I started wholly focusing on the royalties. I began contacting Amazon and asking questions. Anyone who has ever tried contacting Amazon author support and asking questions, is laughing at me now. I am the butt of all your laughing entertainment in this chapter. I might have written three books at this point and published two of them, but I knew nothing about publishing, Amazon, royalties, or how anything worked. I was about to be schooled.

I decided to keep it simple and focus my questions with Amazon on my royalties for Australia and Canada. I did this because I had such amazing sales rankings in those two countries and had many screen shots to prove it. However, my sales reports were not showing any sales in Australia at all, and only a few in Canada. How is this possible?

So, I asked Amazon this. I asked, "How is this possible?" How can a book achieve a Best Seller status and not sell any copies? Good question, yes? Well the answers were not as good. I received lots of deflection and off-topic replies by employees who were obviously using standard copy/paste responses and had difficulty with the English language.

By this time, I also received my first royalty payments that were only a tiny fraction of what I was expecting. I was devastated, shocked, confused, and terrified. I had spent all my cash and used all my credit on marketing. I needed some return for my investment. It was not to be.

Amazon paid my royalties based upon their royalty reports. While most first-time authors would have been thrilled by my royalty payments and sales, I was so upset that I was beet red and on the brink of a meltdown. I would not remotely comprehend how all the marketing and activity I saw, did not result in bigger sales.

I also could not comprehend Amazon's explanations of why I had NO sales in Australia, despite it making it into the Top 100 books in the entire country two or three times. Same issue in Canada. Plus, there were lower sales in UK and USA than I expected.

At this point, I need to say that I am not accusing Amazon of any wrongdoing, or anything inappropriate. They provided sales reports. I would have to prove all the sales. I obviously cannot do that. I cannot go to Australia and find every person who ever bought the book. In fairness to Amazon, they eventually provided an explanation of the discrepancy, by saying the sales were not included in the Australian numbers because they were included in another pool of sales they called "extended distribution." I then asked someone there for a detailed accounting and breakdown of all my "extended distribution" sales, and they refused, saying they could not do that.

It was all very confusing to me because Amazon appears to run a very solid and legitimate business, and accounting of all sales. I would not assume otherwise. They certainly paid me some money for the USA and UK sales, and continue to do so. In fact, I believe my sales/royalties recently are correct and accurate. I have no absolute proof to believe they have ever done anything incorrectly, but I have relayed my thoughts and experience above. The bottom line is that the money never came.

Again, let me repeat. The money I was looking for and waiting for never came. Not only did my ship not come in, but it sank. I was busted and broken. I had two books I thought were selling fairly well, but I had nothing to show for it. I had no cash, and I had no credit remaining. I had taken a fairly good situation from the casino winnings, written three books, and then ruined my life by banking on their financial success.

I could say Amazon this or that, but there is plenty of stupidity to go around. I was inexperienced and naive regarding the publishing business, and how Amazon works. I had bet the farm and lost. I blew it. Game over. I shelved my career as an author in that moment.

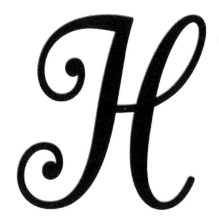

CHAPTER TWENTY-TWO

The Unexpected

Here I sat in this expensive apartment totally broke with limited income. I had stopped playing poker because I stopped winning. I had spent every nickel I had marketing books that did not produce the royalties I expected. I had weakened my client base by spending almost a year writing three books. I had nothing and had no prospects. I was screwed.

I felt stupid and like a loser for letting myself down and putting myself in such a horrible position. I felt if I had not written the books at all, I would have been much better off. At least I would not have spent all my casino winnings and used up all my credit lines. I was sitting in an "okay" situation before the books, and now my life was ruined. Again. How many times has my life been ruined in this story? I lost count.

I was quite depressed and contemplating what I should do, and what might happen to me. Since my daughter never moved in with me as expected, I should probably leave the expensive apartment for sure. Maybe move back into a small one bedroom in the ghetto. Or maybe move to a shack in the middle of the desert. Or maybe move into my vehicle. Or maybe die. Choices, choices. I felt the books were my last real effort and hope toward fixing my life and having a decent life. I did my best, but my best was not good enough. I lost hope inside. I never lost love or hope for those in my life, or my clients I was helping. But I lost hope for myself.

However, there was one thing to look forward to. It was summer, school just got out, and Angel was coming down to visit me for ten days. Although I knew my life was screwed and maybe over, I was really excited to see her and spend time with her. She has always been medicine for my soul. Her presence always made me feel better. So, I decided to put my doomed existence aside for ten days and enjoy her visit.

I excitedly drove to the airport to pick her up. I arrived a little early and waited for her to arrive and come down to baggage claim. FINALLY, I saw her coming down and walking toward me. I smiled in excitement. She looked at me. She walked up to me and said, "Don't talk to me." This was not the greeting I expected. I hugged her and asked her what was wrong. She just said, "I can't talk. Just take me home." So, I claimed her luggage and walked us to the car without saying a word to her. She got into the car and said nothing to me the entire one-hour drive home. I remained silent while I wondered what was going on.

We arrived home and she went directly into her room and closed the door. That was it. I thought to myself that I guess this visit was going to suck. But I didn't know why. I gave it several minutes, and then knocked on her door and walked in. I asked her to explain to me what the problem was.

She started telling me how upset she was about everything in her life. Apparently, she was really suffering at home up with her mother. She and her mother were not getting along. She and her siblings were not getting along. She didn't like people in the school up there, and she was having problems with people on her cheer team. To top it off, her boyfriend had just broken up with her. She was totally destroyed inside in every way. It was as if she held herself together just long enough to land in Los Angeles, then allowed herself to fall apart.

She looked at me and said, "I don't want to ever go back." I was like, huh, what? I thought she was just coming for ten days to visit. I asked her directly, "Do you mean you want to stay here, and live here, and move here?" She replied, "What part of I don't want to ever go back up there don't you understand." Anyone who has a teenage daughter knows this is standard attitude operating procedure. After a while, you don't even take offense. You take as normal teenage daughter conversation. So, I just replied to her that I wanted to make sure I fully understood. So, I said, "After all this time, you are finally ready to move down here and go to school here?" She said, "Yes." I said, "Okay, we will make it happen. I won't make you go back."

After our conversation, I left her room, closed her door, went out to sit at my desk, and I just stared in disbelief. This was what I was praying for and wanted her entire life. This was my dream come true, to finally have my daughter living with me. I wanted nothing more than this. But this was the absolute worst moment for her to do this. A year ago, or even six months ago, I had money and could have handled this no problem. But now I was totally broke and headed toward losing my home. There was no way I could handle this now and take care of her. No way. But I just told her she could stay, and I would not send her back. Anyone else see a problem here?

The next day I told my parents what had happened. I confessed to them I had major problems with the book royalties, and I was in a horrible position financially. I told them I did not feel I could handle having Angel here financially. I was going to have to find another solution. Perhaps I would send her back up there, but I would move up there with her, so she would have my support. I would not leave her hanging or just send her back alone. But surely, I could not handle supporting her here on my own without help.

My mother quickly said, "Whatever you do, DO NOT SEND HER BACK." I was like, "Huh? Didn't you just hear me that I am broke and can't do this?" She repeated, "DO NOT send her back." She then said she would talk with Dave and they would help me make this work. So, I kind of shifted gears in my head and thought, huh, okay so maybe I am doing this after all.

My parents got back with me quickly and said they would certainly help. I asked them for some money up front so that I had some breathing room to operate. They sent it immediately without hesitation or debate. I thought, "Umm, okay, I guess my daughter is living with me now."

The next item on the agenda was how to handle her mother. I felt Angel needed to tell her mother herself. It would do no good for me to tell Luci. Luci would just scream at me and demand to talk with Angel anyway. Understandably, Angel was not eager to tell her mother that she was not coming back home. Her mother had sent her down here with one suitcase, expecting to have her back in ten days.

As Angel's ten days were nearing an end, I insisted that Angel needed to tell her mother now. So, she did. It did not go well. Luci was understandably shocked and upset. She felt betrayed by Angel because Angel said nothing to her in person before she left. She insisted Angel come back home as planned, and then could move down to me at the end of summer. Angel insisted she was not returning back up there at all. It was quite unpleasant and nasty. I ended up speaking with Luci, and she was surprisingly calm and reasonable with me. Luci admitted that things had not gone well in Montana for Angel, and that she was not surprised that Angel had decided to move down to me. Luci said to me, "She is yours now." The conversation ended and I hung up the phone. I played back in my mind that one sentence, "She is yours now," over and over. Those were the words I had wanted to hear for over ten years. Finally, I had heard them. Finally, I had reached the promised land. Finally, I had what I have been wanting all along. I had my daughter.

But there was no victory dance. I was very humbled by the fact that I was totally screwed. I was not expecting this. I was totally unprepared and unequipped to handle this. Plus, I had no money and little income. What I would soon realize is that I also had no time. Parenting Angel would turn out to be a full-time job.

Angel was no Angel. She was a handful. My perfect little Angel that never gave me a single problem before moving to Montana, was now completely different after living away from me for four years. She acted like she had raised herself, gone to college, and was used to living in her own place under her own rules. All at age 16. I was not used to this. She and I had always been close, and she ALWAYS minded me and complied with my requests. Now all of a sudden, she was completely ignoring me and doing whatever she wanted. It was unfortunately obvious to me that I had to start being "the mean parent" instead of the best buddy. This hurt my soul, but she was out of control, and I had to reel her in.

So, as I learned of her riding around with friends in fast expensive sports cars at 100 mph, doing donuts in the school parking lots, being out at random parties doing who knows what, I was very concerned. I was even more concerned by some of the friends she was hanging out with. Therefore, I started restricting her movements. Angel hated this. She hated me for doing this to her.

I went from being her "Daddy best buddy hero" to being her sworn enemy. She stopped talking to me and would violate my rules whenever she felt she could get away with it. I was heartbroken. I wondered whether this arrangement was really going to work. I cursed the last four years she had lived in Montana, as it clearly had turned my perfect daughter into a monster. I really was not sure how to handle everything. I was supposed to be the "expert" on giving clients advice on handling teens, and I was getting my ass kicked by my own daughter.

On top of monitoring and chasing after Angel, I had a long list of tasks I had to do in order to complete her move. I had to make sure she was enrolled in school for the coming year, plus set up medical care, dental, eye, medical insurance, driver license, car insurance for her to drive my car, and the list goes on and on. I was so overwhelmed I truly could not deal with it. Angel was proving to be a full-time job that I could barely keep up with. In addition, I still had client sessions to do. Plus, I had a home that needed to be cleaned and maintained. Don't forget about grocery shopping and so forth. I really couldn't do it at first. I was making myself physically ill with the stress and schedule. I was not sleeping well, and all my routines had been destroyed.

All of you mamas and dads out there that have been doing this all along for years, and especially with multiple kids, I just want to say my hat is off to you. Much respect. I totally get it now. I used to laugh when I would see a mother in a grocery store looking all haggard, worn, and walking dead. But now that was me. I was that person. It was no longer funny.

So, one day, I was limping around the house in sweatpants, un-showered, little sleep, and with a mild flu type illness. I looked horrible and I felt horrible. I heard a knock on my door. This quickly turned into a loud pounding at my door. I looked to see who it was, and it was two Sheriff's Department deputies.

Now mind you, I had never once in my entire adult lifetime had the police pounding at my door. I was not "that guy." I was always the "quiet as a mouse guy." But, then again, I never had a teenage Angel living with me before. I knew right away that it had to be related to Angel. She was not home, and I quickly assumed that she had been pulled over in some car with friends speeding or doing "donuts," or something. I assumed they were there to return my daughter to me from the back seat of their police cruiser. So, I opened the door and greeted them nicely. They said, "Is your daughter Angel here?" I replied no, and I thought it was weird they asked that, since I assumed they had her with them. Thus, I became concerned this was far more serious. They asked if they could come inside and look for themselves. I told them of course they could. I led them to Angel's room, which was a mess. I will also remind you that I looked like some kind of dirty crack addict who was coughing, un-showered, and completely caught off guard, and thus acting nervous and stupid.

The two officers looked around her room (and found nothing of interest I guess). They then told me why they were there. They asked me if I knew where she was. I told them she was with a friend. They told me they had received a call from one of her friends that Angel said she was going to take a handful of pills and hopefully not wake up.

This made no sense to me and I did not believe it. They asked me what pills she had access to. I told them she had some anxiety pills prescribed by her doctor in Montana. However, I could not find all of them when they asked me to produce them. They asked me if I could have Angel return home so they could talk to her. By this time, I was physically shaking. I was very nervous and starting to get upset. I was confused. I was sick from my illness. I was feeling very off guard and unsure of what was happening.

I called Angel and she immediately answered. I asked her to come home. She asked why, and I told her because there are police standing in my living room. She then started to cry. This is when I knew that something was really wrong. She said she didn't want to come home. I told her that she had to. The officers then took the phone and told her that if she didn't come home, they were going to have the entire police force out looking for her until they found her. I was just dumbfounded by what I was hearing, and all the drama. Angel agreed to come home.

Angel arrived home within several minutes. When she walked in the door, I knew she was not right. She seemed different, or distant or something. The officers asked to speak with her alone. After several minutes, the officers told me that Angel had admitted to taking a large handful of the anxiety pills. I was obviously very shocked and could not fully process what was happening. I felt really stupid. Dealing with kids, counseling, and suicide prevention is a huge part of my job. How could I have been so unprepared, inept, and stupid, that I could not handle my own daughter, or even see any warning signs.

It wasn't long before my home was filled with the Fire Department medical first responders, then the actual ambulance EMT's, and then more police just to round things out. They explained they were taking her by ambulance to the children's hospital emergency room and I should obviously follow. Before they could even finish speaking, they had my daughter out of my home and onto a stretcher that was being shoved into an ambulance. I ran into my room and struggled to put some acceptable clothes on, and grabbed my wallet, phone, and whatever I might need. During the entire drive to the hospital, I was in total disbelief over what was happening. Did my daughter really try to kill herself? Was she in danger of dying? What was I going to tell her mother and my parents? What a horrible, irresponsible, awful, useless, stupid, and blind parent I must have been.

I arrived at the emergency room and she was already set up in a room. She was awake and seemed fine. They had hooked her up to machines and were giving her an IV. Doctors and nurses came in and out, and there was a security guard watching us from outside, in case she tried to hurt herself again, I guess.

I sat in a chair looking at Angel as she was propped up in the bed looking at me. I was coughing, felt I might faint, and looked like I was dying because of my own illness I had going. I actually thought of telling the nurses that I needed help myself, but I knew they would then admit me as a patient, and I had to remain free to deal with Angel.

Angel and I just looked at each other. I knew to remain calm and not to say anything rash. She then said to me, "Well I guess you are going to send me back up to live with my mother now." I looked at her and said, "Never. I will never send you back up there." Angel looked surprised by my response. She knew that she had been nothing but trouble since she arrived, and she figured that certainly this was the last straw, and my perfect excuse to get rid of her. But I knew to show her that I had her back 100%, and there was nothing that could make me change that. In that moment. That one moment. That one interchange. Everything changed. I felt the energy change. I felt the entire world shift. I knew, in that moment, that I had my daughter back again.

We looked at each other the same way we used to look at each other when she was younger. She looked at me like her "daddy hero," and I looked at her like my perfect little girl. We smiled and I laughed. She then laughed. She said something about how we should not be laughing since we were in the emergency room, and she just tried to kill herself. I said, "Yeah I know, but we are here together, and we will deal with all this together." I then asked her why she did it. She opened up and told me everything. She explained how she was freaked out by the change, she was upset from her interactions with her mother, and she had been having a major problem with some of her friends here. What was not said, but was the huge elephant in the room, was how she and I were not getting along, and were totally against each other. I knew in my heart that what likely put her over the edge was the fact she no longer had her daddy to confide in. In fact, for the first time in her life, we were pitted against each other. So, she just couldn't take it anymore. She had reached her breaking point, and she just did not care anymore. She took the handful of pills without thinking clearly of the consequences. She took them out of anger and frustration, and just wanted to go to sleep. She did not care if she woke up or not.

And so there it was, I fully understood. I did not even blame her. If I were in her shoes, I would have felt the same way. I explained to her that we could change things, fix things, and make them better. I told her we needed to be on the same team again. She agreed. Finally, we were back to how we needed to be. We spoke openly and lovingly about little things, big things, and unimportant things, in the emergency room that night.

After an entire night in the emergency room, many evaluations and assessments, they agreed to release her into my care, under my watchful eye. We went home and both slept for half an eternity. It took her a week or so to feel okay. Taking a handful of anxiety pills makes you very sick, for anyone who needs to know this. But she recovered and so did our father/daughter relationship.

For those wondering, yes, I told her mother what happened the very next morning. Luci started crying when I explained everything. I also felt the energy with Luci shift. She became more docile and reasonable. Instead of attacking me, she almost seemed like she was being supportive. My parents were also supportive and offered the continued help again.

However, there was another problem. I had been unable to get the medical insurance situation set up before this incident. In the emergency room, I was unable to produce proof of medical insurance for Angel. I was shown an estimate of cost, had to sign consent forms, and other forms taking full responsibility for the costs. Of course, all the numbers I was shown basically added up to one trillion dollars. Honestly, I did not care. I was already at the point of financial ruin. So, I actually kind of chuckled and said, go ahead, bill me as much as you want.

Thus, I was double triple quadruple screwed financially. I knew I would never recover. But I had my daughter and she was safe. I was fine with that. It's hard to explain. There is this moment in life sometimes when you just reach a point of surrender. That point comes with a sense of defeat, but it also comes with a sense of relief when you just drop the burden right where you stand, and do not carry it another inch forward. That's what I did.

Going forward, I focused on my daughter, and improving her wellness. She started hanging out with much better friends, we started going to Disney together every weekend again, and she started minding my rules. Finally, we were in a better place where we could move forward together. So that is what we did. Life became calmer, and more normal. School started and she got into the groove of school. We have remained in a good place together as a family, as father/daughter, and as buddy/buddy. However, the time constraints and all the issues with the finances have not gone away. The struggle is real.

In the meantime, Angel scored a victory in convincing me to let her get her own cat. She somehow produced this tiny one-week old orange tabby that someone had rescued from out in the street. It was presented to us as a female, so she named it Ginger.

We took Ginger to the vet and had her checked out. The vet told us she had all kinds of issues, such as fleas, ear mites, and tar on her claws. Wonderful. Not. But we took care of her and soon fell in love with her.

One thing though. Eventually, I realized that she was a "HE!" I'm not a vet, but I noticed she was developing balls and a micro-penis. So, the cat everyone, including the vet, thought was a girl, was a boy. But we were already fully invested in HER, and her name. So, we decided she identifies as a female rather than a male. Does this mean we have the first transgender cat in our area? Perhaps. So, we still call her a her, even though she is a him. Nothing in my world is ever simple. Not only that, but we are convinced she is part squirrel because of her crazy behavior, or at least very feral at the minimum.

Despite the crazy female cat that is actually a male, and is actually more like a squirrel, things seemed to settle into a decent routine. That is until everything changed again. Angel went up to Montana for a visit. Apparently, she had an amazing time, because when she got back home, she announced she was thinking of moving back up to Montana. Silent pause. Face palm. She cited a few reasons, including my difficult financial situation, her having to struggle more in this school, and her missing some of her friends up there. I of course was devastated upon hearing this news. I felt I had sacrificed a lot to make this work, and now I would end up with nothing, AGAIN.

Well fortunately, this is where the villain of the story would become the hero who saves the day. In a shocking move, Luci called me, and we had a very pleasant, reasonable, constructive conversation about the situation. Luci agreed Angel's change of heart seemed to be a bit premature and possibly misplaced. Thus, Luci said she would put the brakes on any immediate move, giving Angel more time to be sure of what she wants, and why she wants it. Finally, Luci and I were on the same page. As for Angel, she is still contemplating where she wants to finish out high school. The unintentional cliff-hanger is a reminder of how life is. Life is not neat or tidy. Life is unpredictable. Life changes in an instant. Life will always change. Expect it.

My recent experiences, especially with Angel and her suicide attempt, made me realize something. It made me realize that all of my experiences in life perhaps could be used in a way to help other people. I thought about how I decided not to release *The Walk-In,* because I would be too embarrassed and humiliated by everything in the book. However, I realized how selfish that viewpoint is. Instead, perhaps I needed to release the book so that others could pull something from it that might change their lives for the better.

After all, I no longer know what sort of future I have. But then again, none of us know for sure how long we have here on this Earth. After some thought, I felt that maybe it was time I made one last courageous stand and let people see my story. Yes, it might be uncomfortable or even harmful to me and some of those surrounding me, but maybe that is not as significant as the many people it could help. The bottom line is that the last decade of my life since the walk-in event, has been about public service. It has been about helping others. It has been about making the world a better place. So maybe in some way this book can do that. Therefore, I made the decision to sit down and finish, then release this book that you are reading right at this moment.

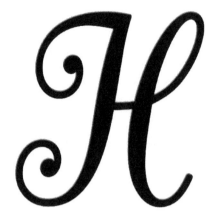

CHAPTER TWENTY-THREE
Contemplation

This story has no ending. That is because my life is not over yet. So, I apologize for the lack of a tidy, tragic, amazing, or happy ending. I didn't write this book to provide an ending. I wrote this book in hopes that others would relate to some of my experiences, perhaps learn from them, and contemplate how to apply them to their own lives. We all need to live our journey and write our own endings.

Hopefully everyone in my life is still speaking to me after this story is told. I value everyone in my life, and here is an update on each of them as of the book's publishing.

My daughter Angel remains the center of my universe. In addition to finishing up high school wherever she decides, she is also contemplating what she wants to do after school. She still does some modeling and is very interested in art and art history. She also has a knack for human psychology and has done considerable research on sociopaths. Yep, she's definitely my daughter. We continue to go to Disneyland together most weekends, and that will hopefully continue for as long as we are blessed to remain together, just as we have done since she was five years old. Angel has grown into a very strong, wise, independent young woman. She is the 2.0 version of myself, and I am extremely proud of her.

Serena remains a dear companion in life. She still lives in Europe with her 50 dogs, to be near her aging mother. We all recently lost her beloved father, who was an amazing man and true inspiration to me, showing me what it means to be a decent and loving human. Serena herself continues to write books and works with many clients all over the world. Despite the distance between Serena and myself, we still speak daily and work closely on projects together. Her endless patience, support, and understanding of me, is what got me to this point.

Gez ended up finally leaving Brazil and traveling all over Europe on a shoestring, along with the help of those he met along the way. He fell in love with a German man, and they are now married and enjoying life in Spain. Gez works there as an English teacher. He is now fluent in Portuguese, English, and Spanish, with an understanding of German. I never got to see Gez again since my last trip to Brazil many years ago. Despite that, Gez and I remain friends.

Luci hopefully continues to evolve into the calmer, and more reasonable person I have begun to see in her. With age, and while Angel has been living with me, Luci has mellowed quite a bit. I rarely have any serious problems with Luci these days, and she can sometimes be quite supportive when it comes to co-parenting Angel. She remains in Montana married to her former nanny boss, now husband of many years. I believe she still hates me and thinks I am a loser, but it's not relevant anymore, as we are coming to the end of our daughter's childhood. I have been encouraging her and Angel to develop a better relationship.

My stepbrother Richie is a financial planning executive, living not far from my parents back east. He ended up being far more successful than I am and is contemplating travel plans and adventures. He also has a beautiful daughter of his own, and he remains a huge sports fan.

My parents are enjoying their well-deserved retirement back east, and we have all been working hard to build upon and improve our relationship. All of their help and support they offered, whenever they offered it, is deeply appreciated. They have been very supportive of Angel and me during recent events. Without their help, all of this would not have been possible.

Larry's cat is still here sitting next to me now. He has been an amazing companion, and I am lucky to have him. Our new cat Ginger is currently in Angel's room in "time-out," as she just tried to climb up the blinds from floor to ceiling. But she is healthy and doing well.

Also, in my life, are my clients, many of whom have become friends. They contribute to my life, as I hope I contribute to theirs.

I did not write my story to prove anything or convince anyone of anything. I do not care if people don't believe some of the things I have said, nor do I care if people disapprove of me or my story. I was also not thrilled to completely humiliate myself and embarrass my family and all those who know me. Just like with all my counseling and life coaching work I do today, my purpose is to use my own experiences, knowledge, and talents, to teach and help others. We learn from our own experiences and mistakes, but it is much better if we can learn from other's experiences and mistakes first, so we do not have to personally suffer the consequences of making those same mistakes. I hope my story serves as food for thought and provides contemplation for others who struggle, suffer, or find themselves stuck in bad situations.

I fully realize people may judge my life. They will judge my story and the things I have done. In my case, I felt I had little control over what happened, and I was more or less riding a destructive tidal wave, while clinging on to a floating pile of trash. But even I had choices and could have done some things differently.

So, go ahead and judge me. Critique me. What would you have done in my same situations? What would you do now? Think. Learn. If judging me makes you a better person, then I am happy for that. Learn from me. Learn from my mistakes. Learn from my journey. If you can make your own life better by looking at mine, then I have accomplished something.

In general, most of my life people have pretty much abandoned me, left me, died, caused me to suffer, or simply left me to suffer. But I love people. I love humanity. I love hope, love, and inspiration. I love the human experience of living. We experience so many sensations and emotions that are priceless and fleeting. I love people so much that I want them to be happy. I want people to experience all those amazing human sensations of hope, love, happiness, joy, excitement, and pride of accomplishment. I want everyone to have an equal chance of having the human experience.

I wanted to share my own human experience, so people could see the breadth and expanse of possibilities. To show how a person could start so low, end up so high, and still end up so low. And then perhaps rise again? How a person can take damage, humiliation, abuse, pain, and still continue, and maybe even thrive. I wanted to show that, despite anything you have been through you can still adapt. You can still live. You must always believe. You must always love. When you stop believing and loving, you stop living.

I know there are people reading this who are in great pain from something in their life. You may have suffered a loss; you may be suffering from depression, addiction, bad circumstances, or bad luck. All these external and internal forces may have then resulted in certain behaviors or bad choices. There are people who will judge you based upon their partial view of your exterior. The struggle is real. I hope you at least feel that I might understand you and relate. You are not alone.

I understand all the different struggles, pain, and suffering. When your circumstances take over your life and your behavior, it can result in destructive cycles, and periods of pain and suffering. Maybe it's just part of your journey, maybe you have your unique reasons for doing what you do, or maybe it is time for you to change. For me, all of the above applied. I had to develop my own coping mechanisms and strategies to help me survive. These are the tools that gave birth to my book, *Rising To Greatness*. I actually used some of these tools myself in my own struggles, and still rely on them today.

We all have pain inside us. Use your pain to fuel your inspirations and your love. Do not be afraid to make changes. Do not be afraid to love. Do not be afraid to try. Do not be afraid to live. Do not be afraid of anything. Eliminate fear from your life. The biggest thing my life journey has done for me, is that it taught me to live without fear. With all that has happened to me, why would I fear anything? Fear is laughable. If something bad is going to happen to you, it will happen to you whether you fear it or not. Do not give it the satisfaction of showing it respect by fearing it.

Show compassion to others. One of the many lessons I learned is that often, the people who could do the most for you, do nothing; and the people who could do something, do less than they could have done; and the people who are not in a position to do much of anything, do the most. You would be surprised how a hug, or a smile can affect someone. It could even save a life. Sometimes a person just needs a sign from the universe that life is worth living.

Teach others your experiences so humanity may benefit from your existence. Maybe in some way you will be contributing to the evolution of humanity.

Live with love. Even if you hate or resent something or someone, still live with love. Love always wins and is far more powerful. Hate always dies eventually. Love is eternal.

Most of all, never give up. If nothing else, my story should illustrate that we never know what will happen. Anything can happen, and it often does. Where there is love, there is hope. When there is hope, you can never give up. Whatever you are going through right now, know that you can make it through. Believe.

See me, Feel me, Touch me, Heal me –

The Who

ACKNOWLEDGEMENTS

I want to thank the following people for their support:

Serena, for your endless love, support, patience, guidance, companionship, and encouragement. Also, thank you for your efforts with the editing and publishing of this book. Without you, I could not have made it to this point.

Angel, for being the center of my Universe, my inspiration for living, and making me the proudest dad who ever lived.

My parents, Mom and Dave, for raising me to have deep character, and coming to my rescue as often times as you have.

Gez, for your love and comfort during the darkest hours of my life when I needed it most; and for showing me I could live again.

All of my cats throughout the years who were often my only source of comfort during lonely times. If only you could have written books of your own...

Thanks to all those who contributed in some way, through beta reading, editing, critique, love, and support.

Finally, thank you to all my clients who have provided support and friendship during my journey.

ABOUT THE AUTHOR

Brian Hunter is a well-known American psychic counselor, author, and life coach based in Los Angeles, California. Brian grew up highly intuitive and had a successful business career. But after a major paranormal event, his abilities increased, and he shortly thereafter became a professional psychic. Brian has been a member of Best American Psychics and was listed as one of the top 50 psychics in the world. Brian has worked with people from all over the world, including celebrities and captains of industry. Brian was an original cast member of the TV series pilot "*Missing Peace,*" in which psychics worked with detectives to solve cold cases. He has also worked as an actor and model in Hollywood and been featured in various movie and TV productions unrelated to his psychic work. Brian's current work consists mainly of life coaching and counseling. However, he also does psychic readings, mediumship, and energy work.

The Walk-In chronicles his own life story, as told by himself.

CPSIA information can be obtained
at www.ICGtesting.com
Printed in the USA
LVHW050126250420
654412LV00012B/1369